A THEORY OF METHOD

HUSAIN SARKAR

UNIVERSITY OF CALIFORNIA PRESS
Berkeley Los Angeles London

University of California Press
Berkeley and Los Angeles, California

University of California Press, Ltd.
London, England

Library of Congress Cataloging in Publication Data

Sarkar, Husain.
A theory of method.

Bibliography: p. 216
Includes index.
1. Methodology. I. Title.
BD241.S32 1983 001.2′01 82-45911
ISBN 0-520-04730-3

Printed in the United States of America

1 2 3 4 5 6 7 8 9

For

Durriya

Contents

Preface

This book commences by proposing a framework for discussing methods. There follows an appraisal of three landmark theories of method with which I disagree. When I am done examining each of these, I shall have left a part of my own theory behind. At the end, the remaining pieces proper to the core of that theory are presented.

To evaluate methods one must know the structure of a method. This is the rationale for proposing a framework for methods in chapter 1. The structure of a method is disclosed in the different and distinct kinds of statements a method makes. Some statements are conventional, some are not. Some are claims of logic, while others are claims concerning the theories scientists should further pursue in theoretical and experimental research. It is clear that no single way of evaluating methods—logic or history—could cover all the various aspects of a method. Against the background of two conflicting claims, one that argues that the social sciences can explain the origin and growth of knowledge, and the other that claims they cannot, I offer a third claim: The social sciences are to be regarded as side-constraints that any method must satisfy. This allows the social sciences to play an important role in method evaluation and yet denies them the status of a method (on my view, a method is not an empirical science).

Chapter 2 reconstructs Popper's theory of method, revealing some of its novel and neglected aspects, such as its leitmotif that the growth of aims and goals is akin to the growth of scientific knowledge. It criticizes

Popper's theory as offering an inadequate account of the complex relationship between method, history of science, and learning; it raises questions about what transforms a second-order tradition, accompanying a society of scientists, into a critical one; it indicates some unresolved tensions between various parts of the theory; and it claims that Popper's theory offers unsound reasons for the thesis that methodological statements are only conventions.

The problem of the logical status of methodological statements is raised afresh. The thesis argued for and defended is that methodological statements, like statements in ethics, should be regarded as normative statements, possessors of a truth-value. To regard them thus is a necessary condition for solving an outstanding problem, namely, Why is a method effective? Or, why is one method more effective than another? By contrast, it is shown that alternative views that espouse the false dichotomy of regarding methods as either statements of conventions or as empirical statements are inadequate for various reasons. For instance, they leave the effectiveness of a method quite inexplicable and mysterious; or they leave no room for progress in method; or they reduce methods to mere historical or sociological reports.

In the next chapter, on Lakatos's theory of method, a distinction is delineated between the logical problem of determining under what conditions one method is better than another, and the epistemological problem of determining under what conditions we can know a method to be better than another. A partial solution to the logical problem is offered which should be acceptable to anyone who regards a method's function as one of capturing the basic preanalytic judgments about scientific theories or decisions in the history of science. In light of the solution to the logical problem, I defend Lakatos against his critics who charge that his theory of method evaluation leads to the following *reductio ad absurdum*: the best method is one that shows every decision in the history of science to be rational—no matter how irrational some are—when viewed under the light of the method in question. Lakatos's position is also defended against critics who argue that his general strategy is unfair and a failure inasmuch as it fails not only to correctly reconstruct the history of methodology but also provides a distorted viewfinder from which to see the relationship between methodology and the history of science. It is also deemed unfair for precluding all-purpose empirical sciences from competing with normative methods. In turn, several criticisms are made of Lakatos's position but none more central than the following: his solution to the problem of arbitration between competing methods, in which he essentially appeals to the normative history of science, is demonstrated to lead to an inescapable and unacceptable paradox.

Chapter 4 on Laudan's theory of method commences by making a logical comparison between Popper's method and Laudan's method—a comparison intended to cast the latter under a cloud and, importantly, to show how methods can be evaluated *without* invoking the history of science. It then advances a theory of how to explain rational decisions in the history of science by relying on a paradigmatic example in which such a decision is made. It is argued that individual rationality requires a consistent adherence to the norms of a plausible method, and that only if a scientist is rational can particular decisions of accepting or rejecting a theory be explained. It next forecasts and forestalls possible objections to that theory. Against the background of the constructive proposal, it is demonstrated that any attempt to use a *current* model of rationality to explain rational decisions of others *in the past* will lead to strange and untoward consequences. If in principle current methods ought not to be invoked to explain or account for these past episodes, or Laudan's so-called preanalytic intuitions, then evidence cannot be adduced in favor of or against contemporary methods by resorting to the history of science. The whole view is encapsulated in the principle of parity. This sequence of arguments carries further my crusade against using the history of science as an arbitrator between methods. At the end, a theory is developed to show that any account of the growth of knowledge and rationality must feature the triple traditions of theories, methods, and theories of method.

The reader arrives at chapter 5 already knowing substantial parts of the alternative theory of method brought to completion here. Other significant parts of the theory, developed in this chapter, are several. To begin with, methods should not only propose ways of appraising theories but they should also give, and be seen as giving, heuristic advice, especially if one wants to assist in and explain the growth and development of scientific knowledge. The thesis is given credibility by portraying the discomforting issues that sprout when the thesis is denied. Furthermore, it is argued that whatever makes it legitimate to give heuristic advice to the historians of science, persuading them to use one method as a historiographical model rather than another, makes it legitimate to give heuristic advice to the scientists, in view of the similarity of their respective tasks.

In evaluating a method, one should not look to the past and see how well that method conforms to what was scientific or rational. One should rather see how effective the method is when it is put into practice, when it is *experimented* with, even when its norms conflict with what we hold to be rational in the history of science. Such a view allows a method more daring departures than the usual historically oriented theory of method evaluation would permit. The rationale for experimenting with a method rests on the claim that the heuristic advice of a method, though a normative statement, is either true or false; and the more false it is, the more likely it is to lead to dead-ends and to the pursuit of unpromising and unfruitful theories. The section ends on a highly conjectural and speculative note. Assume, it says, that contemporary methods of evaluating scientific theories had been espoused by scientists in the past, what realistically possible history of science would have ensued? The happier the history, the better the method.

Our forms of reasoning evolve, and they often conflict with forms others favor. To understand that conflict and slow change, and to find a fair way of settling conflicts, I invoke the technique of reflective equilibrium. A certain usage of that technique, which would teach us that at bottom such conflicts in reasoning are mere social and political disputes and so should be resolved accordingly, is given the treatment it deserves. The appropriate usage of that technique shows, besides much else, that a methodologist need be concerned only with contemporary science and scientists; it also enables me to state precisely the difference between the theory of method I propose and the theories I oppose.

Finally, if one is asked, What are the chief concerns of a methodologist? it would be correct to reply, "Four: his concern is to evaluate a theory at a given time; to evaluate a theory over an interval of time; to evaluate the rationality of a decision of accepting or rejecting a theory at a given time; and to evaluate the rationality of a scientist." My task is to add one more problem to the classical list of issues and to provide a tentative solution. The problem is, Under what conditions is a scientific society rational? Just as John Rawls draws a distinction between principles that govern individual justice and the principles that govern just institutions, so I draw a distinction between principles that govern individual rationality and the principles that govern group rationality.

Again, just as Rawls claims that the primary subject of justice is the basic structure of society, so I suggest that the primary subject of rationality in science ought to be the basic structure or form or organization of the scientific community whose members are engaged in the pursuit of common (partially overlapping?) goals, such as the search for truth. No method should be acceptable if it fails to propose a solution to the problem of group rationality.

When the classical view is reread *as if* it addressed itself to the problem of group rationality, one discovers serious faults in it. My provisional answer to the problem is that a scientific society, composed of a variety of subgroups engaged in a common enterprise of reaching shared goals, is rational if, and only if, the competing subgroups are pursuing the scientific tasks under the rubric of multiple methods, and not just multiple theories (indeed, the latter turns out to be an unintended consequence of the former). Two case studies drawn from the history of optics and medicine, respectively, serve as illustrations of that view. I explain how a scientific group, envisaged in such a view, will remain stable and why it has a better chance of making more rapid scientific progress than a group envisaged on the classical view.

It is a measure of our grim neglect of the issue of what makes a scientific society rational that, while we have a host of concepts and categories—ad hoc, corroborated, empirically progressive problem-shift, monster-barring, disconfirmed, effective problem-solver, nearer-to-the-truth, and so on—with which to describe and evaluate our scientific theories, we do not have a single concept to discuss the rationality of a group. This book ends on the theme of group rationality, to which my next work will be devoted; I hope. Whatever deters me by the magnitude of the task is only slightly overmatched by the promise of not inconsiderable philosophical gain by exploring this hitherto unknown and unplotted philosophical territory.

Acknowledgments

Too many philosophers have contributed to this book to make it, so one might think, nearly fault-free and conclusive. It would be a bit innocent to assume that such is the nature of a philosophical tract that teases and confronts some of the most cherished, and deeply embedded, theses of nearly every major philosopher of science working in the field of methodology since 1959. Therefore, I follow the wise tradition of apportioning credit and blame unevenly: to Gerd Buchdahl, Brian Ellis, Paul Feyerabend, Ian Hacking, Larry Laudan, Grover Maxwell, David Miller, and John Watkins goes the credit, and my gratitude, for what is correct and useful; I take the blame for what is not.

John Watkins, who read sympathetically the penultimate draft of the manuscript in its entirety, was quite critical of the earliest version of chapter 1; the latest version was fashioned by keeping in mind his general concerns. He especially opposed the idea in the last chapter that methods should give heuristic advice. Sir Karl Popper was very generous in endorsing my defense of his views as well as the arguments of section I of chapter 4; understandably, he did not endorse the arguments of chapter 2.

To Paul Feyerabend and the late Grover Maxwell I owe thanks for comments and encouragements on the chapter on Lakatos. At least in the case of Feyerabend, this should not be construed as constituting agreement; indeed, Feyerabend thinks that there is less to the paradox presented here than meets the eye, but he spared me the detailed arguments.

Ian Hacking's gentle but uncompromising criticism of an earlier draft of chapter 4, which was discussed in his seminar in 1979 at Stanford University, led to the version that is before the reader. The first section of that chapter also greatly profited from the careful and extensive written comments of David Miller.

Brian Ellis was the first to encourage me in 1978 on the topic of group rationality, the final part of chapter 5. He suggested then that the topic would be better served if I found some examples from the history of science to illustrate my arguments, something I was unable to do until a few years later. Gerd Buchdahl's editorial gifts were brought to bear on the penultimate version of that topic, as well as on some others, and they set the tone of what I have subsequently written. Larry Laudan urged, and rightly, that I recast the original section on heuristic advice and, far more importantly, that I cast a wider net.

These were the specific suggestions and recommendations I received, but then there were papers and preprints, letters and talks, and gut reactions and gestures, which molded my thinking in ways, I am sure, I am the last to appreciate.

Thanks are owed to the National Endowment for the Humanities for a summer 1979 fellowship that gave me an opportunity to be a member of Ian Hacking's seminar on "The Importance of History to Philosophy of Science." That fellowship enabled me to spend one of the happiest periods of my academic life at Stanford University; chapter 4 is a child of that summer. To Louisiana State University I owe thanks for a summer research award in 1978 and also for sundry partial travel grants which made it possible to write and present portions of the book, in its various stages of development, at several meetings. Thus, section I of chapter 4 was presented at the American Philosophical Association (Pacific Division) meeting in Portland, Oregon, in March 1981; and the final section of the book on group rationality was read that same year in December as an invited paper to the American Philosophical Association (Eastern Division) meeting held in Philadelphia, Pennsylvania. A much earlier version of that paper was read at the Australasian Association for Philosophy meeting held in Canberra in August 1978. Earlier in the same month a crude version of the theory of how to explain rational decisions in the history of science (ancestor of chapter 4, sec. III) was read at the meeting of the Australasian Association for History and Philosophy of Science held in Sydney.

The penultimate draft was completed in late August 1980. What followed were dark and treacherous months. I did no work on the book until early December 1981. If nothing else, when I returned to work on the book fifteen months later, I had gained a much-needed distance and perspective on the issues and problems on which I had been engaged for a long time. During these incredible months I was a recipient of much kindness, encouragement, and goodwill. For all these I am very grateful. What I owe Ian Hacking I cannot repay. Between mid-December 1981 and mid-June 1982, I worked incessantly and intensively on the manuscript, revising large poritons of it, adding new material, and finally completing it.

This is the time to acknowledge my other debts: to Warren Eyster, friend and novelist, I owe sage literary advice; to John Baker for things whereof one cannot speak; to my parents for teaching me by example of what I ought to be to my children, Casim and Ashifa; and to *them* I owe thanks for providing me with excuses for delaying this project. When Dylan Thomas dedicated his *Collected Poems 1943–1952* to his wife, Caitlin, he wrote in the *Note*: "These poems, with all their crudities, doubts and confusions, are written for the love of Man and in praise of God, and I'd be a damn' fool if they weren't." My book is humbler. Moreover, the doubts are obvious; the crudities and confusions are, I trust, less so, and fewer. But it, too, is dedicated to someone's wife—mine—for I would be a damn fool if it wasn't.

Finally—but how shall I thank a country?

Husain Sarkar

Baton Rouge, Louisiana
June 13, 1982

1
A Framework for Methods

What is a theory of method?

A theory is about the world; a method is about theories; and, a theory of method is about methods.

In brief: we propose a theory to describe and explain the world or parts and processes in it. We do so partly to provide a basis for practical actions so that their order is least in conflict with the causal order of the world. In other words, a theory functions as a worldpart selector or correlator of worldparts or worldprocesses: in its light we pick one worldpart over another, or one worldprocess over another, and we correlate one worldpart or worldprocess with another part or process rather than with a third. A true selector or correlator will prevent our stumbling. An approximately true selector or correlator will prevent our stumbling more frequently than a selector that is less true. In part we propose theories simply out of curiosity, in the hope of deepening our understanding of what is intrinsically important to understand, as if understanding per se did something for us.[1] We then propose a method to serve as a theory selector; to help us reject ones that might prove fatal to our goals and aims, and to find or select ones that will further those ends. Our methods, of course, are as conjectural about evaluating a theory as are our theories about the world's causal order. As a consequence, we next propose a theory of method to solve at least one problem about methods.

The problem is utterly important. *What criteria should be proposed to enable us to judge between rival methods?* In the past, the focus of philosophical attention has been on theories, and not on methods. We have asked, What is the nature of a scientific theory, and how is it distinguishable from a pseudoscientific theory? What is the structure of a scientific theory? What is the nature of explanation, statistical and otherwise? What distinguishes a lawlike statement of a theory from an accidental generalization? What is the empirical content of a scientific theory? Which terms of a theory are observational and which are not? Can the language in which observation statements are couched be free of context and conjectures? If not, what consequences will it have on our favored notions of progress, verisimilitude, and rationality concerning theory choice? Under what conditions is a theory (phenomenological thermodynamics, Newtonian mechanics) correctly reduced to, derivable from, or regarded as a limiting case of, another theory (statistical mechanics, special theory of relativity)? What is the role of experimental design? When is a theory ad hoc? When is a theory confirmed or corroborated? When is one theory better than another, logically and epistemically? What are the conditions under which a theory is acceptable? Allied closely with the metaphysical issues of realism and antirealism is the following query: How does a scientific theory relate to the world, on the one hand, and to theory users, on the other? To be sure, these questions do not offer their own separate and sealed-off domains of inquiry but rather foretell that their domains overlap. What is more to the point, they all focus on scientific theories, and not on methods.

In order to deal with the foregoing philosophical problems and a host of other, similar ones, Paul Feyerabend, Bas C. van Fraassen, Clark Glymour, Thomas Kuhn, Imre Lakatos, Larry Laudan, Karl Popper, Hilary Putnam, and others proposed various methods or methodologies. As their sharply conflicting methods solved the problems differently (for instance, compare the erstwhile realist method of Putnam with the antirealist method of van Fraassen; or, the methods of Feyerabend and Kuhn, on the one hand, with the method of Popper, on the other), attention was turned—at last—to the problem of evaluating methods, and philosophers began to search for an interesting and complex solution. This book is about that problem.

Much turns on the solution to the problem. To begin with, the solution would enable us to judge which of the competing methods is the best one. By providing norms for individual scientists and scientific groups to subscribe to, and by guiding their scientific activity, the best method would tell us a great deal, though by no means all, about individual and group rationality.

Some have claimed that such a method would provide the best model of historiography and so should be a matter of considerable importance to historians. A historian of science qua historian works, implicitly or explicitly, with some methodological point of view that enables him to decide what problems, theories, and decisions or actions to consider. Without such a view he could not, in principle, proceed with his work. A historian interested in presenting the tale of the rise and fall of the theory of spontaneous generation in the seventeenth and eighteenth centuries will have to decide whether the Paracelsian theory, which used its postulate of 'Mysterium Magnum' to explain why organisms were spontaneously generated, was pseudoscientific, scientific, or metaphysical; whether the Cartesians on the Continent were rational in rejecting Descartes's mechanical hypothesis which claimed that spontaneous generation occurred when heat acting on putrified matter agitated the particles to form an organic being; whether the recent anatomical and microscopic findings ought to have undermined the belief in spontaneous generation; and, whether the experiments of Spallanzani in 1765 should have been regarded as clear and crucial tests of the theory in the version of Needham and Buffon.[2] These are decisions a historian of science has to make on methodological grounds, decisions that cannot be simply read off the historical facts. Thus, a historian of science is well advised to use the best method as his historiographical model. This is essentially the view of Joseph Agassi[3] and Imre Lakatos.[4]

Others have claimed that a discipline such as the sociology of knowledge or cognitive sociology is parasitical on the best method or model of rationality in the following way. A best model of rationality will distinguish between those beliefs of an agent that are rational and those that are not. The rational beliefs can be clearly and satisfactorily explained on the model, and what cannot be so explained is then turned over to the cognitive sociologist. The latter will then try to explain why the agent held those irrational beliefs, in terms of the social, psychological, economic, and institutional circumstances in which the agent found himself. A sociologist of knowledge trying to understand why, in England in the late eighteenth and early nineteenth centuries, mining and the science of geology went their separate ways when intercourse between them would have resulted in enormous mutual benefit, may find that miners opposed innovation, pursued their rule-of-thumb practice, and accepted, uninformed by a theory, crude generalizations based on practice, such as that coal is seldom found under the mountains of solid limestone or sandstone, or that it is a good sign to meet with dry earth of particular colors. On such a slender basis, advice on the location, nature, interruptions, and complexities of minerals and metals was given. The sociologist would explain the irrational beliefs and the irrational organization of the group as a lack of genuine interest in geological science on the part of the elite members of the Geological Society of London (founded in 1807); the failure of the mining industry to generate an extensive class of technologists, educated and trained surveyors, assayers, prospectors, and managers (unlike in Germany); the attitude of the British laissez-faire system which prevented a national mines' survey, if not a full mines' commission; and, finally the paucity of formal and technical education, and books.[5] Thus, the job of the sociologist of knowledge is defined by the best method or model of rationality. This is essentially the view of Larry Laudan[6] and Imre Lakatos.[7]

Most, if not all, philosophers of science agree on this much as an indispensable part of the solution to the problem we are considering: a method should be judged in the light of the history of science. Failing to conform to the rational episodes in the history of science is considered a serious inadequacy in a method, and squaring up with such episodes is regarded as a necessary condition for the acceptance of a method. Some may even argue that it is also a sufficient condition.

When moral philosophers are engaged in the task of constructing an ethical theory, they take, as the dictates of their intuitions, certain situations and actions to be just, moral, obligatory, and so on. Their task is to emerge with an ethical theory that will show that their preanalytic, intuitive judgments concerning the morality of those situations and actions are correct. The intuitive judgments are, of course, neither inviolable nor infallible; a powerful moral theory that accounts for a wide array of our moral judgments can show why certain such judgments, which we hitherto took to be correct, are incorrect after all. Philosophers of science are engaged, or claim to be engaged, in a parallel task. They must come up with a method that will account for the preanalytic judgments concerning the rationality of accepting or rejecting scientific theories. These judgments may be as follows: it was irrational to accept Ptolemy's theory after 1750; it was rational to accept Darwin's theory of evolution after 1880; it was irrational to accept the theory of continental drift in 1925; it was irrational not to accept the double-helix structure of

DNA after 1965; it was rational to accept the special theory of relativity after 1925; and so on. To be sure, a powerful method that accounted for a wide variety of such preanalytic judgments concerning rationality may show the inadequacy of some other preanalytic judgments that we hitherto took to be correct. Preanalytic judgments, in this case as in the case of ethical theory, are not free from fault and error. Here, as there, a balance has to be found, or restored, between the claims of a *current* method and our preanalytic judgments of the rationality of decisions of the *past*, decisions concerning the acceptance or rejection of theories. This is the view that dominates and has dominated the discussion and debates in methodology. I shall dub it, in light of its invocation of the history of science, the *backward-looking view*. To show that this view is erroneous and too narrow for solving other methodological problems is my most important and central concern.[8]

Prima facie, the backward-looking view is implausible. No plans of military strategies proposed today are rejected on the grounds that they do not conform or square up with the military decisions (even the best ones) of the sixteenth or seventeenth century. The problems and needs are vastly different, perhaps more complex, and call for strategies that may have little connection, if any, with the earlier strategies. Likewise, it is not obvious why the methods we adopt today must in some sense conform or square up with the methods (even the best ones) of Buridan or Descartes. Although our understanding of the history of science, the social structure of science, and the nature of science and rational action is profoundly improved as a result of the work of contemporary methodologists, the influence is not nearly as direct as is claimed by those who hold that social sciences are parasitical on the best method. Lending insight is one thing; giving an explanation of an agent's act—not in terms of the model of rationality *he* held but rather in terms of the best model of rationality *we* hold—is quite another. It is important to understand why between 1850 and 1860 the cell theory of Schleiden and Schwann governed the researches of scientists in microscopic anatomy; or, why Aristotle's theory of motion came increasingly to be doubted among physicists in the Middle Ages. However, it is also indispensable to understand the situations and decisions of these scientists and physicists in light of their methods, their reasons, and their fundamental scientific goals and aims, and not by ours.

Finally, I shall also suggest that our methods ought to be proposed in the same experimental spirit as informs our best scientific work and ought to be judged and evaluated in accordance with their efficacy in practice. I shall call this the *forward-looking view*. What I mean is simple: given, for instance, that we wish our theories to achieve the goal of truthlikeness, we should use a method in our practice that claims to lead us to that goal more effectively than any other method; we should make decisions of acceptance, rejection, and modification of theories in accordance with its claims and norms. We can then measure the performance of a method over a reasonable interval of time. The success of our practice would then say more about the efficacy of that method, compared with its rivals, than would any so-called success at squaring up with the rational segments of the history of science. If it fails us in practice, success elsewhere would count for little, if at all. What is more, such a view of evaluating methods and of discovering and deciding on the best method permits more radical departures for a method than is allowed on the alternative view.

To be sure, providing criteria for determining the best method is not the only problem facing a theory of method. Indeed, the problems in this domain, as elsewhere, are interlaced, and in order to solve the central problem, a theory of method must deal with others, such as, What is the structure of a method? What is the nature of a methodological statement? Ought a method to yield heuristic advice? How is the success, or relative success, of a method to be explained? What is the relationship between goals and methods? How do theories, decisions, and methods relate? How, exactly, does a method serve as a historiographical model? What, precisely, is the matching relationship between a method and the history of science that enables the latter to arbitrate over a methodological dispute? What is the tie between methods and the social sciences? These are the problems, among others, that will share the limelight; extant solutions will be examined and new ones proposed, in the hope that rubbing competing solutions together will lighten up the dark spots in this problem area.

A minimally interesting theory of method must now also urge us to focus attention on the problem of group rationality. To be acceptable, a method will have to seriously consider and answer an array of such questions as, When is one scientific group, composed of various subgroups (in short, the structure of a scientific society), rational? How is rationality to be understood in this context since the usual notion of rationality is reserved for characterizing individual scientists and their decisions to accept or reject theories? What bearing does the rational structure of a scientific society have on the rationality of individuals in that society? (The answer to the converse question, What bearing do rational individuals have on the rationality of the structure of a scientific society?, seems self-evident but, I shall argue, it is not.) What impact does that structure have on the ways in which theories are evaluated, accepted, and pursued? Or, on the ways in which fundamental goals and aims are molded and modified? How is the structure of a scientific society or scientific group to be understood for present purposes? What gives a subgroup in a scientific society its identity? What differences among subgroups will ensure that the scientific society is composed of subgroups of depth and distinction rather than of subgroups that are only trivial variants of one another? Why should there be distinct subgroups at all, why not one single subgroup that coincides with the group? Why is such a group not rational? Or is it? What are the unintended consequences for the growth of scientific knowledge when differing, dynamic subgroups of a scientific society compete with or complement one another? If we are to decide which method is the best one, these questions too must now be answered, and are answered, if only provisionally and as a start.

Discussion between methodologists is often at cross purposes, as when it centers around how well or how badly they have solved the problems or succeeded in reaching aims and goals allegedly shared, when in fact they have neither many aims nor many problems in common. Some attack methods as pandering to mob psychology (so says Lakatos about Kuhn),[9] some maintain that their opponents have missed the main point of scientific activity (so says Kuhn about Popper),[10] some charge that the empirical facts that methods bring forward in support of their methodological claims are irrelevant (so says Popper about Kuhn),[11] some argue that the problem of demarcation others pursue is a pseudoproblem (so says Laudan about Popper),[12] and, finally, some maintain that the whole enterprise of methodology rests on a mistake (so says Feyerabend).[13]

In view of these crossing aims, it is important to have a clear picture of the main connecting lines. I have thus provided a framework for methods to show how the various disparate parts of a method are linked. This in itself would not solve a single methodological problem, but it will achieve its main purpose: to bring into sharp relief the roots of disagreement among rival methods; and to reach surprising but preliminary and promising conclusions on which to build later. Following this, I shall propose two ways of picturing the relationship between methods and the social sciences.

I. A FRAMEWORK FOR METHODS

A method has three distinct components. I shall christen these the *objective component*, the *normative component*, and the *illustrative component*. The objective component of a method defines core concepts and solves logical problems; the normative component yields advice about accepting or rejecting theories and defines rational decisions; and last, the illustrative component draws on the history of science to illustrate the claims and concepts of the method.

As a first approximation, an objective component of a method deals with the following kinds of problems: What is it for a theory to be scientific? What is the empirical content of a theory? Under what conditions is the empirical content of T greater than, less than, or equal to, T'? Under what conditions is T nearer to the truth than T'? Under what conditions can a theory be said to have progressed over an earlier theory? An objective component defines a concept of a method, and the definition often serves as a solution to some such aforementioned problems. In Popper's work, for instance, testability or falsifiability is a central concept in the definition of science: a theory is scientific if, and only if, it is testable or falsifiable. The definition in turn answers the question, or solves the problem, What makes a theory scientific? I leave aside for now the question, How can a mere definition solve a problem?

Among the key concepts defined in various methods are the following: negative heuristics, positive heuristics, mono-theoretical model, ad hoc, progressive problem-shift, degenerating problem-shift, pluralistic model, corroboration, concept-stretching expansion, monster-barring, monster-adjustment, exception-barring, research program, paradigm, normal science, disciplinary-matrix, research tradition, and problem-solving effectiveness. Some of these concepts are ill defined or inadequately explained, whereas others are tagged with crisp definitions. For instance, no unambiguous single definition of *paradigm* or *normal science* can be culled from Kuhn's work, the centrality of these concepts in his method notwithstanding. In Popper's work, by contrast, the concept of the empirical content of a theory, T, is clearly defined as the class of its potential falsifiers, and a *potential falsifier* in its turn is defined as a basic statement which contradicts T. In some methods the definitions of concepts are closely linked as in a system; in others they hang loose.[14] One need hardly add that the more clearly the connections between components in a method are expressed—particularly if they form a deductive system—the easier it is to see how criticisms of one definition of a concept are transmitted to definitions of other concepts. The more distant the connections, the more difficult the task of criticizing and evaluating a method.

The objective components of a method are exhaustively divided into two parts: the *logical part* and the *conventional part*, respectively. The logical part deals with problems, such as the old and new problems of induction, the paradox of confirmation, the issue of contrafactual conditionals, the problem of verisimilitude, and the problems of incommensurability and content-comparison. Consider the problem of verisimilitude: when is one theory nearer to the truth than another theory? The problem does not call for a simple settling convention; what is at stake is a matter of logical fact. Popper's conjectured solution to the problem was that T is nearer to the truth, or has a greater degree of verisimilitude, than T' if, and only if, the truth content of T is greater than the truth content of T' and the falsity content of T is equal to, or less than, the falsity content of T'; or, the truth content of T is equal to the truth content of T' and the falsity content of T is less than the falsity content of T'. Except where T is true and T' is a consequence of T, this solution is false, for two false theories cannot be compared with respect to their verisimilitude.[15] In short, the logical part of a method's objective component contains statements that *do* have a truth-value.

The conventional part deals with problems the answers to which can be neither true nor false. To explain why the conventional part contains statements that presumably have no truth-value, consider Lakatos's definition—let us call it *d*—of a series of theories in an empirically progressive problem-shift. A series of theories is in an empirically progressive problem-shift if, and only if, (1) each subsequent theory contains the unrefuted content of an earlier theory and is itself the result of adding an auxiliary hypothesis to the previous theory in order to accommodate an anomaly; (2) some novel consequences are theoretically derived from any member of the series that could not have been derived from an earlier member; and (3) at least some of these novel consequences have been empirically tested and found to be corroborated.[16] Is *d* true? The question clearly seems odd. Of course, it is not at all odd and perhaps it is very important to ask if any specific series of theories in the history of science satisfies that property. An answer to that question must be a bearer of a truth-value.

What properties are significant, and why? To appreciate the thrust of the question, consider the following rather quaint definition: A theory T is α if, and only if, there are two other theories, T' and T^*, such that T explains precisely two facts more than does T' and precisely three facts more than does T^*. Now, granting that it is a matter of fact whether or not any theory in the history of science satisfies property α, why should such a strange definition hold our interest? Why is it methodologically important? Alternatively and more generally, what is the significance of any member, singly or collectively, of the conventional part of any method? The importance of this question cannot be fully gauged until we have understood the normative components of a method and have introduced a problem.

Among the most significant parts of a method are its normative components. The normative components of a method are exhaustively divided into two parts, too: the *acceptability part* and the *evaluative part*. The acceptability part of a method lays down the conditions under which theories classified in one way or another by the method's conventional part can be accepted. Problems relating to acceptance or rejection of theories are crucial for a method to solve. There are three clear and important senses of acceptance that should be recognized and classified. First, we may accept a theory in the sense that it is the best of all the contemporaneous and competing theories. For example, in 1980 we may accept the big-bang theory over others such as the steady-state theory; in 1620 we may have accepted the Galilean theory of motion and its sun-centered view of the universe over its rivals. Or, second, we may accept a theory in the sense that it is the best theory on which to rely for practical purposes or actions such as building dams, satellites, and bridges. Finally, and importantly, we may accept a theory in the sense that it is the one that promises to yield very interesting results if further theoretical and experimental research is done from its vantage point, such as further investigation into general theory of relativity, cultural materialism, or sociobiology. Three senses of rejection follow as a corollary.

The acceptability part of a method gives advice, heuristic or otherwise, to the scientists. As examples consider the following: "Pursue or accept for practical action the theory that has the highest degree of corroboration," where *degree of corroboration* has been defined by the conventional part of the objective component of Popper's method. Or, "Do not accept a theory as the best of all contemporaneous and competing theories if it is in a degenerating problem-shift," where *degenerating problem-shift* has been defined by the conventional part of Lakatos's method. If the recent conjectures about certain species of early dinosaurs—namely, that they had mammalian characteristics—are marked by a low degree of corroboration, Popper may advocate rejecting these conjectures for further theoretical development and experimental tests. Not all methods give advice on all three senses of acceptance. While Lakatos's method gives advice on what to regard or accept as the best theory, it explicitly denies giving heuristic advice concerning the theory to accept for further theoretical and experimental research.[17]

The evaluative part of a method defines rational action. Since the rationality of actions is closely connected to the acceptance or rejection of theories, it follows that an act is rational, according to a method, if, and only if, it is carried out in accordance with the injunction laid down in the acceptability part. Corresponding to the three senses of acceptance or rejection of theories we have three senses of rationality. In Popper's method, a decision is rational if a non-ad hoc theory is accepted; it is considered irrational otherwise. If the neutrino hypothesis, at the time when it was suggested, was ad hoc, then the scientists who accepted the hypothesis at that time, its after-success notwithstanding, were acting irrationally. On the Lakatosian method they were not. Lakatos's method says that an ad hoc theory can be accepted if it is tacked onto a highly successful research program. On this view, a scientist who accepted the neutrino hypothesis even during the period in which it did not yield any testable result was still acting rationally.

We can now return to the questions, What properties referred to in the conventional part of a method are important, and why? We see that they are important solely because they aid in formulating clearly the kind of advice to be given about acceptance or rejection of theories. On the face of it, α does not seem to be a significant property for giving advice in the way in which *empirically progressive problem-shift* appears to be. We can now say that the significance of these properties or concepts is *determined by the efficacy of the advice* they help to formulate. Two things should now be clear. First, the evaluation or appraisal of the conventional part cannot be made independently of the way in which it appears in the advice-giving acceptability part of the method. Second, prima facie, answers to problems such as which theory should be accepted or rejected for further theoretical research do not call for mere stipulations. Unlike the conventional part, but like the logical part of a method, normative components have a truth-value. The logical part can be evaluated in its own right (since the answers it proposes to logical problems are either true or false). That part, however, also enters significantly into the acceptability part. For instance, the notion of verisimilitude can and does play a central role in giving advice about accepting a theory in the first sense.

Linked to the problem of determining significant properties is another problem I wish to propose. It is, I think, a fascinating problem, one that should concern not only methodologists but metaphysicians (realists and antirealists alike) as well.

It is common realist talk that a language-speaker can construct a symbolic representation—briefly, a theory—of his environment because he causally interacts with it. Unless our theories about the world are in significant parts true or approximately true, our scientific, and especially our linguistic success, cannot be explained. Hilary Putnam states:

> That science succeeds in making many true predictions, devising better ways of controlling nature, etc., is an undoubted empirical fact. If realism is an *explanation* of this fact, realism must itself be an over-arching scientific *hypothesis*. And realists have often embraced this idea, and proclaimed that realism is an empirical hypothesis.[18]

If we trace the history of physics from Kepler to Galileo to Newton to Einstein, we are struck by the overwhelming possibility of convergence in scientific knowledge. The convergence seems to occur in the following way: A later theory (Einstein's) implies, with due modification, the approximate truth of the theoretical laws of an earlier theory (Newton's), and it does so by the difficult route of preserving the mechanisms of that earlier theory.

To give substance to the idea of realism as an empirical hypothesis by forging a connection between the explanation of the success of knowledge and the theory of truth, as well as to make sense of the idea of convergence of scientific knowledge, Putnam, following Richard Boyd, has claimed that (*a*) the theoretical terms of our mature scientific theories typically *refer*, and (*b*) the laws of such theories are typically approximately *true*.[19] He has argued that scientists' actions and decisions can be partly explained by their true beliefs in (*a*) and (*b*), and partly by their effective strategy, namely, to propose mechanisms from which the approximate truth of earlier theories will follow. Putnam claims that this shows that 'truth' and 'reference' have a causal-explanatory role and that, as he says, (*a*) and (*b*) "are premises in an *explanation* of the behaviour of scientists and the success of science."[20]

In what follows, I am not interested in disputing that 'truth' and 'reference' play the role that Putnam accords them;[21] nor am I interested in arguing that convergence in fact does not take place often enough to be worthy of serious consideration;[22] nor in arguing that Putnam's way of preserving reference of theoretical terms across successive theories is implausible.[23] Rather I wish to argue that (*a*) and (*b*) are simply not *sufficient* to explain the success of science. That science is successful is a far more plausible, uncontroversial, and weaker hypothesis than the claim that science is both successful and converges. I wish to argue that the realist's explanation of even the weaker hypothesis is quite inadequate because it omits an important ingredient (something an antirealist would have to take into account, too).

What is that ingredient? Boyd himself points out that the scientists' adoption of the above-mentioned strategy was also important inasmuch as it led to significant discoveries; and he conjectures that the strategy is effective (true?) because (*a*) and (*b*) are true. Strategies, however, are nothing but the normative components of a method the scientists espouse; and there are other norms that also guide scientific practice, activity, and research, which are varied and wide-ranging and at least as deep and significant as the single strategy or norm that Boyd suggests. The methods that led the historical stage from Kepler to Galileo, and then from Galileo to Newton, and so on, did not have merely a single principle or norm (i.e., to preserve older mechanisms and yield as approximate truth the laws of earlier theories); there were other norms, too. Other methodological decisions were made in the light of which a budding theory was molded and marked; other considerations, metaphysical and otherwise, had to be taken into account in view of the current method. Between two distinct, contemporaneous or successive, scientific societies or groups, and often in a single society,[24] the methods espoused by scientists were far from the same. Later methods were not merely modified versions of earlier ones but were often radically different. It is these complex methodological considerations and conjectures that have provided the passage from one major scientific theory to the next.

So, part of our success in science has been due to our *methods*. From Bacon forward, the claim has been made that it is the espousing of the effective or true norms that make success in science possible. The normative components of a method give advice, intricate and complex perhaps, about accepting or rejecting scientific theories (or, indeed, what to count as science), and if the advice is sound, the scientist will be successful. If the advice is unsound, he will fail. The success of our scientific endeavors makes it imperative that we throw in a true or effective method, or an approximately true or effective method, in the explanatory package. But it is not at all obvious that terms in the normative component of a method typically refer, as do terms such as *electron*, *photon*, and *gene*. If they do refer, what terms of a method refer and to what do they refer? If they do not—and this is the problem I wish to introduce—*how shall we account for the effectiveness or truth of our methods used in science?* To put it differently, the success of our theory is evidence that it matches the world; the problem is to make sense of the matching relation. The frequent success of our decisions in accepting or rejecting (in various senses) a theory is our evidence that the method yielding such decisions is effective or true; the problem is to make sense of its effectiveness or truth (and hence how it matches to what we know not).[25]

This also closes the link with the problem of determining significant properties referred to in the conventional part of a method. Science is partly successful because we make right decisions; our decisions are based on the evaluative part of a method which in turn is based on the conventional part. In short, the success of science must at some place point, in part, to the significance of those properties defined in the conventional part of a method.

Finally, let us turn from the objective and normative components of a method to consider the illustrative component. This component consists of the historical examples used to illustrate or illuminate a methodological point. These examples may be drawn from the history of science or they may be fabricated, as they often are. Lakatos offers rather potted historical accounts of the careers of Prout's theory that all atoms are compounds of hydrogen atoms and of Bohr's early theory of atomic structure, to illustrate various key concepts, such as positive and negative heuristics, ad hoc, progressive problem-shift, and research program.

Laudan invokes Cartesian metaphysics and uniformitarianism in geology to illustrate his concept of a research tradition.

Interesting difficulties quickly arise when examples, fabricated or otherwise, are looked upon not merely as illustrations but as evidence. They become enormously significant when we turn to the task of evaluating methods. Thus, for an empirical or descriptive approach in method, such as Laudan's, distorted case studies or fabricated examples are evidence against that method. For a conventional approach in method such as Popper's, the function of examples can only be illustrative. For a quasi-empirical approach in method such as Lakatos's, historical examples need not always tell against the method; the method may sometimes tell against the history of science from which examples are drawn. Lakatos says, "In writing a historical case study, one should, I think, adopt the following procedure: (1) one gives a rational reconstruction; (2) one tries to compare this rational reconstruction with actual history and to criticize both one's rational reconstruction for lack of historicity and the actual history for lack of rationality."[26] Without knowing when the example at hand is being used merely for illustrative purposes and when it is being cited as evidence, it is difficult to state when a method is at fault for failing to be historically sound or when the history of science referred to by the example has failed to be rational. Whether as evidence or as illustration, the illustrative component, strictly speaking, is not an essential part of a method; thus, *a method can now be correctly and clearly defined by its two parts, namely, by its objective and normative components.*

Inevitably, we are led to conclude that a theory of method must carefully consider the four distinct parts of a method if it is to be useful, for the ways of evaluating one part of a method are significantly different from the ways of evaluating another part. Popperians need to show that all methodological problems focus on, or are reduced to, logical problems. This cannot be done. For instance, the problem of determining which theory should be accepted for further theoretical development and experimental testing (i.e., which theory holds greater promise) is not a straightforward problem in logic; nor is the problem of deciding which theory to accept for practical purposes. Popper argues that we ought to prefer the theory that is most severely tested, one with the highest degree of corroboration, for practical purposes, but he refrains from saying that such a theory is more reliable than a theory with the least degree of corroboration. Preferring one theory over another in such a context, however, is to conjecture that the theory espoused is more reliable than the rest. To say this, Popper might contest, is to show that one has failed to understand Hume's result; but, equally, not to provide a justification for espousing a theory in the practical context is to have failed to provide a proper theory of rationality.[27]

In contrast, Laudan needs to show that all the problems in methodology can be settled by using the history of science as arbitrator. This cannot be done, either. Adolf Grünbaum has discovered an interesting difficulty in Popper's method.[28] Popper has claimed that the content of a theory is central; if one theory succeeds another in the history of science, and the later theory entails as a logical consequence the earlier theory, we prefer the later theory partly because its empirical content is greater than that of the theory that went before. If we have two mutually incompatible or contradictory theories, however, such as Newton's and Einstein's, we can no longer justify preference for Einstein's theory by that route, for Einstein's theory cannot entail Newton's theory *simpliciter*. How then should the preference for Einstein's theory be explained? Popper claims that the question-answering capacity of Einstein's theory is greater than the question-answering capacity of Newton's theory, which is why the former should be accepted over the latter.[29] Grünbaum shows, however, that there are questions to which only Newton can provide answers; questions, moreover, that cannot even be formulated in Einstein's theory inasmuch as they make different presuppositions. The purpose here is not to detail this problem, nor to evaluate competing solutions,[30] but rather to provide a case in which no amount of citing of the history of science can solve or dissolve the problem raised by Grünbaum. (It is interesting to note that while Laudan concerns himself exclusively with epistemological problems in order to avoid troublesome logical problems, Popper avoids other problems, where the history of science *may* be used to judge the adequacy of the solutions in favor of the logical problems.)

Finally, some parts of a method are parasitically dependent on others: thus, the acceptability part of a method is dependent on the conventional part, while the evaluative part is dependent on the acceptability part. The framework should enable us to see clearly how the various parts of a method are linked, how criticisms of one part affect other parts, and why logic, or history of science, or the social sciences, cannot be used alone, to the exclusion of all else, to decide on methodological issues across the board.

II. METHODS AND THE SOCIAL SCIENCES

What is the relationship between methods and the social sciences? I wish to characterize two distinct views, both inspired by Robert Nozick.

The First View

"I have a theory," says Thomas Kuhn, "of how and why science works."[31] He then offers a method that he claims is, in the ultimate analysis, sociological.[32] To the extent that a nonprescriptive method is an explanatory model explaining the history of science, it is akin to social sciences such as psychology, sociology, political science, and economics, for portions of these sciences also aim to explain at least parts of the realm of science as do, for example, the sociology of knowledge and the psychology of learning and discovery.

On the first view, there are three distinct, mutually exclusive, and exhaustive types of explanations of the realm of science. The first type fully explains the scientific realm in terms of a nonscientific realm. If this type of explanation were possible, it would be the most important and fundamental. The second type views the scientific realm as emerging from a nonscientific realm but not as reducible to it. The third type of explanation grants science its own autonomous realm.[33]

Kuhn clearly was offering what he hoped was a fundamental explanation. A sociological theory of science is an explanation of this type, as it proposes sociological mechanisms or societal relations captured in laws by which the content of theories and the phenomena of a scientific tradition's emergence, sustenance, and decay, and the eventual birth of a new tradition can be wholly explained. The contents of myths and categories in primitive societies are often explained in this fashion. When a Burmese Kachin is asked what he is doing when killing a pig, he replies, "Giving to the *nats*." Leach informs us that *nats* are magnified, nonnatural men and that their world is populated by chiefs, aristocrats, commoners, and slaves. The task of the anthropologist is not to evaluate and explain the myth in terms of truth, explanatory power, empirical content, and such (or to explain it away as prelogical) but rather to see the myth as rooted in human behavior and organizations. As Leach puts it, "*Nats* of Kachin religious ideology are, in the last analysis, nothing more than ways of describing the formal relationships that exist between real persons and real groups in ordinary Kachin society."[34] The myth reflects the social structure, not the world.

Durkheim and Mauss maintain that the genesis of the categories in primitive societies, or of the change in these categories, is to be found in group structures and relations or in changes in those structures and relations. Individuals are more powerfully oriented toward groups than toward nature, and this orientation leaves its imprint when categories are formed in an attempt to understand nature. Consequently, to understand primitive forms of thought one should deal with the regular recurrence of social activities such as ceremonies, feasts, and rites, as well as the clan structure, and spatial configurations of group meetings. Some, taking this cue, suggest that the Chinese feudal structure and the rhythmic alternation of concentrated and dispersed group life serve as a basis for their conceptions of space and time.[35] Others have recently argued that even the content of mathematical theories should be explained sociologically.[36]

A fundamental explanation would not invoke the aid of the autonomous norms or principles of theory selection espoused by a scientist or a group of scientists. On the contrary, from the viewpoint of a fundamental explanation the espousing of such principles is a by-product of the sociological and psychological conditions that govern perceptions, motives, values, ideologies, and relations between individuals and groups. Perhaps the sociological and psychological factors can, in their turn, be explained biologically.

What of fundamental explanations that altogether bypass principles of selection? Are they preferable to the types of fundamental explanations that yield these principles as consequences? Ludwick Fleck, in commenting on Gottstein's history of syphilis from the time it errupted suddenly in 1495 and spread across the whole of Europe (the French mercenaries fighting in Italy being the chief carriers) to the twentieth century, marvels at the metamorphosis of the thought style, and ends with the conviction that there is no linear development of thought, just a change from one thought style to the next. He advises epistemologists "who regard their task exclusively as the treatment of the question of 'right' or 'wrong' knowledge" to take heed of this fact.[37] "The general structure of a thought collective," says Fleck with emphasis, "entails that the communication of thoughts within a collective, irrespective of content or logical justification, should lead for sociological reasons to the corroboration of the thought structure."[38] The acceptance of a theory, on this view, is ultimately explained in terms of sociological powers and pressures, *not* in terms of methodological principles. Darwin's theory of evolution was accepted in the final third of the last century because the social conditions in 1860 and after, unlike in 1840, were stable; Darwinians were extremely respectable members of the Victorian society; Darwin's associates controlled the major scientific journals and societies, like the Royal Society, the Geological and the Linnaean societies, and the Zoological and the Entomological societies.[39] In short, methodological principles are left as unexplained danglers; a theory would have been accepted without these principles so long as those social conditions and power structures in scientific communities prevailed.

A fundamental explanation of a different sort may not bypass principles of selection but rather may explain how and why they came to be espoused. I present my argument by analogy. At one time, the major problem for sociobiologists was to explain how a moral principle—in particular, the altruistic principle—came to be espoused. It was assumed that altruistic behavior would promote another's genes at the expense of the genes of the organism performing the altruistic act. Such an organism thus would have been selected against in the fight for survival, so that one might expect that by now such a trait would have disappeared; but the trait prevails. Why? Sociobiologists, such as Robert L. Trivers, have argued that in fact the moral principle of altruism can be explained on the basis of evolutionary principles. In brief, the theory of kin selection shows that altruism assures the reproductive success of one's own genes, at the least, and the theory of reciprocal altruism shows that the altruistic organism is a direct beneficiary in the long run.

By analogy, one can argue that methodological principles can be explained on evolutionary principles as well. Certain methodological principles are accepted over others since they enable us to select theories that are true, and reject ones that are false. Such principles would enable us to let our theories perish in our stead.[40] Thus, evolutionary principles will yield the methodological principles scientists accept, and the methodological principles in turn will yield an explanation of why scientists accept certain theories in favor of others. This would raise some questions: How could the proliferation and a succession of methods in the history of science be explained on evolutionary principles, when the interval of time in which this has occurred is so small? Or, are the differences in methods mere surface differences to be explained away? Does such a fundamental explanation attempt to derive a methodological-ought from an evolutionary-is? Note: some may regard the present example of explaining, via evolutionary theory, how methodological principles came to be espoused as an explanation of the second type, namely, an explanation that shows how methodological principles emerged from or are emergent properties of, but are not reducible to, appropriate biological causes and conditions.

This first view, then, sets the direction for analyzing modern science and its growth as older myths and categories have been analyzed. Attempts have been made to explain in a fundamental way the rise of scientific institutions in seventeenth-century England (Merton); psychoanalytic theories have been offered to explain part of the work of scientists such as Newton (Manuel); and finally, Marxian theories of science have been offered to explain the rise and fall of scientific traditions (Bernal). I do not find this a viable approach for various reasons. My task here, however, is not to evaluate this relation between methods and the social sciences; it is to delineate a part of the first view.

A method intended as a fundamental explanation is simply one of the social sciences. A nonfundamental explanation, at least of the third type, and of the kind offered by Popper, grants science its own autonomous realm. It explains science in terms of logic, content of theories, verisimilitude, and such. Whether one theory is nearer to the truth than another or whether a theory explains more than another is a matter of logic and is quite independent of sociological matters. Of course, this kind of explanation offers no empirical laws; no lawlike regularities govern this domain. Thus, such a method has little to do with the social sciences; and it may even claim that its results and the results of logic are presupposed by the sociology of knowledge, and that the latter could not function without these results. Popper is right, I think, in condemning the social sciences for claiming to be the proper tools for explaining science or its growth. His point is strengthened in a deeper way by seeing precisely how, why, and where any purported explanation of the first two types fails.[41]

A purported explanation, fundamental or otherwise, may fail in various ways: it may be *fact-defective*, *law-defective*, or *process-defective*. It would be fact-defective (or law-defective) if the initial condition (or law) it invoked was false, although if the initial condition (or law) had been true the phenomena being explained would have come about. A purported explanation would be process-defective if the process *P* it suggests did not in fact bring about the result being explained, although if some other process had not done so, then *P* would have (with the usual qualifications to avert some obvious and some not-so-obvious objections).[42] I shall call a method *norm-defective* if it grants science its autonomous realm yet fails to explain things as they *in fact* happened in that realm, although if the norms had been true or had been espoused by the scientists in question, then the phenomena the method purported to explain would have come about.

Nozick claims quite rightly that even if fundamental explanations are defective, to the extent that they are plausible they seem to illuminate and deepen our understanding of the realm being explained. (Let us ignore intractable and as-yet-unanswered questions such as, What makes a false explanation plausible, and how does it illuminate?) Nozick goes on to say, however, "These things could not be said as strongly, if at all, about nonfundamental explanation."[43]

I disagree. A nonfundamental explanation can illuminate, too, and that possibility makes the problem of evaluating methods not only more difficult but also interesting and intriguing in surprising ways. Hitherto, the strategy among methodologists has simply been to show *not* that a given method is norm-defective but rather—a far weaker claim—that the method that grants science its autonomous realm fails to explain things as they *in fact* happened in that realm; no more. For instance, a common complaint of Feyerabend's is that very few scientists were Popperians and that very little can be explained in the history of science by Popper's method. Galileo used propaganda, psychological tricks, adopted ad hoc strategems, proceeded counterinductively, and ignored the rule of consistency.[44] True, let us grant. Popper might reply that at worst his method is norm-defective. If scientists had adopted his linchpin principle of falsification and what goes with it, instead of the methods they did use, then progress in the history of science would not only have occurred as it did but perhaps might have occurred at a faster rate. Popper could then cite, as indeed he does, the history of post-Ionian science when the critical tradition dissipated and science suffered. To argue successfully against Popper's method one has to show considerably more than that his method is norm-defective; one has to argue that even if the norms of Popper's method had been espoused, for instance, in the various periods when science stagnated, Popper's method could not have helped. This has hardly been done. Thus, prima facie, it is illuminating to be confronted with a plausible story of how science could have progressed successfully in the way suggested even though in fact it took a different path, just as it is enlightening to be offered a contrafactual, state-of-nature story in political theory that purports to explain how the state could have arisen, although in fact it arose in a different way.

Of course, it is important to see how such a contrafactual claim is made. What form will (must?) it take? What constraints must be imposed in order to render such an account plausible? Which of two norm-defective methods should be preferred, and why? When we have a defective fundamental explanation of the realm of science and a norm-defective nonfundamental explanation of it, which one should we prefer? How, in this case, is the truth-value of a contrafactual claim to be determined?[45] Why should a norm-defective method be condemned? If it should not be condemned, how can the history of science, as it occurred, be sufficient or necessary to evaluate methods?

The Second View

There is an obvious initial plausibility in the claim that methodological norms should not conflict with facts about human potentialities and weaknesses. Ascertaining what the human potential is and what our collective capacities are, is presumably the task of the social sciences, such as psychology and economics. So, if a method enjoined a scientist or a group of scientists to pursue science in a way that they could not possibly pursue, given their various limitations as expressed by the laws of the social sciences, we would be right in rejecting such a method.

I suggest that we regard the developed social sciences not as something integral to any particular method, nor as methods themselves, but rather as *side-constraints* on methods in general. This would be analogous to a situation in ethics.[46] On one view, a moral theory that aids in decisions when pursuing moral goals is minimally correct only if it does not violate individual rights in the pursuit. The rights of individuals function as side-constraints on those decisions. On such a view, maximizing goals is wrong even if we attempt and succeed in minimizing the violations of rights. We are urged, in short, not to be utilitarian with respect to rights, not to read rights into our goals. We are free to make any decision on the basis of a moral theory, once that theory satisfies the side-constraints. Such side-constraints leave ample room for several conflicting moral theories and do not naturally guarantee the survival of only one morally correct alternative.

Similarly for methods. A method that aids in decisions when pursuing methodological goals, such as maximizing interesting truth or solving problems, is minimally correct only if it does not violate the laws of the social sciences. These laws function as side-constraints on those decisions. The laws being necessary, there is no question of trying to minimize their violation, for violation in this case is an impossibility. To be sure, violations of some laws are more detrimental to the pursuit of science than are others.

Using a revised clinical method in which the role of language communication is made less significant than in his earlier clinical method, Piaget studied the problem of classification in children from ages two through eleven. He discovered that in stage 1 (two to five years) the child fails to use a defining property for classification. In stage 2 (five to seven years), the child succeeds in using a well-defined property and can even construct hierarchical classification, but fails to understand inclusion relation. In stage 3 (seven to eleven years), where concrete objects are involved, the child succeeds in understanding the concept of a class, relations between members of classes, and the class inclusion relation. Stages 1 and 2 are termed *pre-operational stages*, while stage 3 is called *concrete operational stage*.

His study of ordinal relations, with children of ages four through eight, led to the discovery that in the pre-operational stage 1 (four to five years), when the child is confronted with several sticks of different sizes, he is unable to order them according to their length. In the preoperational stage 2 (five to six years), the child is able to order them with some minor success, but not entirely. Experiments with sticks, dolls, and such reveal that the judgment of the child is dominated by spatial relations, and that his grasp of one-to-one correspondence is very weak. In stage 3, the concrete operational stage (six to eight years), the child is successful in all the various tasks.

Interestingly, the child may be at stage 2 in one sequence while at stage 1 in another. Furthermore, in what is called the phenomena of *horizontal décalage*, the child may display different levels of achievement in relation to problems that call for similar mental skills. For instance, a child may master the concept of the conservation of substance and discontinuous quantity, which he does around six or seven years, but not the concept of the conservation of weight, which he generally acquires around nine to ten years. Or he may have the latter concept but not the concept of the conservation of volume, usually acquired around eleven or twelve years. The stages are not sharply defined but rather one stage slides into the next. The ages at which the stages may occur may vary: not all Genevan children attain stage 2 of number development at six years; and children in Martinique lag behind Genevans by approximately four years. Perhaps eventually we will discover laws about why a child moves from one pre-operational stage to the next and then to the concrete operational stage. Piaget has a theory that calls for various factors to explain why the child makes the transition: these factors are maturation, physical experience, social transmission, and equilibration.[47]

What is important here is to note that Piaget's investigation into the development of the child's conception of number and mental imagery also confirmed the same general result: there are invariant sequences of stages of learning. If a child could ask himself how he ought to proceed to understand the world and then give a reply, his reply would be goal-defective if it contravened Piagetian laws. Less picturesquely, from the point of view of the theory of a child's education, this result is of considerable consequence. One cannot skip stages. One cannot learn a skill learnable only at a later stage. But the theory of a child's education is certainly in very significant parts normative, inasmuch as it deals with the problem, What *ought* the child to be taught?

Like children, scientists may have certain limits imposed on the way in which they seek to understand the world, given their neurophysiological structures, their theoretical beliefs,[48] and the powerful social and political conditions in which the beliefs were learned and fostered. Perhaps they, too, need to move through invariant stages.[49] An attempt to influence the behavior of scientists pursuing their various activities, or an attempt to make them change or cast off theories in certain ways that conflict with these limitations, will not succeed. Part of the task of the social sciences is to discover and delineate these limits; the task of a method is to stay squarely within them.[50]

The second view relating methods to social sciences can be expressed in another way, in terms of an analogy with differential equations, beginning first with an example that will not do. A theorem assures us that for a first-order differential equation, given the boundary conditions or side-constraints, there is not only a solution but a unique solution to the problem. In the analogous case, we would assert that given the side-constraints of the social sciences on methods, the solution to the problem of deciding which is the best method would be a unique one. This is an unacceptable consequence, for a number of alternative ways, even trivial and inefficient ways, of pursuing science are possible within the perimeter defined by the social sciences.

Consider, however, a nonlinear differential equation, where even if the side-constraints are specified, we do not have a unique solution to the problem, but a family of different solutions each satisfying the same constraints. By analogy, if our present knowledge as established in the fields of psychology, sociology, economics, and political science serves as a side-constraint on methods, and methods serve as solutions to problems about effective ways of reaching goals, then more than one method can solve the same problems. The analogy can be used in a different direction as well. The singularities of a solution depend on and vary with the boundary conditions. Thus, when one set of conjectured social sciences laws, acting as side-constraints on methods, is replaced by a different set, owing to the growth of our knowledge in these areas, weaknesses that were thought to infect a method in one place may turn out not to be weaknesses at all, while the new laws may show a different defect elsewhere in a method.

There is potentially a large payoff to the social sciences as well, for methods may pose new and probing problems for them. A norm that demands too frequent a rejection of theories may raise interesting questions for the social sciences about the creative capacities of scientists. This benefit to the social sciences will largely accrue and will significantly increase when methods attempt to answer questions pertaining to the problem of group rationality: namely, under what conditions is a group rational? Methodological norms will be suggested in the light of postulated group goals, and these norms will pose problems, such as, What are the conditions of stability and cohesiveness of a scientific group? What sociological conditions prevent the fulfillment of a group norm? What defense mechanisms in individuals and groups work to forestall criticisms of a theory? And, how, if at all, can these defense mechanisms be broken down?

It should be quite evident that this approach to the relation between methods and the social sciences indicates the necessary condition a method should meet if it is not to be goal-defective. Other criteria will be needed to pick the best method. Where every method violates some side-constraint, we will pick one that violates the least significant and the least number of side-constraints. Among the problems that will have to be solved on this view are, What constitutes a significant side-constraint? How are side-constraints to be weighted? How shall we arbitrate between a powerful method that violates an insignificant constraint and a trivial method that contravenes none? We are also assuming that although methods may be proposed with different goals in mind—one pursuing truth, another pursuing a goal which has little to do with truth—the activities in pursuit of these goals have enough in common, are structurally similar, to be touched more or less equally by the limitations expressed in the side-constraints. This is not only a plausible assumption but quite a significant one. It shows that when we are evaluating radically different (incommensurable?) methods, the solution to the problem of stating the necessary conditions a method should meet is not altogether impossible.

On the second view, one no longer needs to speak of falsification or corroboration of methods, as if methods were empirical facts confronting other empirical facts, but rather to see methods as hemmed in, constrained, or restricted by facts in ways the view suggests. What is perspicuous is that the second view offers significant advantages to someone who sees important parts of a method as normative statements that, unlike statements of convention in a method, are bearers of a truth-value and, unlike empirical statements, are neither descriptive nor explanatory. They show, rightly, that the social sciences have no bearing on those parts of a method that attempt to solve logical problems. Between two polar views, one that claims that the social sciences have nothing to do with methods (epistemology is logic) and the other that claims that methods rest squarely on these sciences (epistemology is naturalized), I find this view to be the mediating one.

2
Popper's Theory of Method

"It is good to remember from time to time that our Western science—and there seems to be no other—did not start with collecting observations of oranges, but with bold theories about the world."[1] What probably prompted Karl Popper's remark was the sterile epistemological tradition that emphasized beginnings and origins and simple observations but ignored some of the best examples and finished products of scientific knowledge. The remark is quite surely prompted by Popper's knowledge of the history of science and particularly by his fascination for the group of early Ionian physicists.

It is indispensable to keep this in mind when dealing with Popper's theory of method, which is both neglected and misunderstood. In some of its substantial claims, I shall argue, it is indefensible; but it issues a set of interesting and intriguing philosophical problems and presents a powerful alternative to the theories of method discussed later in this book.

Popper himself has never quite fully developed his theory of method. There is, of course, chapter 2 of *The Logic of Scientific Discovery*, several important remarks in *Conjectures and Refutations*, and his response to Imre Lakatos's objections in *The Philosophy of Karl Popper*. These do not add up to a systematic theory of method. In reconstructing Popper's theory, I have not felt constrained to these sources, and I have used Popper's ideas in other philosophical realms and adapted them to the problems a theory of method has to face. Some of these sources are: "Back to the Presocratics," "Towards a Rational Theory of Tradition," "What is Dialectic?," the 1961 Addendum to *The Open Society and Its Enemies*, volume 2, the last chapter of *The Poverty of Historicism*, and the one-page "Preface to the Second Edition," of *Conjectures and Refutations*. I am far more interested in the theory of method that results in and is consistent with his overall aims and goals than I am in the boring exegetical question, Did Popper really *mean* that?

Before presenting the usual story of Popper's theory of method, I begin with an account of his method. In his desire to distinguish Freudian theory of psychoanalysis, Adler's theory, Marx's theory of history, and their ilk from such theories as Einstein's general theory of relativity, Popper proposed his method whose key concept was the concept of falsification. In brief, if a theory is falsifiable, it is scientific; if not it is unscientific, mythical, or metaphysical. A theory is corroborated if it passes a severe test. The degree of corroboration of a theory is a concise report of the result and evaluation of the critical treatment the theory has received in its career. This report consists of the manner in which the theory has solved the problems, the severe tests it has undergone and passed. For theoretical and pragmatic purposes, it is better to choose a theory that has the highest degree of corroboration (which has nothing to do with the promise of success or likely success in the future). There is growth of knowledge when a succeeding theory explains everything earlier theories could, and makes novel predictions as well, at least some of which have been successful. The key concept in explicating the notion of the growth of knowledge is the concept of verisimilitude. In the classical sense of incorrigible knowledge, we can never know. For all our desire and attempts to discover more and more interesting truth, we never may. The best we can do is to conjecture that we have a true theory or a theory that is nearer to the truth than any other theory.

Popper's theory of method claims that, unlike scientific theories, a method is neither true nor false but is simply a convention. Clearly, it cannot be claimed that one method is truer or has a greater degree of verisimilitude than another method. Nor can it be claimed that successive methods are converging upon a true method. Methods, like conventions, are to be judged by their fruitfulness and by their distance from absolute rightness.[2] Hence, much of the burden of Popper's argument rests on clarifying the twin notions of 'fruitfulness' and 'distance from absolute rightness.'

A method is fruitful provided it is consistent, is able to solve some of the problems it sets out to solve, does not conflict with other philosophical theories needed to solve other problems, and generates interesting problems. A method is not a piece of empirical science; it is on a par with conventions. Conventions, however, unlike scientific theories, cannot be supported, tested, or criticized by empirical observations or claims. A methodological decision or proposal *creates* a norm; it does not depict or describe one.[3] A methodological statement does not say what *is* the case but rather what *ought* to be the case. Thus, a methodological norm must be kept separate from the facts of history of science and such. One does not entail the other. As a consequence of the cluster of these claims, *history of science cannot be used to criticize methods*. It follows, so claims Popper's theory of method, that we must find nonempirical criteria for evaluating competing methods. Perhaps Popper's emphasis on logic is best understood in this light.

This is Popper's theory of method. How elaborate, if at all, is his theory, and can it be reformulated to overcome certain major objections? To answer these and related questions, I shall first turn to an illustration from the history of science. Next, I shall try to reconstruct, explain, and systematically connect the various theses of Popper's theory of method. In particular, I shall argue against the cardinal feature of his theory—that statements of a method are statements of conventions—and show that it is not even necessary for Popper to stake such a claim. After the reconstruction, I shall raise a series of objections to it. These objections pertain to the problems of the nature and growth of aims, their relation to methods, and the nature of the relationship between methods, history of science, and learning. Finally, I shall state the problem of the logical status of methodological statements and present some major alternatives. I shall argue that when a method is regarded as empirical or conventional we are led to intractable problems, but that when a method is regarded as normative, with an attendant truth-value, various pieces of the puzzle seem to fall into place.

I. ILLUSTRATION

As usual, Popper makes a bold claim: "I want to return to the simple straightforward *rationality* of the Presocratics."[4]

Three ingredients are important in our story of the birth of cosmological speculation at the hands of three Ionians, Thales, Anaximander, and Anaximenes. These ingredients are: problems, solutions, and a methodological tradition; the last being easily, in Popper's view, the most important of the three. Happily enough, it is that tradition which serves the main point of the illustration.

Aside from their interest in cosmogony, the Ionians were engaged in several problems of cosmology, including, What is the structure of the universe? Out of what is it made? What is its ground plan? Related to these cosmological problems were the methodological and the epistemological problems, namely, How can I know what is the stuff and structure of the universe? What are the constraints on an adequate theory? This relation signifies a close tie between scientific theories and a methodological tradition. A stronger claim might declare that the history of science cannot be understood without the methodological tradition and, conversely, the methodological tradition cannot be understood without its accompanying history of science.

Thales suggested that the earth was supported by water. This simple claim enabled him to explain earthquakes. He argued on the basis of an analogy: just as a ship shook in stormy seas, so also the earth shook when the water it rested upon became turbulent. He conjectured that the primary element out of which the various forms of organic and inorganic matter in the universe were constructed, and did not just originate from, was water. Plants and animals need water; food and semen contain moisture; solidified water is like rock; and, evaporated water is like air. Thus various phases of matter—solid, liquid, and gaseous phases—could be explained in terms of the various states of water. Hence, it was plausible to conjecture that the source and substance of all things lay in this primary element.

If Popper had wanted to support the thesis that scientific theories are formulated on the basis of observations, the illustration could not have been more poorly chosen. For, Thales's theory was not only false, it was not likely even based on observation (in the way in which one might say, "All blue litmus paper when dipped in acid turns red," is based on repeated observations of blue litmus paper turning red when dipped in acid). Indeed, the situation is worse when we consider Anaximander's theory. Anaximander claimed that the earth was suspended freely in space. This conjecture contradicts all our experience and observations and could not have been based on them.

For Popper, however, the single most significant part of this tale is that Anaximander was able to offer a rival theory by *criticizing* Thales's theory. Anaximander refuted the theory thus: if, as in Thales's theory, we use water as the support for the earth, we would be obliged to find a support for the water, and a support for that support, and so on—an unwelcome infinite regress. Anaximander conjectured that the earth was at the center of the universe because the earth had no reason to move either up, down, or sideways. Its being in the center was reason enough, a natural state of affairs, and only when a departure from such a state occurred was an explanation called for.[5] In place of Thales's primary substance, water, he put the unlimited indeterminate (*apeiron*), tacitly introducing the notion of infinity; the indeterminate is one and in motion. It contained the opposites, hot and cold, wet and dry; these, together with "all the heavens and the worlds," as Simplicius informs us, came from the indeterminate and sank eventually back into it.

Not aptly described as the poor man's Anaximander, Anaximenes in turn arrived at his theory by criticizing his predecessor. Whereas Anaximander postulated the indeterminate as the primary element, Anaximenes postulated something determinate and unlimited, the air. He accounted for the cosmological and cosmogonical facts on the basis of the condensation and rarefaction of this elemental substance. Dilated air was the source of fire, condensed air was the source of solid substance, and a spectrum of the density of the air at which the sun struck was the cause of the rainbow. Furthermore, he was able to account for a host of astronomical and meteorological phenomena in terms of those two basic processes and one elementary substance.

In the light of this episode in the history of science, Popper makes at least three significant claims. First, the inductivist method is wrong in emphasizing the primacy of observation over theories and wrong in emphasizing the role of "I-see-orange-now" in epistemology over more substantive examples drawn from the history of science. Second, inductivist historiography is utterly inadequate inasmuch as it would eliminate or distort some of the most important episodes in the history of science by emphasizing observations and only currently accepted theories. Third, and by far the most important, Popper's focus of attention was not the three ancient scientific theories, or the family of shared problems, or even the general commitment that an explanation of natural phenomena must be in terms of natural phenomena and must not invoke gods and their psychological characteristics. Rather, the attraction for

Popper was that major theories rose and fell and could only have done so in a climate where criticisms were not only tolerated but were invited. One might say, a scientific society is an open society. It is not the society of Homer, Hesiod, and the Pythogoreans, wherein basic beliefs and tenets were beyond question. It is the society of Thales, Anaximander, and Anaximenes. What is more, the criticisms were not directed at the margin, but at the roots, of each theory. The fundamental entity in Thales' explanation was water; but not so for Anaximander. The fundamental entity in Anaximander's explanation was the indeterminate; but not so for Anaximenes. Even if the break Thales succeeded in making with his past was momentous, the break that his successors made from him was only slightly less so. Yet, alternative world pictures were woven within the same scientific community and in a relatively short period of time (approximately between 615 B.C. and 520 B.C.). The trial-and-error method, the attempt to propose testable explanations, and the permissibility of refuting conjectures are what made possible the growth of scientific knowledge, or at least a succession of major theories.

Thus Popper claims, "My thesis is that what we call 'science' is differentiated from the older myths not by being something distinct from a myth, but by being accompanied by a second-order tradition—that of critically discussing the myth."[6] It follows significantly that if the principle of testability or falsifiability deals only with the *form* of the statement alone, then it is not enough, for the same statement *S* asserted in a society that lacks the second-order tradition (method) Popper speaks of, can be asserted as well in a society that has that second-order tradition. According to the usual or the standard interpretation of the principle of falsifiability, *S* is scientific in both societies, if it has a specific form;[7] whereas, if we take into account the much broader picture Popper has delineated—which includes, at least, a critical methodological tradition—then *S* may be scientific in one society but need not be in another.

How and where was this critical tradition found? Aside from this important historical question which Popper has raised, there is another vital question. According to Popper, the critical rationalist tradition was "invented only once."[8] After two or three hundred years this tradition dissipated and science suffered. It was rediscovered and reinvented by Galileo and science prospered. Popper states this boldly and briefly. The vital question is, What significance do these *historical* episodes, particularly the momentous discovery of rational critical tradition, have for Popper's *method*?

I close this section with what I take to be five telling problems: (1) Are Popper's historical conjectures correct? (2) If they are correct, and Popper takes them to support his method, in what way does his theory of method differ from that of, say, Imre Lakatos, which he criticizes as naturalistic? (3) If they are not correct, then would Popper regard his method as justly criticized? Or, how should his incorrect historical account be seen to be related to his method? (4) Popper views methods as mere conventions that are neither true nor false; how then can his methods be supported by anything as empirical as the history of science? (5) Since in his account there are two distinct traditions—namely, the scientific tradition and the second-order methodological tradition—which of their histories supports Popper's method? Or, do only the histories of both traditions together do so? If the scientific tradition does not progress even if the critical rational tradition was adopted, would that tend to be a criticism of Popper's method? Or, if the scientific tradition progressed even if the critical tradition was not adopted, would that provide a compelling argument against his method?

II. POPPER'S THEORY OF METHOD

I shall begin by discussing Popper's view that methodological claims and decisions are conventions that are neither true nor false. I shall conclude that it is quite consistent with his overall view and reasonable for Popper to claim that methodological statements possess a truth-value. Finally, I shall present the remainder of Popper's theory of method, reconstructed and woven together from strands drawn from his entire corpus.

Popper has throughout maintained the thesis of critical dualism. The thesis is that natural laws are distinguishable from norms even though they both share important characteristics, namely, they are both criticizable and both are governed by their respective regulative ideals. Norms are conventions or proposals, albeit not arbitrary ones, and as conventions they are to be judged by their fruitfulness or their consequences. Norms cannot be derived from, or reduced to, facts. Norms can be proposed, broken, and replaced, and they are neither true nor false; they are either good or right. In contrast, a natural law can be either true or false and if true cannot be broken, changed, or replaced (at least not as a direct consequence of our doing).

Now, granting his distinction between norms and facts, Popper's arguments do not sustain his claim, (*T*), that norms are neither true nor false. First, Popper states that norms cannot be derived from or reduced to facts.[9] This does not show that norms cannot be true or false. For instance, scientific theories cannot be derived from or reduced to singular observation statements, but Popper does not say that theories are neither true nor false. So, Popper's Humean claim that an ought-statement cannot be derived from an is-statement is quite consistent with a denial of (*T*).

Second, Popper claims that natural laws cannot be broken or transgressed but that normative laws or commands can be broken.[10] This claim, however, is quite compatible and consistent with a denial of (*T*). Indeed, that a law cannot be broken may be an inadequate characteristic to highlight the difference between a natural law and a methodological norm. One cannot break the rules of bridge without ceasing to play the game, but it would hardly warrant the claim that the rules of bridge are either true or false. Furthermore, nonarbitrary decisions can be incompatible, too. In special cases, where one such decision is the negation of the other, there is surely a prima facie case for claiming that only one of the two competing proposals is true rather than saying that only one of the two competing proposals is good, right, or fruitful.

Third, one asymmetry between norms and facts is that norms always pertain to facts and that facts are evaluated by norms; these are relations that simply cannot be turned around. Popper himself has argued, however, that when decisions or norms contradict certain natural laws, they have to be given up or regarded as inadequate or pointless.[11] Thus, facts do pertain to norms; if they did not pertain to norms they could not contradict them; if they contradict norms, then norms are false. In a broad and reasonable sense of evaluation, facts evaluate norms by acting as side-constraints on them.

None of my criticisms of Popper's arguments in support of (*T*) should be construed as attempts to undermine any of his important objections to biological naturalism, ethical positivism, or psychological or spiritual naturalism.[12] My claim so far has been simply to show that it would be quite consistent for Popper to claim that norms can have a truth-value. Here, in brief, let me suggest how Popper might weave in with his other methodological theses the claim that norms can be either true or false.

The powerful moral force and arguments of *The Open Society and Its Enemies* and Popper's distaste for the myth of the framework make it quite puzzling why he should not claim that his moral principles—such as, "Minimize suffering (human and nonhuman),"—are his conjectures about the true principles of morality or justice, principles that are, like conjectured scientific theories and the ultimately true scientific theory, denizens of Popper's World 3. Popper's conjectures could be false, but arguments and experiences would have to be provided to show why they are false. Arguments in the sphere of morality must then be carried on in a fashion similar to the way in which they are conducted in the science that Popper approves of.

The regulative goal of our scientific theory is absolute truth; our hope is to discover a scientific theory that depicts it. Likewise, the regulative goal of morality is absolute goodness or rightness; and our hope is to discover a system of morality that would capture it. To complete the parallel, the regulative goal of method is the absolutely correct way of appraising and evaluating the theories of science and the giving of heuristic advice concerning them; our hope is to discover such a method. Popper speaks about seeking absolute right and discovering principles of morality; he would then presumably speak about seeking and discovering the true or correct method. But that which is not objective—that is, independent of my creating it in the act of proposing it—I can neither seek nor discover.[13] I can only legislate it by convention. Finally, when Popper says that we certainly can make progress in the realm of morality,[14] he can give an account of progress in method that is analogous to the account of progress in science: one methodological proposal, *M*, is better than another proposal, *M′*, if, and only if, *M* is more like the absolutely correct method than is *M′*.

Let me proceed from a very different route to arrive at the same scene. Popper's social engineer is no historicist. The social engineer does not pay attention to the origins of social institutions, their development, their present and especially future significance, or to the intentions of their original founders. Instead he will ask, "if such and such are our aims, is this institution well designed and organized to serve them?"[15]

Clearly, whatever the answer to *this* question, it is either true or false. There is a fact of the matter involved, if for no other reason than that it is the task of an empirical social scientist to answer it. But Popper also rightly claims that "in institutions normative laws and sociological, i.e., natural, laws are closely interwoven, and it is therefore impossible to understand the functioning of institutions without being able to distinguish between these two."[16]

This important insight I expand as follows: if the functioning of an institution is effective inasmuch as the aims are reached or the desired state is maintained, then the efficacy of the institution is attributable to the fact that the institution is designed to dovetail with the natural laws, such as sociological laws, and to the fact that sound normative proposals are espoused by the members of the institution. If the aims are not reached or the desired state not maintained, then this may be because the norms are not efficacious or the designing of the institution conflicts with the natural laws. The key idea in my explication is this: at best, the meshing of an institution's design with the natural laws (and there are presumably several mutually incompatible ways of doing it) is a necessary condition for that institution to function effectively. *What is also needed are effective norms.* The question the social engineer will ask, then, has to be reformulated to read, If such and such are our aims, is this institution, with its normative laws espoused by the members of that institution, together with the natural laws, well designed and organized to serve them? Again, whatever the answer to this question, it is either true or false.

The above question easily prompts another one, (*Q*), which is most significant to our present discussion: If our aim is truth or nearness to truth, is a given scientific institution, in which the members make evaluations of theories and give heuristic advice on the basis of their methodology together with the natural laws, well designed and organized to serve them? Once again, to be sure, there is a fact of the matter involved, not just a convention, in answering the question.

Popper says, "It is perfectly true that our decisions (norms) must be compatible with the natural laws (including those of human physiology and psychology), if they are ever to be carried into effect; for if they run counter to such laws, then they simply cannot be carried out."[17] Now suppose we have competing methods that are consistent with natural laws, including, for instance, the laws of psychology, physiology, economics, and sociology. It is quite unlikely that all methods save one are inconsistent with natural laws. We may then ask, Which of the competing methods will be most conducive to our aim of more and more interesting truth or verisimilitude? But we may also ask a prior question, namely, by virtue of what set of characteristics of methodological statements is one method successful and another not? If methods are either true or false, then the effectiveness of a method can be explained on the grounds of its truth (although, admittedly, it is *very* difficult to establish exactly what the truth-conditions are). However, if like Popper we maintain that methods are conventions lacking in truth-value, the greater effectiveness of one method over another appears to be completely mysterious. Finally, even if methods are neither true nor false, we are far more interested in the relationship between goals, institutions, natural laws, and methods than we are in a method in isolation; and it is by no means obvious that statements about *this* relationship lack a truth-value, too. To be sure, no institution is foolproof; not even the best ones, as Popper himself says. But he is surely conjecturing as a *true* answer to the question, (*Q*), formulated above, that an institution that allows for criticisms in ways proposed in his method has a better chance of making scientific progress than ones that allow for criticisms in a manner suggested by other methods. If that is not what Popper means, how is his claim about the fruitfulness of his method to be understood? How shall we understand his institutional theory of progress?[18] Or, how, indeed, shall we understand his example of the Ionians and their tradition of rational criticism which successfully generated rival, major theories?

To build the rest of Popper's theory of method, let me begin with the oft-quoted passage from *The Logic of Scientific Discovery*:

> "Definitions are dogmas; only the conclusions drawn from them can afford us any new insight," says Menger. This is certainly true of the definitions of the concept of "science." It is only from the consequences of my definition of empirical science, and from the methodological decisions which depend upon the definition, that the scientist will be able to see how far it conforms to his intuitive idea of the goal of his endeavours.[19]

This is entirely too general to be of much help, but it does say the following (where *M* is some method): (*i*) Test the consequences of *M*'s definition of science. (*ii*) In the light of *M*, find out how useful or successful were the decisions that were made. This is to be determined by seeing if the consequences and decisions referred to in (*i*) and (*ii*), respectively, square up with the intuitions of the scientists. By way of illustration, one consequence of Popper's definition of science is that astrology is excluded as science, as is much of psychoanalytical theory as well (insofar as they were unaccompanied by a second-order critical tradition).[20] The decision to regard the Eddington experiment of 1919 as a crucial severe test of Einstein's general theory of relativity was useful and sound.[21] Both these consequences square up with the scientists' intuitions, and thus redound to the credit of Popper's method.

Elsewhere, in comparing his system to the inductivist position, Popper says,

> We may consider and compare two different systems of methodological rules; one with, and one without, a principle of induction. And we may then examine whether such a principle, once introduced, can be applied without giving rise to inconsistencies; whether it helps us; and whether we really need it.[22]

This statement introduces other parts of his theory of method: (*iii*) If a method has a principle of induction, check for possible inconsistencies. To be sure, this criterion is too specific, though it is harmless to consistent but noninductivist methods such as the conventionalist method. But one may generalize to capture Popper's intention: check to see if a method has rules that lead to internal inconsistencies or permit the acceptance of an inconsistent theory. It is arguable that Laudan's method, which regards the notion of truth as irrelevant in the evaluation of theories, leads in some situations to the acceptance of an inconsistent theory over a consistent one.[23]

(*iv*) Test to see whether a particular methodological rule helps us or whether, if seen in its context, it is vacuous. Popper is here evaluating the rule of induction. He conjectures that a rule of induction simply shifts the problem on to a different plane. For instance, such a rule may have to be justified in its turn, to use *oldspeak*, and this leads to an infinite regress of a vicious kind. Thus, no rule should be introduced that simply dislodges a difficulty at one level only to reintroduce it at another. Laudan, to give another example, abandons the notions of truth and verisimilitude in favor of the notions of problem-solving and problem-solving effectiveness. However, he gives us no philosophical theory that stipulates the conditions under which a scientific theory may be regarded as having solved a problem. If, as seems likely, such a theory cannot be provided without tacitly assuming or invoking the notion of truth, at least, then the old problem will crop up again at a different place.[24]

(*v*) Test to see if we really need the methodological rule under question to solve our problem. Again, Popper has the rule of induction in mind. Popper claims to have solved the problem of induction and to have shown that the principle or rule of induction is not needed, whereas inductivists who still seek for justification of knowledge in their epistemology need to postulate the rule of induction, which leads to unnecessary and unsolvable problems.

It is important to recognize that whether or not a particular methodological rule is needed depends on what our epistemological problem is. It may well be the case that if two methodologists have different problems (perhaps based on different goals), then one and the same principle may be useful to one methodologist and not to another. Laudan, unlike Popper and others, regards the problem of demarcation as a pseudoproblem. He claims that rationality in science, and rationality in other intellectual disciplines that do not fall within the rubric of scientific activity, share a lot in common. For Laudan the important problem is what distinguishes a well-founded claim from an ill-founded one.[25] If we are to evaluate methods, it is imperative that we be clear on what are their goals and problems.

Now if, as I argued earlier, it is consistent and reasonable for Popper to claim that (*vi*) methodological statements are either true or false and are not merely conventions, then what Popper says of philosophical theories can be usefully adapted to his theory of method. Popper regards philosophical theories like idealism or phenomenalism, on the one hand, and realism, on the other, as incompatible or inconsistent with one another. They cannot both be true, says Popper, even though they are both irrefutable. The question naturally arises, How shall we assess the relative merits of these philosophical systems? Popper might have said the same thing about methods. Lakatos's method and Kuhn's method, for instance, cannot both be true, though they may both be false, even if they are both irrefutable. Then, the criteria Popper offered for evaluating philosophical theories could be translated to apply to methods.[26] In what follows I do just that.

Popper's theory of method can be extended thus: (*vii*) Check the methodological problem-situation before evaluating the answers that *M* proposes. Perhaps the success of the attempt to formalize deductive logic inspired similar attempts to formalize inductive logic. But no formal algorithm for testing a theory, as for discovering it, exists. Moreover, Nelson Goodman showed that such theories of confirmation immediately lead to inconsistencies unless we first distinguish, in the language in which the hypothesis is formulated, projectable predicates from non-projectable ones. Here, as in the case of the Bayesian method, in which prior probabilities which cannot be determined mechanically have to be assigned, the judgment of a seasoned scientist is indispensable. So formal methods have given way to less formal ones.[27]

(*viii*) Check the answers proposed by other methods and make a comparative evaluation. When several methods are in the field, the problem of evaluation is not straightforward. It is important to see if other methods have succeeded where *M* has failed, and if other methods have failed where *M* has succeeded. Carl Hempel's famous paradox of ravens has infested standard theories of confirmation. "All ravens are black" is a hypothesis that is 'confirmed' by a red button, a green zucchini, and a petunia, inasmuch as they 'confirm' the contrapositive of the hypothesis. A quarter-century ago, John Watkins argued that Popper's method of falsificationism is not riddled by this paradox because Popper's method insists that only serious but unsuccessful attempts at falsifying a hypothesis can count as corroborating: a nonblack object poses no serious threat to the falsification of the hypothesis in question.[28]

(*ix*) Prefer a simpler solution to one that is unnecessarily complicated and artificial. Popper sometimes complained that Lakatos often sprouted too many distinctions such as ad hoc_1, ad hoc_2, ad hoc_3, and so on, whereas Popper worked with only one definition of ad hoc. As with scientific theories, so in the case of methods; simplicity is hard to define.

(*x*) Check to see if *M* conflicts with other methods or metaphysical systems needed for solving other methodological problems or metaphysical ones. Laudan's method, which discards the concept of truth and verisimilitude, makes it quite difficult to retain the much-needed metaphysical theory of realism or to retain large areas of philosophy of language in which causal theories of meaning and reference play a central role, and which may be crucial in averting the specter of incommensurability. For the sake of completeness we add two points discussed before: (*xi*) Check to see that if *M* was adopted by a given scientific community, its goals are reached effectively (or more effectively than by any other method); and (*xii*) check to see if *M* proposes norms that conflict with the known laws of psychology, physiology, sociology, and so on.

There is one last intriguing and puzzling strand in Popper's theory of method: (*xiii*) "Now it appears that in order to apply this method we must already have *some aim*: we err if we stray from this aim. (A feedback thermostat depends on *some aim*—some definite temperature—which must be selected in advance.) Yet though in this way some aim must precede any particular instance of the trial and error method, *this does not mean that our aims are not in their turn subject to this method*. Any particular aim can be changed by trial and error, and many are so changed. (We can change the setting on our thermostat, selecting by trial and error one that better satisfies some aim—an aim of a different level.) And *our system of aims not only changes, but it can also grow in a way closely similar to the way in which our knowledge grows.*"[29]

Popper claims that the virtue of his method lies in its applicability to the growth of knowledge *and* to the growth of aims. He would also claim that not only is his method supported by the early history of physics or physical theories in Ionia but it is also supported by the history of fundamental goals and aims espoused in the ancient world. Thus, Popper would argue, the goals or aims of Homer and Hesiod were critically evaluated (perhaps unconsciously) and replaced, not simply by other goals but by *better* goals, just as the early cosmological theories of Homer and Hesiod were replaced by better cosmological theories of Thales and Anaximander after due critical evaluation.[30] This picture becomes not only complicated but, in a sense, fascinating. Unfolding the complex relationship between goals or aims, theories or myths, and methods or second-order traditions is important because it leads to issues that are fundamental in unforeseen ways.

III. QUESTIONS AND CRITICISMS

Suppose that in the history of science a community of scientists, S_1, adopted for itself (intentionally or otherwise) certain aims or goals, conjectured and proposed several theories to reach these goals, and discussed and evaluated their theories in the light of their method or second-order tradition. A succeeding (or contemporaneous) community of scientists, S_2, adopted for itself (intentionally or otherwise) different aims or goals, conjectured and proposed several theories to reach *its* goals, and discussed and evaluated their theories in the light of *their* method or second-order tradition; and so on down the history of science. In the chart on page 43 (which does capture some of Popper's claims), the superscripts distinguish one group from another; the subscripts distinguish one goal, theory, or method from another goal, theory, or method, respectively.

Popper, as we know, contends that it is not merely the logical form of a theory that makes it either scientific or unscientific; it is only with the advent of the *critical attitude*, exemplified in the adoption of a critical second-order tradition, that science is born and nurtured. It was the Ionian physicists who gave this tradition its finest hour, and with the withering of the tradition, science as it was known disappeared, not to resurface until the Renaissance.[31]

A glance at the chart immediately raises several important questions. In particular, what were the goals of those in the tradition of Homer and Hesiod that were distinct from the tradition succeeding it? Assuming that truth-seeking was a common goal shared by these two traditions, how did their other, differing goals dovetail with the goal of truth to give each tradition its own distinctive character? More generally, do we have any criteria for distinguishing one set of interlocking goals (theoretical and practical) from another such set? How are priorities among goals set? Do we have any criteria that would distinguish one second-order tradition from another? How loosely are goals or aims and second-order tradition tied? Do second-order traditions generally evolve slowly? Can we envisage a new critical tradition that breaks away as sharply from an earlier tradition as the tradition set by Thales broke away from the tradition preceding him?

The last question is particularly important. Popper has argued that he is far more interested in the simple and general ideas of falsification, testability, critical tradition, and so on than in a more complicated network of ideas.[32] Even if Popper's broad and general idea of a critical tradition is true, however, it is at best only a necessary condition for the growth of knowledge, not a sufficient condition for it (certainly, Popper has not argued for the condition being sufficient). Galileo broke from an earlier tradition, says Popper, just as Thales and his followers broke away from the tradition preceding them; they both established a critical tradition, and as a consequence opened up the possibility for the growth of knowledge. Let us grant, for the sake of argument, that both these new traditions had a common element, namely, a critical attitude. This common element, let us further grant, was necessary and sufficient to stimulate and produce a rich set of scientific theories among the Ionians. Why should we assume, however, that in a different historical milieu, with different goals and methods, a critical attitude alone was sufficient for the production and permeation of the scientific heritage that began with Galileo? Alternatively, one can grant Popper's remarkable claim that "there can, I believe, no longer be any doubt nowadays about the astonishing similarity, not to say identity, of the aims, interests, activities, arguments and methods of, say, Galileo and Archimedes, or Copernicus and Plato, or Kepler and Aristarchus (the 'Copernican of

Scientific Community	*Goals/Aims*	*Myths/Theories of*	*Second-Order Tradition*
S_1	$G^1_1, G^1_2, \ldots, G^1_n$	Homer Hesiod	M^1_1 [Uncritical Tradition]
S_2	$G^2_1, G^2_2, \ldots, G^2_n$	Thales Anaximander Anaximenes	M^2_1 [Critical Tradition]
S_f	$G^f_1, G^f_2, \ldots, G^f_n$	Plato Aristotle	M^f_1 [Uncritical Tradition?]
S_i	$G^i_1, G^i_2, \ldots, G^i_n$	Ockham Buridan Albert of Saxony Oresme Pierre d'Ailly	M^i_1 [Uncritical Tradition?]
S_k	$G^k_1, G^k_2, \ldots, G^k_n$	Copernicus Rheticus Praetorius Maestlin Brahe Kepler	M^k_1 [Uncritical Tradition?]
S_m	$G^m_1, G^m_2, \ldots, G^m_n$	Galileo	M^m_1 [Critical Tradition]

antiquity')";[33] but even making this assumption (a false one, I think), why should we accept without further argument the notion that enormously dissimilar scientific institutions embedded in common second-order traditions produced the same happy result? In effect, the question to be raised is, If such and such are our goals, then is the scientific community, S_i, well designed and organized to serve them if its accompanying second-order tradition contains only the common element of a critical attitude. This is a question we treated earlier.

Like our scientific theories, our methodological norms or traditions become more articulated and sophisticated and hence changed. Later second-order traditions are responses to specific problems that arose in the earlier scientific and methodological traditions. In brief, Popper's simple and powerful idea of a critical tradition is akin to a genus; the species exhibit a rich variety of the mode and manner of critical conduct and attitudes. There is not one unique and unconditionally correct answer across the historical board to questions such as, Under what conditions would you give up your theory? I am suggesting that the schools of Thales and Galileo could have both attempted to answer similar questions and yet would have come up with correct, different answers in the light of their differing scientific and methodological heritage, not to mention their differing goals and aims. Thus, even if Popper finds support for his method in the Ionian scientific tradition, it is not obvious that his method can be supported by citing later critical traditions. Paul Feyerabend's well-known conjecture is that the Popperian critical tradition would have arrested the growth of scientific knowledge had it been espoused by Galileo or Copernicus.

There is also the following problem. Popper says that "while we have a logical criterion of progress in science—and thus of rationality—we do not seem to have anything like general criteria of progress or of rationality outside science."[34] It follows that later second-order traditions, which are typically theories outside science, do not constitute progress over earlier such traditions, and thus no problem of rationality can arise in the selection and adoption of second-order traditions. But Popper's theory of method is meant to *help* in arbitrating over competing methods and so should be unacceptable. If, however, Popper could be urged to regard a method as a norm that is either true or false—a view that he could consistently adopt given his other views on methods—the task of specifying *progress in method* would not be entirely hopeless from within the Popperian framework.

Question: What does it mean to say, as does Popper, that one goal or set of goals is better than another goal or set of goals? What sense can be made of the claim that a system of aims grows? Epistemologically speaking, when can one know that one goal is better than another? Or, when can one know that one goal is replaced by a better goal? To my knowledge, Popper is the first to speak about the changes, critical evaluation, and adoption not only of theories but of aims and goals as well. Still, his point is no less perplexing than it is interesting and important. It is perplexing because it is very hard to make any clear sense of it. It is interesting because goals and aims, like theories, are not arbitrarily espoused or shed, and yet we have virtually no theory to explain that fact. It is important because *without proposing an answer to this question, a theory of method fails at a deeper level. For methods are dependent on goals, and acceptance or rejection of theories are dependent on methods. As a consequence, arbitrary espousal of goals and aims leaves open the charge of arbitrary acceptance or rejection of theories.*

All theories aim at truth or nearness to truth, and so any two theories can be compared (grant for the sake of argument) to see which one is nearer to the truth. But what do all *goals* aim at? Indeed, what does a single goal aim at? While it makes sense to say, for example, that a scientific theory aims at interesting truth, it is nonsense to say that the goal of truth itself aims at anything. To be sure, I am speaking of ultimate and fundamental goals, which Popper refers to as beyond rational argument. Subsidiary goals may be postulated to fulfill a higher goal, as in Popper's example of the thermostat, and one may recognize an entire hierarchy of goals. Popper's claim about the application of the trial-and-error method to the discovery and testing of goals, and his claim about the growth of goals, are best understood as applied to all save the ultimate goals within a given hierarchy.

Bearing in mind the complex questions and the absence of answers, it may not be unwise to start by proposing a highly conjectural and intuitive solution to the problem. Is there, like the true theory, a (reachable?) objective goal or set of goals, *G*, that scientists in any given tradition in the history of science have been trying to capture as they have been trying to capture the true theory? If so, could not *G* then be used as a yardstick by which to measure which proposed sets of goals are nearer to it? In the ultimately true scientific theory, let us say there are *n* basic terms, which hook on to the *n* basic parts and processes of the universe. At this fundamental level, it is an all-or-nothing affair: either the basic terms in the theory latch onto the basic parts and processes of the universe or they do not. If heat is molecular motion, then current theories of heat are more fundamentally adequate (now it is merely a matter of knowing more about molecular motion) than are theories that regard heat as a substance. If organisms have evolved, then current evolutionary theories are more fundamentally adequate (now it is merely a matter of knowing more about the mechanism of evolution) than are nonevolutionary theories such as the theory of the fixity of species. These comparisons are to be distinguished from comparisons of two theories whose terms latch onto the same fundamental parts and processes but conjecture different things about them, or about one of them, as when one says that evolution proceeds in a punctualist fashion and the other says that it proceeds gradually. Various scientific theories also may hook onto only some, but not all, of the fundamental and basic parts and processes of the universe; the more such parts the terms of a theory hook onto, the better the theory is compared to its rivals; or, the more its basic terms fail referentially, the worse it is.

Likewise, let us say that there are objectively *n* basic and fundamental goals that the ultimately correct method captures. At this fundamental level, it is an all-or-nothing affair, too: either the basic postulated and conjectured goals of the method capture the fundamental goals, as does the ultimately correct method, or they do not. If truth is a basic goal, then current methods that postulate that goal are fundamentally more adequate than methods that ignore or discard it. This is to be distinguished from comparisons of two methods both of which postulate and conjecture truth as a goal but make different guesses about it or its nature, as when we have different accounts of truth in terms of correspondence or coherence, respectively. What is more, these latter methods need not have latched onto all the basic and fundamental goals but only to some of them. In that event, one can argue that the more fundamental goals a method captures, or hooks on to, the better it is; or, the more its postulated and conjectured goals fail to refer to the objective goals, the worse it is compared to its rivals.

Thus, very schematically, if G^*_1, G^*_2, G^*_3, . . . , G^*_n, are the basic, objective goals a method ought to capture—and are captured by the ultimately correct method—then, one might argue, the scientific society of Thales, Anaximander, and Anaximenes is better than the society of Homer and Hesiod partly because (say) only one of the latter's conjectured goals, G^1_1, captured a basic goal, while G^1_2, G^1_3, G^1_4, . . ., G^1_n failed to capture any of the other existing, objective goals. The Ionians, however, captured more of the objective goals. The scientific society of Copernicus, Rheticus, Maestlin, and others was better than that of the Ionians partly because (say) more of the former's conjectured fundamental goals captured the objective, fundamental goals than did the conjectures of the latter. Similarly, the scientific society to which Galileo belonged succeeded because it captured more basic goals than did its predecessor or because fewer of its postulated goals failed to refer.

In short, in terms of fundamental goals, one method can be better than another in either of the following ways: other things being equal, the method captures more fundamental goals than do its rivals. Or, they both capture the same fundamental goals but the first method characterizes the nature of the goals correctly, or more correctly, than the other method, as (arguably) when a Quinean method incorrectly dismisses the notion of verisimilitude as based on a false numerical analogy,[35] while a Popperian method correctly retains the notion. Or, finally, a trade-off between capturing fundamental goals and characterizing them correctly shows that, on balance, the first method is better than its rival. Thus we can account for the growth of fundamental aims and goals.

Such an account makes the discussion about aims a matter of objective fact. It remains fallibilistic in approach, that is, any postulation of an aim is a conjecture of what a basic, objective goal is. The conjecture could be false, as can be our conjecture that one scientific society (of Thales) is goalwise better than another scientific society (of Galileo). It allows for the possibility that we can take a step backward, as we would if (assuming truth is an objective goal a method ought to capture) we ignored truth, as some methods do; so there are no guarantees to progress. It raises the question about the nature of goals (akin to the question about the nature of numbers), and of how to weigh the various goals if an adequate account of how to appraise methods in respect of its goals is to be developed. It also raises the question about what concept or concepts should be utilized to characterize and evaluate goals, analogous to the concepts of truth and verisimilitude used to characterize scientific theories. Finally, it raises the most important question of how to explicate the correct capturing of basic goals and the success of scientific practice, and why in pursuit of wrong goals we are sometimes successful. A theory that attempts to answer these questions will also tell us which goals and aims to pursue or preserve and which ones to discard.

In *The Logic of Scientific Discovery*, Popper says, "My criterion of demarcation will accordingly have to be regarded as a proposal for an agreement or convention. As to the suitability of any such convention opinions may differ; and a reasonable discussion of these questions *is only possible between parties having some purpose in common. The choice of that purpose must, of course, be ultimately a matter of decision, going beyond rational argument*."[36] The footnote to this passage adds, "I believe that a reasonable discussion is always possible between parties interested in *truth*, and ready to pay attention to each other." In effect, Popper's theory of method disallows any comparison between Popper's method and Laudan's method; for the fundamental goal or aim of falsificationism is truth or verisimilitude while the fundamental goal or aim of the methodology of research traditions is problem-solving, a methodology that has little use for the notions of truth, confirmation, corroboration, and so on. From the vantage point of Popper's theory of method, methodological incommensurability is then a real threat. To escape this consequence, perhaps the conjectured solution will be heeded more seriously. In any event, we can no longer ignore the problems posed by aims and goals.

Dubbing the methods that are on par with the empirical sciences as 'naturalistic' (to which, Popper would say, much of the work of Thomas Kuhn and Imre Lakatos belongs), Popper admits that a "student of the logic of science may well take an interest in it, and learn from it."[37] *His* method, however, is not naturalistic; it is conventional. "What I call 'methodology' should not be taken for an empirical science. I do not believe that it is possible to decide, by using the methods of an empirical science, such controversial questions as whether science actually uses a principle of induction or not."[38] But the notion of method is *far broader*, as the framework for methods revealed, than this remark would lead us to believe. For instance, appraisal and heuristic principles enshrined in a method are *not* principles of pure logic by any means; the notion of rationality is encompassing enough not to be solely tied to logical issues. Hence, even if it is true that questions pertaining to the principles of induction can be settled by resorting to logic alone, it still leaves open the possibility of settling such questions as, Was Popper's principle of corroboration ever used in science? by probing more deeply into the history of science, recent and past.

However, in "What is Dialectic?" it appears that Popper has abandoned the position of *The Logic of Scientific Discovery*. According to Popper, scientific method is a trial-and-error process carried out consciously and systematically; but, he says, this trial-and-error method is nothing but a good description of human activity in general and scientific activity in particular. The dialectic of thesis, anti-thesis, and synthesis "describes fairly well certain steps *in the history of thought*, especially certain development of ideas and theories, and of social movements which are based on ideas and theories."[39] It is of interest to note that Popper concludes that "Dialectic . . . is, therefore, an empirical descriptive theory,"[40] *because* the method of trial-and-error is. Conclusion: Isn't Popper's method naturalistic (at least in part)? If not, how could conventions *describe*?

It is Popper's treatment of the trinity of the history of science, methods, and learning that I find most puzzling. What distinguishes Popper's theory of method from the theories of method of his students and contemporaries is his insistence that the history of science has little to offer a methodologist since, among other things, his problems are logical in nature. He asserts that "to me the idea of turning for enlightenment concerning the aims of science, and its possible progress, to sociology or psychology (or, as Pearce Williams recommends, to the history of science) is surprising and disappointing."[41] It follows that one cannot cite events from the history of science as refutations of Popper's method of falsificationism.

One cannot say, "Look, Popper, you propose such and such aims and such and such criteria for the growth of knowledge, but in the history of science scientists proposed different aims and different criteria. Don't say it can't be. Look and see!" To a careful reader, Popper may seem to be setting up a one-way street: a methodologist can contribute to the work of a historian, but the historian has nothing to contribute to the work of the methodologist.

What contribution can the methodologist make? Concisely and clearly Popper states "two logical criteria" in the light of which we can adjudge science to be revolutionary, progressive, and cumulative. First, a new theory must contradict its predecessor and, second, it must always be able to explain fully the success of its predecessor. This means, claims Popper, that "in the field of science, we have something like a criterion for judging the quality of a theory as compared with its predecessor, and therefore a criterion of progress. And so it means that progress in science can be assessed rationally. This possibility *explains* why, in science, only progressive theories are regarded as interesting; and it thereby *explains* why, *as a matter of historical fact, the history of science is, by and large, a history of progress*."[42] To the historian of science interested in explaining certain segments of the history of science as progressive or eager to explain why certain theories in a given period flourished, Popper's first historiographical lesson is obvious.

Further, like other methodologists after him, Popper has discussed, although briefly, the problem of what impedes the growth of scientific knowledge. He has proposed two chief obstacles: ideology and economics. Like Popper, I shall focus on the ideological obstacle. An ideology is broadly defined to include "*any non-scientific theory* or creed or view of the world which proves attractive, and which interests people, including scientists."[43] (Note: this is broad enough to include methodological goals, directives, and commitments, often woven into a theory.) Two scientific revolutions, Copernican and Darwinian, initiated a new ideology, changing, as they did, man's view of himself in the universe. "The most widely recognized of the ideological obstacles is ideological or religious intolerance," says Popper, "usually combined with dogmatism and lack of imagination. Historical examples are so well-known."[44] He discusses briefly one such example: Aristarchus's theory of heliocentricism. Popper notes that the charge of impiety can hardly explain why the theory was neglected. Indeed, when social circumstances could not have changed much, it was proposed again by a respected astronomer, Seleucus. Historiographical lesson number two: when ideas that conflict with the major theories of the day are neglected, look for the reigning repressive ideological dogma (including methodological dogma).

Now, what contributions can the historian of science make to the methodologist? I quote a remark of Popper's again: "A student of the logic of science may well take an interest in [the history of science or empirical science], and learn from it." Recently, he claimed that a "great deal can be *learned* about obstacles to progress from the history of these neglected ideas."[45] I am unclear about what sort of learning this is. The point can be so expressed: if there is in principle something a methodologist can learn from the history of science that would lead him to revise his method, then Popper is wrong in immunizing his method from criticism by the history of science. For instance, one may find that ideology, such as Copernicus's or Gilbert's, sometimes aids rather than hampers the growth of knowledge.[46] Furthermore, if Popper allows the history of science to test his method, the least he must do is revise his thesis that a methodological statement is conventional. If, however, the study of the history of science cannot, *in principle*, force us to revise our method, then what precisely is being learned? Indeed, what is the nature of this learning that is so opposed to the nature of learning taught in *Objective Knowledge*?[47]

Or, look at it this way. Popper's argument against the verificationist's method is that it is mistaken because it excludes those systems in the history of science that we typically regard as "the theoretical systems of natural science."[48] Popper must presuppose—and indeed he does—that we have a preanalytic judgment concerning which theories in the history of science are scientific and, by implication, which are not. In fact Popper makes his point and preferences explicit. "If I define 'science' by my criterion of demarcation, then anybody could propose another definition. A discussion of the merits of such definitions can be pretty pointless. This is why I gave here first a description of great or heroic science and then a proposal for a criterion which allows us to demarcate—roughly—this kind of science."[49] His examples of great science are the theories of the Ionians, Aristarchus, Kepler, Galileo, Newton, and Einstein; the theories paradigmatic of nonscientific theories he notes are Marxism and psychoanalytic theories.[50] This allows his critics to retort that they have preanalytic judgments about a vaster, or different, area of the history of science than that which he considers. By their lights, Popper is mistaken for reasons similar to the ones he gives against the verificationists. Presumably, these preanalytic judgments of his critics reflect the intuitions of the scientists, too.

Two relatively-lesser points: First, Popper has claimed that whereas Lakatos's theory of method is trapped in an infinite regress of a vicious sort, his theory is not.[51] It is difficult to see how or why this is so. Lakatos claims correctly that in order to evaluate a scientific theory one has to move up to the level of method; to evaluate a method one has to move a step higher onto the level of meta-method. At this point, it will be argued, one has now to move a level higher to evaluate a theory of method, and so we inescapably climb levels *ad infinitum*. We need not, however, move any higher; after all, says Lakatos, we need to stop somewhere so we may as well use the plane of meta-method as the agreed-upon stopping point. Popper argues that since he is a conventionalist he does not fall prey to this vicious regress, nor does he need to block the threat of regress by an artificial ploy. If we do not agree on the specific conventions Popper proposes, however, or we accept different conventions on the same level, we must rise to a higher level of conventions. Now if we agree on these higher-level conventions, well and good. But we need not agree; thus, the threat of infinite regress is a potential threat for Popper's theory of method, too.[52] In Popper's method, observation reports are conventionally accepted, to stave off regress, for purposes of falsification; but these reports, on Popper's view, are not sacrosanct, even if rarely questioned. They too can be doubted and tested. Lakatos might analogously argue that agreeing on higher-level conventions is not necessarily keeping them safe from questions and criticisms; but, we may question these conventions, like the aforementioned observation reports, only as a last resort or in a dire situation.

Second, Popper proposes that one should check the claims (*i*) and (*ii*) of his theory of method against the intuitions of the scientist in order to determine how fruitful his method is. Indeed, it has been claimed that Popper's method, especially the historically oriented theory of corroboration embedded in it, does greater justice to the intuitions of the scientist than earlier atemporal or ahistorical theories (although, it is argued, it is not as successful as the methodology of research programs).[53] And, yet, Popper has maintained that the choosing of scientists is arbitrary, and that such an arbitrary choice enables us to carefully select only those scientists who confirm our methods.[54]

IV. THE LOGICAL STATUS OF METHODOLOGICAL STATEMENTS

Any theory of method must confront the problem of the nature of methodological statements, for the way we view the logical status of such statements will profoundly affect the way we view an acceptable theory of method. Some, such as Francis Bacon, Auguste Comte, John Stuart Mill, Brian Ellis, and Larry Laudan, have claimed that methodological statements are *empirical*. Others, such as Popper and Lakatos, have claimed that they are *conventional*. I shall argue that methodological statements should be regarded as *normative* statements, statements that are bearers of a truth-value. As is usually the case, the strength of the view proposed and defended is to be measured against the successes and failures of the alternative views.

Empirical

To say that a methodological statement is empirical is to claim that it may tell us something about the world—in this case, about the behavior of the scientists. For instance, the methodological statement,

"Do not propose ad hoc hypotheses," says in effect, on this view, that scientists as a matter of fact do not propose ad hoc hypotheses (given such and such goals). Even this is ambiguous, however, since it could mean either that methodological statements describe some lawlike regularity in the behavior of the scientists (Comte, Ellis) or that methodological statements describe specific ways in which scientists do behave without implying any lawlike regularity (Laudan).

The latter position is easier to illustrate than define. One discovers what specific values and goals the scientists being studied held; one conjectures what method they espoused as the one that would lead most effectively to their goals; and then one explains the behavior of the scientists in the light of that method. Briefly, the Ptolemaists' goal was to propose a theory that made use only of circular motion and that would best predict the phenomena of the heavens. As such, it was permissible to design an ad hoc, separate deferent-epicycle model for each planet, although the motion of the sun and the moon (then regarded as planets) could be approximately explained with the help of a single deferent. Such separate models accounted for the retrograde motion of a planet and the irregular intervals of time consumed in successive journeys around the ecliptic. Minor irregularities—such as Venus not always attaining the maximum deviation of forty-five degrees from the sun, and the nonuniform motion of the sun which took six days longer to move from vernal equinox to autumnal equinox than it did to move from autumnal equinox back to vernal equinox—were corrected by using minor epicycles that moved differently, in speed and in direction, than the deferent on which they were mounted; finally, the plane of the circles was tilted and adjusted until the northern and southern deviation of the planets from the ecliptic could be explained.[55] By contrast, the Copernicans adopted a different goal, for they not only wanted what the Ptolemaists sought but they also desired a theory that described the world, a theory that was not only an instrument of prediction but a piece of information, too. Hence, ad hoc devices were avoided and hypotheses that were empirically testable—in principle, if not in practice—were suggested. Divergent methods explain divergent practices.

To be sure, we are not to assume that the Ptolemaist or the Copernican actually used the term 'ad hoc,' or that he had carefully defined a similar methodological term, or that he had carried out his scientific activity fully consciously and explicitly in the light of his methodological commitments. It is not essential to make such claims in order to conjecture that he implicitly held such a method. As is usual with empirical inquiry, a historian or a methodologist might make mistakes in his conjectures about the goals and norms of the scientists he is studying. On the view discussed here, he neither evaluates their behavior, nor claims that there is a lawlike regularity in such behavior, nor argues that only one method is possible and was actually used in the history of science. He simply submits a historical, sociological report.

We now turn to the more interesting claim that methodological statements are scientific statements that tell us how, as a matter of lawlike necessity, scientists accept or reject theories.

Brian Ellis remarks in his *Rational Belief Systems*, "In many epistemologies it is assumed that man is a rational agent applying (or perhaps misapplying) certain a priori principles of reasoning to what is given to him through experience to construct his system of beliefs about reality."[56] Ellis finds this view in direct conflict with the scientific view that regards man as a physical organism. Man's beliefs, his reasoning, and his reaching a conclusion are causal processes or brain-states resulting from such processes. It is the shape and structure of man's belief system that should be explained. This explanation should not be wedded to a dualistic metaphysics, such as Popper's, invoking free agents or a priori rules of reasoning. Ellis is concerned only with the first step of the inquiry, namely, with how rational men think. Eventually, of course, the underlying neurophysiological theory will have to be found, but first attention has to be paid to the structure and dynamics of belief systems, about which he thinks much can be said.

Ellis rejects the a prioricity of the laws of thought (the phrase is used advisedly) and regards them as empirical in the way in which we regard Newton's first law of motion. To be sure, his position is psychologistic, as he himself says, but it has the virtue of being sophisticated in a way that Mill's theory was not. Ellis's theory of rational belief systems attempts to provide an adequate theoretical basis for modalities and conditionals, and it does so without the usual arsenal of classical semantics such as possible worlds, similarity and accessibility relationships between possible worlds, identity across possible worlds, and so on.

Since he regards his task as scientific in nature, one of constructing *scientific epistemology*, he proceeds like a scientist. He seeks the fundamental laws of rationality governing an ideal rational agent, just as a physicist seeks physical laws governing an ideal physical system or as a chemist seeking laws governing ideal gases. He discovers that the laws governing the structure of ideally rational belief systems or governing an ideal rational agent holding such a system of beliefs turn out to be the laws of logic. He refers to these as the laws of rationality, for on his view they are one and the same.

An ideally rational belief system is one that is in equilibrium against severe internal criticism and discussion. As with real gases, so with ordinary rational agents—they are far from ideal. Belief systems of rational agents nearly always fail to be ideally rational belief systems since the stock of acquired beliefs is customarily growing and, as a consequence, threatening to overthrow the system of beliefs held in disequilibrium. Deviations from the equilibrium are explained away as one would explain such deviations in economics or physics, and the task is just as complicated. The chief point is that the physical ideal of a rational belief system is useful in explaining ordinary belief systems.

One might add, on behalf of Ellis, that the laws of logic or rationality, once they took into account the dynamics of our belief systems—about how they change, grow, and evolve—would eventually explain much of the history of science in which men have held certain combinations of beliefs that we would intuitively regard as rational. In Ellis's metaphor, various belief systems in the history of science should be more "likened to an ecological system than to a building." But various ecological systems should be ideally explained on the basis of only one set of ecological, biological principles. Likewise, various rational belief systems in the history of science should be, in principle, explainable in terms of the laws of rationality or the laws of logic. Should we succeed in such a venture, at the very least we shall have exhibited an uncanny unity of the sort Newton demonstrated when he explained the terrestrial and the celestial phenomena on the basis of one set of physical laws.

"I do not believe," says Ellis, "that it is just an accidental by-product of human evolution that we have these ideals, or that our having them has been culturally determined. Our rationality has almost certainly been a major factor in our survival as a species. Therefore, it is probable that our having those ideals of rationality is genetically determined."[57] He goes on to add that we do not know how these ideals contribute to our survival and that we are unlikely to know that, or come nearer to knowing that, until we have first learned a great deal about the causal role of belief systems in determining human choices and actions.

It is more than evident that on Ellis's view the objective and the normative components of a method, which a rational agent espouses and which aid him in making choices, thus determining a subset of the range of human actions, must be (a central?) part of a rational agent's belief system. The method, like the goal and laws of logic, must be genetically determined and the statements in a method should be regarded as expressing a lawlike regularity. How could they be otherwise, if they are genetically determined? How could they be otherwise in a view that bans a priori principles?

Of what importance, then, is the study of the history of science to a methodologist? Assuming that scientists are rational in their problem-solving or fact-explaining activities and that their rational behavior is susceptible to a lawlike generality, by paying close attention to the historical development of science a methodologist may latch onto the methodological law (or laws, more likely). Statements such as, "Other things being equal, scientists prefer the best-tested theory," will be a methodologist's conjecture of how scientists behave in a lawlike manner. Such conjectures can then be tested against the history of science, or against the actual practice of current scientists. In the limit of this type of inquiry, the laws of method expressed in its two main components and incorporated in an ideal rational belief system must be derivable, as a consequence, from the laws of rationality.

To get a different perspective on the claim that methodological statements are empirical, let me present an analogy. In order to learn a language, a couple of prerequisites are necessary: we must have an appropriate organization (brain structure, nervous system, etc.) with which to receive and decode language signals, and we must be exposed to a community of individuals in which language is spoken; indeed, a lack of exposure to such a community may well cripple our ability to speak. These two factors together bring about our ability to speak a language fluently without our knowing what basic and fundamental principles (depth grammar, if you insist) enable us to effectively execute this task. Notice that I did not introduce any particular language, just as later in the analogy I will not introduce any specific or particular scientific theory or scientific problem.

As in the speaking of a language, so also in doing science. In order to solve a scientific problem or to know something about the world we live in, we need two things: *(a)* we must have internalized basic and fundamental principles for rejecting or modifying proposed theories about the world; and *(b)* there must be a set of scientific problems to work on, or a scientific community to work in. Only *(b)* can activate *(a)*. An organism not engaged in solving scientific problems would leave the innate principles dormant or unexercised; if we view problem-solving activity broadly, then this is not an option an organism has. By contrast, an organism that lacked such internal principles would make guesses about theory selection that were so random that its chances of hitting the target (truthlikeness, say) would be utterly remote. To this Ellis would add that if our survival as a species was due partly to our making right choices in theory selection, we could not have survived if we lacked internalized correct principles of theory-choice, or if the principles were not genetically determined, or if we had to depend on the risky trial-and-error procedure to find the right principles of theory selection to deal with our hostile environment. The task of method or scientific epistemology, then, is to try to uncover these lawlike, basic, and fundamental principles.

Having delineated the claim that the logical status of methodological statements is empirical, and that such statements express lawlike regularities, it is reasonable to ask, How sensible is it to view method in such a fashion? First, Ellis's theory insofar as it concerns the dynamics of belief systems, with which we are primarily concerned here, is largely programmatic. No case has been made to show how in a specific case—let us say, in the overthrow of Ptolemy's astronomical theory in favor of the Copernican theory—the theory of rational belief systems can be used to explain the actual transition of our belief systems.

Second, it is difficult to see how a statement of method could be derived from the laws of logic. By a law of logic Ellis does not mean sentences of a formal language such as, "$P\ v\ \text{-}P$." He means something like this: *(S)* "There is no rational belief system on the language L_O in which any sentence of the form '$\alpha\ v\ \text{-}\alpha$' occurs with an F evaluation." This law of logic is regarded as a framework law useful in the process of explaining, but it is not descriptive any more than an ideal physical law or gas law describes how a real physical object or gas in nature behaves. But *(S)* is like a statement *(S′)*: "There is no rational belief system on the language L_O in which any sentence of the form 'α is the least corroborated of competing theories, and it should be accepted as our knowledge of the world' occurs with a T evaluation." How is S' to be derived from S, or from some such a statement as S? If it cannot be derived, and S' is central in explaining rational action, what status is conferred on S'? It is a plausible conjecture that statements like S are far too general to aid in explaining rational behavior in the history of science—in explaining, as

Ellis would put it, the dynamics of belief systems. We may grant that the laws of logic may be, at best, necessary conditions, but they hardly constitute sufficient conditions.

Third, it is even more problematic how conflicting methods espoused by scientists in the history of science and used by them in their decision-making processes, could be derived from the laws of logic alone; so, should we conclude that conflicts between methods are to be explained away as more apparent than real?

Finally, the approach that regards methodological statements as conjectures about the world has the following very unintuitive consequence, namely, that we already know implicitly, at least, whatever we need to know about rational behavior; there is no room for progress in method. We are so programmed that these basic and fundamental principles that we have internalized cannot possibly lead us astray (remember, we are dealing with lawlike necessities and not just accidental regularities). The best that can happen is that if we do discover the true method we would know explicitly what basic and fundamental principles we had been operating with implicitly hitherto. Knowing them explicitly, however, does not lend extra help in our task of doing science, inasmuch as we are unlikely to learn language more effectively than we do now if we should ever discover the rules of depth grammar. To argue otherwise is to be saddled with an unsupportable claim, namely, that lawlike internalized rules operate more efficiently when an organism is conscious or aware of them than when it is not. The move that a principle consciously held can be checked and criticized is impermissible, for we are dealing with lawlike regularities that cannot be changed or altered, except perhaps biologically.

Conventional

The claim that methods are conventions is, as we have seen, Popper's. How are conventions to be evaluated generally? How are we to evaluate conventions that specifically pertain to scientific activities?

The fact that red rather than avocado is used for the stop signal simply exhibits an innocuous convention, just as staying on the right instead of the left marks an uninteresting divergence of traffic conventions. Such "competing" conventions can hardly be evaluated. Clearly, Popper's idea of a conventional methodological statement is not on par with conventions about the colors of traffic signals. His notion of conventions must involve ways that touch, affect, and change scientific activity. Could methods then be mere conventions?

Imagine: after the publication of Ernst Mayr's *Systematics and the Origin of Species* in 1942, scientists were divided into two groups of evolutionists. The first group held the hypothesis that evolution occurred in slow, measured steps in an entire population; this hypothesis was called the *gradualist* hypothesis. The second group held that evolution occurred in spurts, that evolutionary changes in populations or established species were minimal, and that the evolution of a species occurred most rapidly at a time when it diverged from its ancestral species, as when it got geographically isolated from the parent species. This hypothesis was called the *punctuationalist* hypothesis. The two groups were not only divided on what was the correct mechanism of evolution but also on the correctness of the method to be used for making decisions about accepting or rejecting theories and auxiliary hypotheses. However, the groups had one thing in common: the goal. Each group was searching for interesting truth or verisimilitude. Imagine, furthermore, that the first group sought to reach the goal by using my method and the second group sought to reach the goal by using Popper's method.

Between 1942 and 1982, the second group, in accordance with the dictates of Popper's method, proposed testable theories, pursued for theoretical and experimental purposes hypotheses with the highest degree of corroboration, eschewed ad hoc strategems, preferred a simpler theory over another because it was more easily testable, attempted severe tests of the theories proposed in novel situations, and so on. Let us say that my method was the direct opposite of Popper's, and so scientists in the first group permitted themselves, for instance, ad hoc moves.

The first case concerned the bowfin fishes, large North American freshwater animals of the Amiidae family. Have the bowfin fishes evolved slowly? asked the second group, and set to search for fossils that would answer the question and test the theory. An excellent fossil record was consequently established in due course. The fossils were found in sedimentary deposits that showed that bowfin fishes—no more than two bowfin fishes existed at any one time—were around for at least 140 million years. For the whole of the Cenozoic era, however, approximately 65 million years, bowfin fishes were noticed to have evolved only marginally, while in the latter part of the Cretaceous period the species only slightly elongated. The first group attempted to save its hypothesis by questioning the fossil record, or by proposing an explanation of the near-absence of evolution in bowfin fishes in ad hoc ways, or by simply regarding their theory as mildly confirmed by the insignificant evolutionary changes that were observed.

But Popper's method urged the punctuationalist to seek to test his hypothesis in new and novel circumstances. So, the lungfishes provided another test. The lungfishes breathe air and are structurally fashioned to withstand droughts. They, too, evolved very rapidly during speciation. Three hundred million years ago their lineage declined to a small number, and that number has remained stable since then. A similar pattern was observed when the second group considered sturgeon fishes, garpikes, snapping turtles, alligators, tapirs, and aardvarks.

Perhaps the most spectacular test of the gradualist hypothesis came when the first shelled animals were discovered at the base of the Cambrian, approximately 570 million years ago. These shelled animals were trilobite arthropods, snails, brachiopods, and a variety of rare, extinct invertebrate marine animals. The first group, in the footsteps of Charles Darwin, postulated the existence of life forms well into the Precambrian in order to give a fair amount of time for these shelled animals to evolve from the simplest and earliest life forms. Viewing it as a test for their theory, the second group conducted a search for such fossils in rocks of early Precambrian, but no life forms were discovered, at least in rocks earlier than the very latest Precambrian age. What did turn up were the trace fossils, fossils that are remnants of tracks, trails, and burrows made by soft-bodied organisms on and within the seafloor. While trace fossils are common in Cambrian rocks, they make their first appearance only in the very late Precambrian. These trace fossils indicate simple tubelike creatures that quickly evolved into a variety of forms as well as into complex organisms by the earliest Cambrian period. These findings corroborated the punctuationalist hypothesis, and strained the gradualist's.

Both groups were aware of the fact that the dinosaurs disappeared during the Cretaceous. How, then, did the mammals evolve after that? It was discovered that the first mammals were small in size and were usually nocturnal. Within a span of 12 million years, most of the living orders of mammals were in existence, including the order that contains modern lions, wolves, and bears; one that contains horses and rhinos; and the order that includes deer, pigs, antelopes, and sheep. These evolved from nothing more than rodentlike, small animals, not all of whom possessed teeth for gnawing. What is more, bats as well as whales also evolved from the rodentlike creature. If evolution proceeded gradually, then the time available to evolutionarily carve out some twenty new orders was utterly small and insignificant.

As urged by Popper's method, the second group pressed their theory harder still. Grant, they said, that the fossil record is unreliable and insufficient (as Darwin had so frequently said when confronted with paleontological findings). A stronger test of their theory should concern very recent (geologically speaking) species that have not escaped their place of origin. Radiocarbon dating techniques confirmed that Lake Nabugabo in Uganda was formed about 4,000 years ago. The fishes in it have been isolated by embayment from their ancestors in Lake Victoria, parent to Lake Nabugabo. If the gradualist hypothesis is right, the fishes will have evolved insignificantly; if the punctuationalist model is right, the fishes will have evolved markedly. The lake was inspected, and it was discovered that Lake Nabugabo held five species of cichlid fishes that were unknown anywhere else, including Lake Victoria, but the lineage of each species could be traced to the species in the ancestral lake. Once again, in the African lake Barombi Mbo, seventeen species of cichlid fishes occur, and twelve of these are endemic. Indeed, seven of these endemic species belong to four genera, and these genera have evolved to a point where it is unclear how they are related to the cichlid species of the adjacent areas. The time the seventeen species in lake Barombi Mbo had in which to evolve, however, was no more than a few hundred thousand years at most, as the volcanic crater in which the lake sat was no older than that.

Examples of severe independent tests conducted by the second group, and the ad hoc adjustments of the first group, can be easily multiplied. Cases can be cited concerning the pupfishes of Death Valley; several species of banana-eating moths of the genus *Hedyleptra*; the "dawn-horse" genus *Hyracotherium* of the Bighorn Basin; the unexpected fossil appearance of angiosperms (including not only flowers but also grasses and hardwood trees), leaves, and pollen; the rate of conspicuous phenotypic changes in Cenozoic taxa; and so forth.[58]

What does this imaginary example show? Overwhelmingly, of course, it shows that the punctuationalist hypothesis is a powerful hypothesis and that the gradualist hypothesis needs to be refashioned, at best. The success of the first theory over a forty-year period, however, is surely in no small part due to Popper's method. Guided by the method, the theories were put to severe tests; in the light of the method, the scientists accepted and pursued some auxiliary theories and rejected others; they made minor adjustments and put the readjusted theory to a new test; their theory developed, and it was in significant part shaped and honed by the method they espoused and in part by their findings and experimental results. How else can the fruitfulness of a method be determined? We must conclude: Popper's methodological rules are more effective than mine, a fact that renders the following conjecture more plausible. Given the historical and methodological tradition the two groups of evolutionists were placed in between 1942 and 1982, there was a *fact of the matter* as to which of the two particular sets of methodological rules and norms would be more conducive to reaching the shared goal of truth or verisimilitude. But if, as Popper argues, methods are conventions, how can a mere convention succeed so well?

Normative

More plausibly, then, it appears that methodological statements should be regarded as normative and bearers of a truth-value. Such a view, at least against Ellisian empiricism, allows for methodological mistakes made in the past and for ones we may be making now; it allows for correcting those mistakes and for improving our method in the future. In short, it makes room for progress in method. Furthermore, it avoids the serious problem that conventionalism runs into when it leaves the success of a method not as a matter of fact but of mystery.

Over a reasonably large interval of time, each scientific society finds itself in a particular historical, social, economic, political, scientific, and methodological tradition whose broad and general features remain stable and constant.[59] Given these, the scientific community is confronted not only with specific scientific problems but also with specific methodological ones, such as, How shall we evaluate the currently proposed scientific theories? What heuristic advice shall we give? How shall we organize as a group? In Popperian parlance, for each scientific society there are *objective methodological problem-situations*. The description of such a problem will draw on the methodological heritage or commitment of the society, and the solution offered will certainly invoke a method. The mere fact that the problem-situations, as well as the solutions, are encased in a particular historical trapping does not make them any less objective. Presumably—and more so for Popper, with his theory of situational logic or situational analysis, than anyone else—

there is an objective solution to such problems after which scientists and methodologists hanker.

Going back to our two societies, the Popperian scientific society and mine, we find that the Popperian society was more successful partly because objectively its solution to the methodological problem was far better than mine. How can this be explained even in a rough-hewn way? Popper offers three ontologically distinct, but causally related, worlds: World 1 consists of physical objects or physical states, events, and processes; World 2 consists of states of consciousness, mental states, and behavioral dispositions to act; and World 3 is more expansive than the world of abstract entities envisaged by Plato and Hegel: it is the autonomous and objective world of theoretical conjectures and claims as embedded in World 1 entities, like journals, monographs, and books. It also depicts logical relations between theories, including their logical consequences, both known and unknown, problems and problem-situations, critical arguments, and the current state of the critical discussion of theories.

Popper's theory of understanding invokes World 3 essentially. To understand Galileo's *theory* of the tides, Popper argues, one has to ask not only what the *problem* was, but also what the *problem-situation* was in which the problem arose. These again must be understood only against a certain *background* and a certain historically given *theoretical framework*. He then proceeds to unravel these World 3 entities, as when he shows that for Galileo the problem of the tides was important because Galileo was deeply interested in the Copernican theory and the fortunes of that theory could improve upon the successful solution of the problem posed by tides. Popper shows why Galileo rejected the rival explanation of the tides, which conjectured the moon's influence on the ocean waters, based on the background of Galileo's rejection of astrology.[60] "It is a fatal mistake," warns Popper, "to believe that there can be an adequate theory—psychological, or behavioural, or sociological, or historical—of the behaviour of scientists which does not take full account of the World 3 status of science."[61]

Popper's World 3 harbors not only scientific works but also those as disparate as the works and theories of art, ethics, and mathematics. There is thus warrant for the claim that *methodological* problem-situations, problems, and their solutions are in World 3, too. What is more, to understand, say, Bacon's methodology, one has to ask not only what the methodological problem was but also what the methodological problem-situation was in which the problem arose. These too must be understood only against a certain background (such as the then-prevailing Aristotelian method) and a certain historically given framework, presumably a framework in which problems of method were in fact discussed or could have been discussed. Indeed, to understand Popper's own deductivist method, one has to inquire not only into the problems that moved him—such as, How is science to be distinguished from metaphysics and, can Hume's problem of induction, duly reformulated, be solved?—but also to uncover the problem-situation (the background and the framework) in which these problems arose for Popper. The delineation of the problem-situation will underscore, for instance, the prevailing attempts of the logical positivists to provide a criterion that would distinguish meaningful sentences from ones lacking sense (and to argue that the criterion also provided the divide between science and metaphysics); it will also underscore the attempts of Carnap and others to provide an inductivist theory of confirmation.

What I wish to emphasize is neither the ontology nor the theory of understanding but the twin claims concerning the objectivity of methodological problems and the truth or falsity of methodological solutions. Methodological statements, like scientific statements, have an objective content that belongs to World 3; and, just as solutions to ethical or mathematical problems can be true, so also methodological solutions to methodological problems can be true or verisimilar.

If one regarded a scientific law as a process law, one might say that we would be able to predict the various states of the solar system at different times on the basis of our knowledge about the laws of physics and the state of the system at any given time. This is possible only because of the stability of the system. If several comets of sufficiently large magnitude were to enter and pass through the solar system, it would disrupt and change the system, perhaps alter the laws applicable to it, and our predictions would unsurprisingly fail. Again, process laws in biology should be understood as explanations of the behavior of biological systems only for periods when there is a closed system. But biological systems are rarely closed for sufficiently long intervals of time. Biosynthetic pathways, individual organisms, breeding populations, ecosystems, and entire species are partially and often open systems. External, environmental influences, not to mention internal, genetic ones, alter these systems in unexpected ways; our predictions and explanations would fail if we did not take into account these radical changes.[62]

Putting methods in place of scientific laws, and stable scientific societies in place of closed physical and biological systems, we see that a methodological solution or an explanation of rational decision depends, for the application of its general rules and norms, on the stability of the general features of the various traditions of a scientific society. What may precipitate a change may well be a new set of methodological rules put to use in place of others, as when Aristotelian method or Baconian method replaced the methods that were in use before. Their immediate impact, clearly, would be first on the scientific tradition and then on the other traditions linked to it. Sometimes, however, the change may come about in a different style; other traditions may become affected first, and they in turn may leave an imprint, occasionally long and lasting ones, sometimes pernicious ones, on intellectual disciplines such as the scientific disciplines. Joseph Needham in his *Science and Civilization in China* argued that science in early China received its support from an unlikely source: the nature-mysticism of the Taoists. In 1368, however, the Ming revolution instituted a mandarin bureaucracy that favored Confucian ideals over the ideals of the Taoists. Confucian ideals were not hostile to the scientists or to their science, so much as they were indifferent to them; so, the net result was the same as if they were hostile. Science declined. The stability of the scientific society of early China was disrupted, as was its character affected, by external social and political forces. Our attempt to explain what transpired in the scientific societies subsequent to the revolution would fail if in our explanatory package we were to invoke the method in use before the revolution. *When new traditions, scientific and nonscientific, have evolved and settled, we may have a new and objective methodological problem-situation*. Thus, such questions as how to evaluate contemporary theories and what heuristic advice should be given will again be asked, but their force and character will be different. If these questions *seem* exactly the same, it is their seeming the same that fosters the illusion that the methodological problems do not change and that unchanging problems must have answers that are valid for every time and place.

The questions are not really the same, however, since the objective methodological problem-situation is not the same. *Altered traditions yield altered problems*. To make these problems and questions look different, all we need do is append statements of the respectively different traditions, however these may have been inspired. Scientists working in China well before the Ming revolution were in a different scientific and methodological tradition from those who lived in the wake of the revolution and from those who lived in a later, more stable period. Scientists working on the continent immediately after Descartes were in a different methodological tradition (a tradition Steno would strongly oppose later) from those who worked before him, and then from those much later after him, especially in England.

In sum, the network of ideas in a given period constitutes the methodological problem-situation, and methodological problems must be understood only in the light of that situation. When the methodological situation is disturbed or disrupted, so to speak, we have a commencement of a new methodological situation or state, which over an interval of time will become stable or hardened. The transition from one methodological milieu to the next may be caused by the difficulties sprouted by the methodology itself; or it may be due to a rising new methodological tradition that has gained a foothold in that scientific society; or it may be due to a massive change in social and political conditions which finally affects the direction of the methodological tradition.

One final point. Though perhaps occurring less frequently, there are conjectures and refutations in methods just as there are in the sciences. Any defense of empiricism that claims that since the discussion of method is remarkably similar to the discussion of science, we must regard statements of method as empirical, too, is ill founded. Consider ethics. Here, as in science, we proceed conjecturally. No one would claim, without the benefit of further supporting arguments, that ethical statements are empirical or scientific, and even less claim that in ethics we propose lawlike statements. Any ethical theory that rendered persons ethical because they have biologically internalized ethical principles would not likely be accepted. We know we have made serious mistakes in the past, and not simply in deliberately doing the wrong thing. Often, we have unknowingly been subscribers to wrong principles—such as, "It is not unethical to own slaves or support the institution of *harijans*"—however well-intentioned our acceptance of such principles might be. In brief, I can claim that methods change and progress as a result of conjectures and confutations, without leaving myself open to the charge that the statements of method are empirical. To repeat, the statements of method are objective, normative, and bearers of a truth-value.

When Popper says, "Profound truths are not to be expected of methodologies,"[63]—or, he might have added, theories of method—I disagree. My reasons are unabashedly Popperian.[64]

3

Lakatos's Theory of Method

In the early 1960s a strong reaction against an excessively formal and clinical approach in philosophy of science set in. To philosophers of science in the formal school, history of science seemed irrelevant since logical analysis of concepts such as 'explanation,' 'scientific law,' and 'confirmation' appeared in a sense to be timeless. An answer to the question, What is a natural law?—like, What is consistency?—if correct, could not be refuted by citing mere history or precedent. But Paul Feyerabend disagreed. "History," he said, "cannot be dismissed out of hand as being irrelevant to the methodologist."[1] So the slogan became, "Practice is primary." Philosophers of science who belonged to the historical school proceeded—though not all of them on as grand and influential a scale as did Thomas Kuhn—"to sketch quite a different concept of science that can emerge from the record of the research activity itself."[2] But these were still *methods*.

In 1971 there appeared a landmark paper offering a theory of method. It was Imre Lakatos's "History of Science and Its Rational Reconstructions," which three years later was followed by his "Popper on Demarcation and Induction," a paper on similar issues.[3] Lakatos's theory of method made a strong impact not only on philosophers but also on the historians of science. For good reason. He not only envisioned clearly some of the problems we face in deciding over rival methods, he offered an exciting solution. I shall argue that for all its brilliance and importance, the attempt is a failure.

The plan of this chapter is as follows. In the beginning, I present and evaluate Lakatos's statement of the problem. After that, certain indispensable Lakatosian preliminaries to his solution are discussed. Lakatos's solution is then examined and several difficulties raised. A new problem is stated, a partial, tentative solution is provided, and in its light criticisms are averted. Next, Lakatos's general approach is defended against recent appraisals of it. Finally, I show that Lakatos's solution leads to an unacceptable paradox, for which a simple, formal model is provided at the end.

I. THE PROBLEM

After briefly citing Popper's method, his game of science, Lakatos asks, How can this game, which is nothing but a conventional set of rules, be criticized and evaluated? Popper had argued that a reasonable discussion can take place provided the parties to it have an agreed common goal; the goal itself, Popper held, was beyond debate. Lakatos then notes that Popper "never offered a theory of rational criticism of consistent conventions. He does not answer the question: 'Under what conditions would you give up your demarcation criterion?' "[4] In the obscurity of a footnote, Lakatos remarks, "Popper's crucial arguments against various inductivist theories of science show that they are inconsistent. On the other hand, he admits that the conventionalist theory is consistent, 'self-contained and defensible,' and concludes: 'My conflict with the conventionalists is not one that can be settled by a detached theoretical discussion.' Is then the choice between (two or more) consistent sets of rules (methods) a matter of subjective taste?"[5]

This forces the problem into the open. One way of criticizing a scientific theory is by arguing that it is internally inconsistent or inconsistent with other well-corroborated theories. But a theory can also be tested against the objective reality, and be criticized for failing to match up to it. Why is a method different from a scientific theory? What criteria do we have to decide between competing and consistent methods? Do we really wish to assert that our acceptance of a method is simply a matter of subjective whim or fancy? If not, why is it that methods enable us to discuss scientific theories in an objective way but the same cannot be done for the methods themselves? Why are they beyond the pale of objective appraisal?

Lakatos's formulation of the problem is unprobing and rests on unnoticed assumptions. In most discussion of theories of method one finds that there is very little awareness of the aims of methods. One can compare two scientific theories if both have a common goal of being aesthetically pleasing. One obviously cannot compare a theory that aims at truth with another that aims at being elegant. Methods may have conflicting goals or aims, too. Indeed, they sometimes do. Popper's method is geared to the assumption that if we are interested in truth, his method will lead to truth, interesting truth, quickly and efficiently, other things being equal. Laudan has argued, however, that truth is irrelevant for many considerations that philosophers of science had hitherto thought depended on truth. He replaces the notion of truth with the notion of problem-solving effectiveness. Laudan would claim that if we are interested in a theory that is an effective problem-solver, then his method will lead to such a theory quickly and efficiently, other things being equal. Again, one method may say something relevant only to the problem of group rationality, whereas another method may offer theories relevant only to the problem of individual rationality. Thus even if methods had a common aim of explaining rationality or proposing norms for doing science, they could conceivably address themselves to entirely different problems.

How shall we compare methods that have such widely divergent goals? How shall we evaluate methods that have different explananda? Ought we to make indiscriminately an a priori assumption that using history of science as a testing ground, irrespective of the aims or goals of the methods, is a reasonable thing to do? It is difficult to see how any adequate theory of method can possibly ignore problems of discovering common goals, weighing their relative importance, providing arguments why the proposed criteria can and ought to be applied reasonably to the methods in question, and so on. However, assume that the statement of the problem, as Lakatos formulates it, is sufficiently clear, precise, and unproblematic.

II. PRELIMINARIES TO THE SOLUTION

Before discussing Lakatos's theory of method, I shall deal with some preliminaries. Lakatos puts these in the following way: "(*a*) Philosophy of science provides normative methodologies in terms of which the historian reconstructs 'internal history' and thereby provides a rational explanation of the growth of objective knowledge; (*b*) two competing methodologies can be evaluated with the help of normatively interpreted history; (*c*) any rational reconstruction of history needs to be supplemented by an empirical (socio-psychological) 'external history.' "[6] To this he adds that each method will demarcate the distinction between normative-internal and empirical-external quite differently.

"Most historians of atomism," writes Robert Kargon in his *Atomism in England from Harriot to Newton*, "deal with their subject as if it existed, so to speak, in a void. In these works, atomism is treated as an ideological development of a few major figures. Absent are truly *historical* relations between men and ideas; all stress is placed upon internal philosophical and scientific developments. . . . Atomism becomes a concept developed by philosophical titans and not *real* men, facing *real* problems—social, political, theological, and personal, as well as scientific."[7] This is the view that takes unkindly to views, such as Lakatos's, that make so much of internal history.

To put it roughly, internal history of science is intellectual history. It is the history of scientific theories, both successful and otherwise; a history of experimental results that confirmed these theories or falsified them; the history of the analysis of central concepts, like gravity, force, and field, which in hand with various modifications of the relevant theories gave the latter their final form, content, and confirmation; and the history of the attempt to render a theory self-consistent, as in the case of naive set theory, or, to render a theory consistent with other well-confirmed theories, as when Lamarck's version of evolution, in the days of Cuvier, ran afoul of confirmed theories about geology, anatomy, and fossils. No internalist says that these developments took place in a void. The absence of social, psychological, and political factors does not constitute a void, for the internalist will claim that these developments took the shape they did against the background and heritage of preceding theories and tests. The method enables a historian, or a philosopher, to reconstruct the succession of ideas, theories, and experimental tests, and to exhibit a growth in objective knowledge. Truth, consistency, corroboration, evidence, and experimental results are concepts not rooted in social and political circumstances and institutions; and, hence, such circumstances are ignored in providing intellectual history.

External history is parasitical on internal history for its problems. Internal history of science is a rational enterprise—if it is not rational, then nothing is—as external history of science is not. The latter is to be explained not in terms of a method but rather in terms of some empirical science with which every method is supplanted, such as psychology or sociology of discovery. To illustrate the point: Even in the face of overwhelming evidence in favor of Mendel's theory of genetics, Soviet scientists and scientific societies rejected it. Here the task of explaining the internal history of science ends, and the task of explaining external history begins. A historian has now to uncover the prevailing social and political repression, the economic conditions of Soviet Russia and the power structure within the dominant scientific communities, to understand and explain why such a theory was irrationally rejected; such explanations can then be confirmed or confuted in the usual way. It is therefore mostly a misplaced protest to cry that the internalists are destroying or distorting the history of science.

There is some justification in the protest, however. Lakatos and other internalists argue that the division of labor between methodologists and social scientists can be precisely drawn. If a certain segment of the history of science has been shown to be rational by the standards of a current method, then that segment is outside the domain of social scientists. If a certain segment of the history of science has been shown to be irrational, then that segment is outside the concern of the methodologist. The task of the methodologist is with the *character* of theories, of the social scientist with the *causes* of discovery, acceptance, or rejection of theories. But this need hardly be. If it was rational to accept Darwin's theory of evolution, together with his theory of natural selection by 1865, it does *not* follow that various scientists and scientific communities accepted it for good reasons rather than for political, social, and economic considerations; if it was rational to reject substance theories of heat, it need not follow that the scientists' rejection of it was *not* due to social and political pressures. It is a brute fact that William Harvey rejected the primacy of the heart in favor of the primacy of the blood; the question is, How shall we explain his rejection? An internal historian of science may explain it by citing Harvey's failure to use that Aristotelian notion of the primacy of the heart fruitfully in his embryological work, work "which lead him to doubt other facets of the heart's primacy." But an external historian of science may cite the political transition from monarchy (heart) to republic (blood) as deeply and decisively influencing Harvey's decision.[8] We cannot always be sure that an external explanation is not lurking somewhere, even if we have a plausible internal explanation; and, of course, the converse is also true. Consequently, there is no a priori way in which we can lay down the conditions that determine those segments of the history of science that need not concern an empirical scientist and those that need not engage a methodologist.

Moreover, if external history comprises merely what is not in internal history of science, as Lakatos assumes, then there is much in external history, I suspect, that is inappropriately characterized as irrational. To the historical problem of why Frege started to work once more on the foundations of mathematics after 1923, this time using the fundamental notions of geometry as the basis with which to analyze and derive other mathematical theories, including number theory and analysis, the answer is, of course, that his use of the theory of classes in *Die Grundgestze der Arithmetic* in developing the foundations of mathematics led to contradictions, as was shown by Russell in 1903. To the historical problem of why Bolzano worked on the analysis of the concepts of continuity and limit, the answer is that he was dissatisfied with the work of Newton, whose analysis appealed to an intuition of continuous motion, and with the work of Leibniz, who merely postulated the concept of continuity. Bolzano wanted to lay a rigorous foundation for calculus by invoking considerations drawn only from algebra, arithmetic, and analysis. To the historical problem of why Adams and Le Verrier worked on the problem of the perturbation of Uranus, the answer is because they wished to rescue a highly successful Newtonian theory of mechanics from a serious problem. These questions and answers are appropriate to internal history: answers to why certain problems were dwelt on have their roots in intellectual history.

In contrast, consider the question, Why did Archimedes work on the problem of designing destructive machines? There is no intellectual context and background from which to answer this question. What happened was that the king of Syracuse "persuaded Archimedes to make for him offensive and defensive machines for every type of siege." To be sure, the analysis of the problem Archimedes was engaged in—whether his formulation was sufficiently sharp, whether he took into account the various extant relevant theories, and so on—is a matter for the historian interested in intellectual, internal history. He will not, however, be able to answer *why* Archimedes was engaged in this problem if he stays squarely within internal history. Correspondingly, the question of why so many contemporary scientists are engaged in energy problems may not be answerable in terms of the intellectual history of their discipline but may reside in the social and economic situation of the times. The answers that external history of science provides in the two cases, however, do not show that Archimedes and contemporary scientists were irrational for working on those particular problems.

The notion of external history, I wish to argue, is even broader than this. Broadly construed, it can meet an objection that can be put thus: Suppose a biologist decides not to conduct basic research in certain areas of biology, such as genetic engineering. If viewed from the limited perspective of scientific rationality, his decision may appear irrational. If we enlarge our view, however, taking in the biologist's ethical and religious goals and beliefs as well, then his action will appear rational rather than otherwise. The action or decision of the biologist can be accounted for without invoking economics, sociology, psychology, or such empirical sciences, by appealing to other normative principles. On the Lakatosian view of external history, confined as it is to being accounted for by the empirical sciences (and ethics not normally being considered a science), the biologist's decision would have to be explained away quite differently, not to say unsatisfactorily.

Interestingly, the issue of demarcating internal history from external history is joined with the issue of whether a scientist qua scientist makes a value judgment. If he does, then the ethical principles that yield these value judgments ought to be part of the normative components of a method. If ethics and method are independent, as I believe, then the manner in which external history can be explained ought to be broadened. This modification of Lakatos's view is quite consistent with his proposals. What is more, Lakatos views the various social sciences as being protosciences, at best, and as offshoots of a "new bad tradition," at worst. It is therefore fair to conclude that explanations that invoke the social sciences would be inconclusive and inadequate, at best; and explanations that invoke ethical and religious norms, in some instances, may be right and adequate. I now turn to the all important (*b*).

Lakatos says, "Whatever problem the historian of science wishes to solve, he has first to reconstruct the relevant section of the growth of objective scientific knowledge, that is, the relevant section of 'internal history.' As it has been shown, what constitutes for him internal history, depends on his philosophy, whether he is aware of this fact or not." So that, "in constructing internal history the historian will be highly selective: he omits everything that is irrational in the light of his rationality theory." This point is culminated in Lakatos's saying, "*History without some theoretical 'bias' is impossible.*"[9]

In terms of our framework for methods, if a historian of science uses a method, *M*, he will consider scientific only those propositions that satisfy the criteria laid down in the objective component; he will ignore the rest. Likewise, he will consider rational only those actions of the scientists that satisfy the criteria laid down in the normative component; the rest he will regard as irrational. This historian's bias, according to Lakatos, is essential and indispensable, and his bias (method, that is) presumably would be reflected in the history he writes.

So far I have merely explained one part of (*b*), namely, how and why the history of science must be normative in nature. I should now explain Lakatos's claim that two methods can be compared and critically evaluated with the help of normatively interpreted history. This is what Lakatos proposes: We take a method, say M_3, which is quite successful, and use it as a model to write normative history. We then use M_1 and M_2 to write normative history. M_1, M_2, and M_3 will each determine internal and external history in the list of their objective and normative components, respectively. Assuming that the methods being evaluated are M_1 and M_2, what we do is the following: We compare the internal history as charted out by M_1 with the internal history as charted out by M_3; similarly, we compare the external history as charted by M_1 with the external history charted out by M_3. We repeat this process with M_2. If we discover that the boundaries of internal history and external history as charted out by M_1 coincide more nearly with those charted out by M_3 than do the boundaries of M_2, we prefer M_1 to M_2.

While each method will have its own unique logical and epistemological problems, says Lakatos, it will also have the problem of trying to account for the normatively interpreted history of science or to explain the discrepancies when compared with it.

III. THE SOLUTION

We have now set the stage to answer in detail the question, How shall we arbitrate over methods? Lakatos cites the following criteria for the selection or acceptance of a method. Briefly, what ensues is Lakatos's theory of method. A method must (*a*) square up with the basic value judgments of the scientific elite; (*b*) reclaim more of external history as internal history; (*c*) predict basic value judgments; and (*d*) lead to the revision of basic value judgments. In appraising his criteria, I defend Lakatos against the criticisms of others, and offer a few of my own.

Lakatos says "if a demarcation criterion is inconsistent with the basic appraisals of the scientific elite, it should be rejected."[10] While there is little or no agreement on a general or universal criterion for the scientific character of theories, there is considerable core agreement over particular episodes in the history of science. The task of each method is to incorporate as much of these basic agreements as it can, and any wide difference between what the method says and what the core agreement—the basic values of the scientific elite—is, reflects poorly on the method.

It is an imperative of Popper's method that the scientist working on a theory should specify in advance what is going to count as a refutation of his theory. If we consider the history of Newtonian mechanics, however, we do not find Newton, or any Newtonian, setting down the conditions under which the theory would be given up. What we find instead is that, far from giving up Newton's theory when Mercury's perihelion falsified it, the scientists made ad hoc moves contrary to Popperian dictums. It is important to note that the scientific elite would have regarded the rejection of Newton's theory under these conditions as utterly irrational. In short, the decision of the scientists of the time was highly rational. These are the basic appraisals of the scientific elite. Therefore, history falsifies Popper's method since it does not square up with the basic value judgments of the scientists.

There is an oddity in Lakatos's criticism of Popper, and it is this: Lakatos says that Popper was right in condemning the psychoanalysts, palmists, and astrologers who did not specify the conditions under which they would give up their theory. Lakatos agrees with Popper that their not specifying the conditions under which they would give up their respective theory was a hallmark of their intellectual dishonesty.[11] If this is so, why was it not intellectually dishonest for the Newtonians to have left unspecified the conditions under which they would reject Newtonian mechanics? A method should at least be consistent (or should it?),[12] and if so, any method that makes it rational for the Newtonians to leave unspecified the conditions that would falsify their theory would make it rational for the psychoanalysts, palmists, and astrologers to do the same. In other words, Lakatos cannot have it both ways: praise Popper for condemning palmists and psychoanalysts for their ad hoc ways, and condemn Popper for not praising Newtonian scientists who adopted similar strategems.

Moreover, to echo Popper's concern, *who* are the scientific elite? Since different groups will reflect sharply differing basic value judgments, we need an answer to that question if we are to capture the "right" basic value judgments in our method. Lakatos does not favor a view that leaves *scientist* undefined since astrologers, or any pseudoscientific groups, could set themselves up as supreme authority.[13] Although Lakatos himself does not provide such a definition, he pleads for dual authority in method where "some of the scientists' basic value judgments can and should be overthrown, especially when a tradition degenerates or a new bad tradition is founded."[14] The aim is to take away excessive authority from the scientists and to emphasize the importance of methodological norms. But this reply cannot work, for several reasons.

The dual-authority view already presupposes that we know who the scientists are whose basic value judgments need to be heeded. Heinz Post claims that an attempt to define *elite scientist* in terms of those who exert influence is not only distinctly sociological, hence making the criteria external, but may be circular as well.[15] One can go further than Post and say that if one can tell whether a tradition is degenerating or progressing without turning to the basic value judgments of the scientific elite, then appeal to the latter is redundant. For no matter how unanimously or firmly held certain value judgments are, if we know objectively the poor worth of a theory because, for instance, it has failed a number of severe tests, then the members of the tradition who consistently hold onto such theories are not to be regarded as scientists. If, on the contrary, one cannot tell if a research program is progressing without resorting to the basic value judgments of the scientific elite, then the final authority must rest with the scientists, making matters distinctly sociological. Perhaps, as I believe, this dilemma is inevitable, and Lakatos is reasonably asking us to strike a happy balance between the two ways of evaluating a theory.

"When a better rationality theory is produced," claims Lakatos, "internal history may expand and reclaim ground from external history." And, "In the light of better rational reconstructions of science one can always reconstruct more of actual great science as rational." Further, "Rational reconstruction of science (in the sense in which I use the term) cannot be comprehensive since human beings are not *completely* rational animals; and even when they act rationally they may have a false theory of their own rational actions."[16]

Some find this seriously objectionable. Richard Hall says, "Nobody would want to say that *all* of science is rational and that *all* of scientists' judgments about science are correct. . . . This seems to imply the possibility of a methodology that includes too much of science as internal."[17] He then proceeds to show how Lakatos's claim can be reduced to a *reductio ad absurdum*. Suppose a method asserts that one ought to accept a progressing research program over its degenerating rival unless the government encourages the acceptance of the latter. Such a method, or a suitable variant, can easily show more of Lysenko's actions or decisions as rational or internal. Hall concludes: "Should we accept this methodology because it includes as internal some of science that Popper and Lakatos relegate to external history? Of course not."[18] In a similar vein, Larry Laudan argues that "Lakatos' approach strikes me as counter-intuitive for a very simple reason: if we take his proposal seriously, then the best model of rationality would be that one which resulted in the judgment that every decision ever made in the history of science was rational. This seems to be a curious ideal to strive after, for just as we are convinced that some scientific choices have been rational ones, we are equally convinced (given 'human nature') that not all of them have been rational."[19]

The objection is puzzling. Lakatos has explicitly claimed that *not* all the decisions in the history of science are rational.[20] On their reading of Lakatos, either the value judgments of the scientific elite regard no action as irrational or these value judgments of the elite are not to be heeded—a disjunction Lakatos did not maintain. The difficulty lies in understanding precisely what Lakatos was claiming when he said that a better theory of rationality will reclaim internal history from external history. Clearly, Hall's counterexample can be sympathetically understood only on a false rendering of Lakatos's claim—namely, showing what is really irrational to be rational—if one is to have a better theory of rationality. It is toward the end of trying to give a correct explanation of Lakatos's claim that I state a problem, propose a tentative solution to it, and show how the objections of Hall and Laudan can be met and why Hall's counterexample is not a counterexample after all.

Among the problems confronting a theory of method is the question, Under what conditions is one method better than another? Separating the logical problem from the epistemological one, we distinguish the two problems confronting a theory of method thus:

(*Logical Problem*): Under what conditions is one method, *M*, better than another method, *M'*?

(*Epistemological Problem*): Under what conditions can we know, reasonably guess or conjecture, that one method, *M*, is better than another method, *M'*?

To solve the logical problem, I need to raise and answer the question, Under what conditions is a method to be regarded as the *best* one? Lakatos would have answered that under ideal conditions, when all the data is in, so to speak, and unanimity prevails concerning the value judgments of the scientific elite, and no revision of these values is possible or necessary, the best method is the one that captures precisely those theories that are scientific and fails to capture those that are unscientific; the best method captures precisely those decisions that are rational and fails to capture those decisions that are irrational. What is a little bit less vague is to say that such a method will explain why all rational decisions (and no others) are rational, and why all scientific theories (and no others) are scientific. It will also explain why all unscientific theories (and no others) are unscientific, and why all irrational decisions (and no others) are irrational. Such a method I shall refer to as *M**. Parenthetically, although it is relatively easy to say in what precise way a method shows theories to be either scientific or unscientific, it is very difficult to say precisely how a current method *explains* actions or decisions of past scientists as either rational or otherwise.

The partial solution to the logical problem is tucked away in an appendix at the end of this chapter, but the essential idea is quite simple. *A method* M *can be better than* M' *if, and only if,* M *is more like* M* *than is* M'. For instance, other things being equal, *M* captures more of what *M** charts as internal history (scientific theories and rational decisions) than does *M'*, as when *M* can explain the scientific character of the special theory of relativity and *M'* cannot. Or, *M* relegates to external history less of what *M** charts as internal history than does *M'*, as when *M'* shows Vesalius's theory of the human anatomy and Linnaeus's taxonomy to be unscientific, and *M* pronounces only the Linnaean theory to be unscientific. Or, when *M* explains more of what *M** charts as external history than does *M'*, as when *M* explains why Marx's theory of history is unscientific and *M'* cannot. Or, *M* retrieves what *M'* incorrectly charts as external history of *M**; and so on.

The solution envisages the possibility of two methods such that the better of the two is able to account for unscientific theories and irrational actions or decisions but cannot account for, or can account for only a few, scientific theories and rational actions.[21] For example, a method may be able to show why astrological theories are unscientific or why adherence to alchemy or to the doctrines of special creation or spontaneous generation, at a certain time, was irrational. It is probable that a developing, immature method or a protomethod is more likely to account for these than for more complex scientific theories and rational decisions such as the theory of the great Darwinian morphologist, Ernest Haeckel, namely, that a single, gastrulalike (an early stage in embryonic development) ancestor is the common origin of all multicellular organisms. Of course, it would be wrong to infer that there are no complex, irrational actions or unscientific theories that a developing method can fail to account for, such as the Latin encyclopaedists' movement of the seventh and eighth centuries inspired by the works of Pliny and Isidore of Seville. To be sure, we would still need an *epistemic* criterion to judge between rival protomethods; perhaps this may help in taking a step toward proposing that criterion.

The solution provides my defense of Lakatos against the criticisms of Hall and Laudan.[22] Lakatos made two claims: (*a*) the more rational actions or decisions a method accounts for, the better it is; and (*b*) the more external history is retrieved and shown to be internal history, the better a method is. Although Lakatos often conflated (*a*) and (*b*), the solution to the logical problem can be used to show that these claims are separate and that they are safe from the lately mentioned criticisms.

The solution can show that M' can improve, come closer to filling the gap between it and M if, like M, it can account for other scientific theories and rational actions as well.[23] Thus, assume that according to M^* it was rational to reject Aristarchus's heliocentric theory at the time, and M can account for this decision. M', however, can neither account for the rational rejection of it *nor* show the rejection of that theory to be irrational. If M' is further developed, then assume that it can account for the rejection of the theory. It is a better method than it was before, and the gap between it and M has slightly diminished as a result. This is what Lakatos meant in asserting (*a*).

The solution also shows that a method can mistakenly or wrongly portray part of internal history as external history, and such a method can improve if internal history is reclaimed from external history.[24] Let us take Lakatos's own examples. According to the justificationist methods, the phlogiston theory and the Bohr-Kramer-Slater theory were unscientific. Popper's method retrieved from the external history of the justificationist method what was internal history of M^*. Again, according to Popper's method, it was irrational to retain and further develop Newtonian theory once the perihelion of Mercury was discovered, and it was irrational to develop Bohr's old quantum theory since it was based on inconsistent foundations. Lakatos's method retrieved from the external history of Popper's method what was internal history of M^*.[25] These examples, and all others, clearly indicate the *manner* of retrieval and the sense of the claim (*b*). It would be wrong to suppose, as did Hall and Laudan, that *any* retrieval is as good as any other. The example of Lysenko is not a counterexample since the fabricated method Hall proposes would have the effect of making external history of M^* to be the internal history; this does not show improvement in a method, it shows inadequacy.

The thrust behind (*b*) is the following generalization: retrieval is from an incorrect method. A method M correctly retrieves internal history of M^* from the external history of M' if, and only if, M' portrays internal history of M^* to be M^*'s external history. Similarly, a method M correctly retrieves external history of M^* from the internal history of M' if, and only if, M' portrays external history of M^* to be M^*'s internal history. No other retrieval by M is correct.

My solution to the logical problem is quite in keeping with the Lakatosian enterprise inasmuch as it retains the basic idea of using normative history of science, M^*, for evaluating methods. However, I emphasize that the solution is a partial one, and this brings me to some of the inadequacies of the solution. The solution is impotent against the following possibilities. First, suppose the internal history of theories captured by M is greater than that captured by M', but that the internal history of rational decisions captured by M is less than that captured by M'. Second, suppose the internal history captured by M is different (nonoverlapping, that is) from the internal history captured by M'. In these instances the solution will not be able to say which method is better. Finally, these difficulties are compounded by the fact that we must distinguish between important scientific theories and less important ones, important rational actions and decisions and less important ones. It is important to retain Newton's theory but not as important to retain all the recent cosmological models. It is important to account for the acceptance of the special theory of relativity but not so important to account for the rationality or irrationality of accepting or rejecting the hypothesis of the theory of group selection, Hamilton's kinship theory, Trivers's theory of reciprocal altruism, and so on. If one method captures more trivial theories and actions but fails to capture some very important ones, while another method captures some very important theories and actions but fails to be clear on some trivial ones, the solution will not be able to say which method is better. In brief, we would have to consider some quantitative and qualitative problems. Though the above difficulties pertain to the logical problem, they also have an obvious bearing on the epistemological problem as well.

This brings us to the last two criteria of Lakatos's theory of method that I shall discuss here. "A theory of rationality," says he, "has to try to organize basic value judgments in universal, coherent frameworks. . . . We should, of course, insist that a good rationality theory must anticipate further basic value judgments unexpected in the light of its predecessor or that it must even lead to the revision of previously held basic value judgments."[26] Thus, two more criteria are added to the claims that a method must square up with the basic value judgments of the scientific elite and must attempt to retrieve internal history from the external history of science. First, a method must *predict* further basic value judgments, although not expected ones, perhaps to ensure independent testability. Second, a method must lead to the *revision* of basic value judgments already held.

What is it for a method to predict values? Is it the task of a method to predict values or changes in values? Consider an example. A century and a half separated Galen and Oribasius, two great medical authors of antiquity. Although this was a period pockmarked with internal and external conflicts and strife that left little time and peace for scholarly activities, it was also an epoch that witnessed a quiet and deepening change in interests and values. Earlier during this period, pagan philosophy and religious movements could count on the broad-based support and participation of the educated public in scientific discussion and debate; the pagan movement was eclectic in style, and science prospered. In the third century, however, "intellectual needs underwent a transformation." The rising movement of Neoplatonic philosophy repressed the earlier rational and eclectic movement in favor of interests, aims, and values more mystical in nature. Not surprisingly, each movement partly nourished the other: pagan philosophy gained new inspiration from

Christianity, and Christianity drew its philosophical arsenal, in its fight against other religious myths and movements, from paganism. Thus, from the fifth century B.C. until the sixth century A.D. Greek science flourished; however, with the advent of Christianity, which had then mastered the Mediterranean world, the values underlying the investigation of a transient world (or, what was then perceived as a transient world) dwindled as men sought knowledge of more permanent things, such as God and the human soul. Science declined, notwithstanding the facts that Christians were not against science and that the last two great scientists of this epoch, Philoponos and Anthemios, were Christians.[27]

Now, what part or component of a method enables it to make predictions about the change in values just described? A method is defined by the objective and normative components: an objective component defines key terms while the normative components advise scientists how they ought to appraise theories and what theories they ought to pursue. Neither component makes any claim remotely resembling empirical claims of the sort needed here to make predictions or prognostications about the future values of scientific societies or about the change in present ones. Moreover, the sciences that enable us to make the predictions about values are really immature sciences, from the point of view of Lakatos. And, as Feyerabend argues, the values a scientist holds are often in a state of flux, held without reason, or rest on serious mistakes, and scientists often have different values given their different theoretical and disciplinary persuasions. From all of this Feyerabend concludes that "common scientific wisdom is not very common and it is certainly not very wise."[28] It appears, then, that a method is not only very ill suited to make predictions but that if it attempted to do so, it could not enjoy a status much better than that of the immature social sciences.

What is meant by the claim that a method should lead to a revision of the basic values? Is a method to operate as a propaganda device? Is it to be used to train incoming scientists in new values? On Lakatosian grounds, one cannot argue that the scientific community is always right, or that if the community did not in fact adopt the values the method commended, it only shows that those values were worthless. This argument cannot be made because it would make nonsense of Lakatos's insistence that scientists are not rational men all the time. There is also a simple and straightforward empirical question: in consulting the chart earlier in this book,[29] can one discern any method or second-order tradition in the history of science and methodology that in fact made even a single prediction about future scientific values or that in fact explained how these new values would have to compete and struggle with older values? If not, were all these methods inadequate? Is there a rationale for imposing a burden on current methods of which older methods were free?

Let us assume, however, that a method, as part of its function, should aim at predicting, changing, and explaining basic value judgments. Why would it be better if it actually did correctly predict values? How would this help us to confirm or eliminate methods? Suppose we are evaluating two methods. The first predicts (retrodicts) that after the twelfth century Arabic science will decline, and the second predicts that that science will continue to grow and flourish. We discover that subsequent to the work of the mystical theologian al-Ghazali, Arabic science declined and intellectuals turned away from contemplating nature, the creation of God, to contemplating God's beauty, a beauty to be recognized by delving deeply into one's soul. We find, too, that "cultural priorities then changed; science tapered; Islamic poetry, architecture, and the arts achieved splendid new magnificence." Our general conclusion about the decline of Arabic science would not be erroneous even if we learned that there were a few bright spots later, such as ibn al-Nafis's discovery in the early thirteenth century of the pulmonary circulation of the blood; or ibn al-Shatir of Damascus' fourteenth-century geometrical explanation of planetary orbits, which bore an astonishing similarity to the descriptions found in the work of Copernicus; or Ulug Beg's mid-fifteenth-century astronomical observations and measurements that rivaled in precision those made by Tycho Brahe.[30] Should we now eliminate the second method and regard the first method as confirmed? Should the second method be rejected on this ground alone? Is it not sound defense of the second method to say that after the twelfth century Arabic science worked with a very inadequate set of values and that in fact it should have opted for the set of values commended by the method in question? If that answer and response are right, would that falsify the first method?

If a method attempts to bring about revision in the basic value judgments, and *succeeds*, the problem may then be that it failed to advocate values that are more effective; or, alternatively, that it advocated values that were not effective at all. One's immediate response is to say that this is impossible: if a method is attempting to bring about changes, it will not predict values detrimental to the interests and aims of the scientific community. But this is far too optimistic. Is there any reason to believe—indeed, isn't there a good deal of reason to believe the opposite?—that a community will adopt those values that it ought to have and will never have values it ought not to have? A method will have two separate parts to accomplish the respective tasks of revision and proselytizing of values. Since these parts are different, and they each have different functions, and each can make judgments incompatible with the other, the possibility of inconsistency is very real. Clearly, (*c*) and (*d*) as criteria for evaluating methods lead to some serious problems.

IV. APPRAISALS OF THE APPROACH

Not to overlook the forest for the trees, let us leave the examination of specific issues in the Lakatosian solution and scrutinize the criticisms of the general overall strategy of Lakatos's theory of method.

Ernan McMullin points to the difficulty of not knowing when Lakatos is using the history of science, warts and all, to confirm methods, and when he is using the history of science as an example of what ought not to have been. He argues that Lakatos notes the difficulty of rejecting any particular theory of rationality in the absence of a more general theory of rationality, but that instead of offering a general theory, Lakatos criticizes particular theories, such as dogmatic falsificationism, by citing the history of science.[31]

It is patently unclear what a *general* theory of rationality is. Is it something from which any particular method is derived, or a theory under which particular theories of rationality are subsumable? Just as it is difficult to tell what precisely is wrong with a particular scientific theory—how its inadequacies are to be accentuated, and how it should be corrected—unless a rival comes along, so also Lakatos might say that the inductivist view was seen as seriously objectionable only in the light of Popper's methods, as the latter view was seen as objectionable only in the light of Lakatos's own method, and so on. We do not know what to do with an objectionable method that has no better rival or no rival at all.

McMullin feels uneasy because of the equivocal role assigned to the history of science, which is "at once emphasized and called upon as evidence, yet is systematically 'reconstructed' in the service of a prior theory of rationality." In short, we do not know if the history of science is being used as evidence or as illustration; one cannot help but worry. But what else should a historically oriented theory of method recommend? No methodologist, Lakatos included, says, "Here are some of the episodes in the history of science, such as Prout's hypothesis and Bohr's early theory of the atom; but regard these only for purposes of *illustration*. They will give you a handle on the basic concepts of my method. But now look at the other episodes in the history of science, such as the Copernican revolution and the Darwinian revolution. We have an intuition that those were scientific theories and that the scientists in those periods were rational in rejecting earlier theories, namely, the Ptolemaic theory and the theory of Lamarck, respectively. If my method does not explain the correctness of those decisions then my method is at fault; if it does, as I claim, then my method is correct and there is *evidence* for it. I have thus stated the precise conditions under which my method is to be accepted or rejected."

As with scientific practice, so with methodology: no well-defined, precise predictions are continuously made; this is only truer in methodology. The task of method construction is not different from theory construction. If certain segments in the history of science are not accounted for as rational, then the methodologist may pronounce them as irrational, our intuitions concerning the rationality of these historical episodes notwithstanding, for he does not take these intuitions to be inviolate. Or, the methodologist may tinker with his method so as to retain its basic form and features and show how he could explain the segment of the history of science that he could not explain before. Or, the difficulties posed to his method by certain segments of the history of science—for example, da Vinci's theory of how sea water got salty, Boyle's theory of why the bottom of the sea is exceedingly calm, Buffon's theory of the formation of the earth in seven epochs, or Michell's theory that earthquakes are caused by a massive, underground, elastic force of vapors—may not be considered sufficiently important or serious enough counterevidence until the major difficulties have first been responded to. Hence, it is always a matter of striking a delicate balance between using the history of science as an arbitrator between methods and using methods to pronounce on the rationality of the history of science. No theory of method that is historically oriented can recommend otherwise.

McMullin made a remarkable claim that the contemporary conflict in the philosophy of science is at the level of the theory of method rather than at the level of method. He thinks that inductivism, conventionalism, falsificationism, and the methodology of research programs share a wide agreement on how to appraise theories and that they would have offered the same advice to the scientists. They differ, however, on how the notion of rationality, the history of science, and method hang together. He suggests that philosophers of science can agree on a theory of method but disagree on a method, as well as agree on a method but disagree on a theory of method.[32] He therefore concludes that it is not the history of science, but rather the recent philosophy of science, that Lakatos first needs to rationally reconstruct.[33]

Most philosophers, I think, agree that the history of science should be used as an arbitrator between methods; their theories of method differ, at most, as trivial variants on that central theme. Their methods, however, are vastly different. Laudan's heuristic advice as to which theory to pursue is different from Popper's; their respective methods would have given not merely different reasons but different advice. Feyerabend's advice to Galileo would have been to ignore Popper's advice; the logical positivist would have advised the scientist to discard metaphysical theories; not so a Duhemian; Lakatos's advice to the scientist as to what to regard as a scientific theory, and the conditions under which a theory should be rejected, would not have coincided with Popper's advice. *It is precisely because the advice would have been different, reflecting the different reasons, that the history of science is called in to settle the differences in method.*

To be sure, there is a common factor: there is a shared pool of common preanalytic judgments and intuitions, such as the transition from the Ptolemaic theory to the Copernican theory was a rational one; Newton's theory was an improvement over its Galilean predecessor; and so on. But other intuitions may vary in emphasis, some may not be too sharp in cases not yet fully explored, others may sharply conflict, and still others (the largest class, surely) may be in an embryonic stage waiting to develop and mature as other hitherto neglected areas of the history of science are studied, old methods more fully developed, and new ones fashioned. Perhaps bearing such less rooted intuitions in mind, Lakatos not only proposed that a method should weave in shared judgments in order for it to be considered good, he also proposed an epistemological criterion by which we will be able to judge whether the method is progressing. This criterion he stated as follows: "Progress in the history of scientific rationality is marked by discoveries of novel historical facts, by the reconstruction of a growing bulk of value impregnated history as rational."[34] At the least, the criterion presupposes that new things are waiting to be discovered, over which rival methods may potentially conflict and settle their claims. Only by ignoring less well-founded and conflicting intuitions and by confusing shared intuitions with reasons and methods could one claim that methods do not conflict, that only theories of method do.

McMullin argues that the structure of reasoning that proceeds in the sciences is different from the structure of reasoning in the theory of method.[35] If so, Lakatos's suggestion that a method should perform a dual function—both at the level of method and, with appropriate changes, at the level of theory of method—is unhelpful. But is it so difficult to see that the structure of reasoning is in fact the same? What corresponds to the observations are preanalytic judgments of the scientists; what corresponds to theories are methods; and what corresponds to the problem of whether a given scientific theory fits in with other well-established theories is the problem of whether a given method, and the quality of knowledge it provides, dovetails with other forms of knowledge, and so on.

If a method, such as the methodology of research programs, fits in with most of our preanalytic judgments concerning certain episodes in the history of science, it will not only be the best method, it will also then function, with appropriate changes, as a theory of method that will enable us to arbitrate between other rival methods. So, if the methodology of falsificationism is falsified, it is not falsified by its own principles but rather by the principles of the methodology of research programs. The falsification of falsificationism is not hastened as it would be if it were judged on its own terms; its falsification is a drawn-out process which entails showing, in part, that the methodology of falsificationism has entered a degenerating phase as defined by that method. Such a theory of method will also rank rival methods just as, in the guise of a method, it ranked rival scientific theories.

Noretta Koertge has different general complaints. She argues that (*a*) the legitimacy of introducing rational reconstructions in the history of science is questionable; and that (*b*) Lakatos has deliberately rigged the competition in favor of normative methods and against certain all-purpose descriptive theories.[36]

Both her claims are implausible.

Reconstructions, say Koertge, are a commonplace in science: there are conservative reconstructions, bold reconstructions, Procrustean reconstructions, and Galilean reconstructions. The interpolation of missing letters by a papyrologist would be an example of a conservative reconstruction. Examples of bold reconstructions include Cuvier's attempt to give the full skeletal structure of an animal on the basis of a single bone and Marvin Harris's attempt to explain human sacrifices as a way of satisfying protein needs. There are Procrustean reconstructions that simply distort the facts to serve and protect a theory; an example might be the stretching of geological and biological facts to safeguard the Biblical theory of the origin of man and the universe.

Just as Galileo introduced ideal laws in the physical sciences, so Lakatos is credited with introducing ideal Galilean reconstructions in the history of science. The law of the pendulum, the gas law, and the law of falling bodies, which ignore such factors as air resistance and intermolecular forces, are typical examples of ideal laws. What saves this kind of reconstruction from being Procrustean is the fact that scientists explicitly list the perturbing influences—'external factors'—that have been ignored and either test the law in cases where the perturbing factors have negligible effects or test it indirectly when the effects are not negligible. In both instances, scientists are able to give approximate estimates of the magnitude of the effects the ideal law in question ignores. This kind of accuracy is "almost always missing in the historical case," laments Koertge. She then asks, "Without some check, how could one compare the legitimacy of competing idealization?"[37]

Providing a list of perturbing influences or forces at the outset, in the way physical scientists do (assuming that they *do*), is well-nigh impossible; the quantitative precision is perhaps not as important as it is deemed to be; and indirect testing can be done without it—indeed, in some historical cases quantitative precision fails to make clear sense.

Suppose we have the following ideal methodological law: scientists ought to prefer the best-corroborated theory. At the outset, what list of perturbing factors can a methodologist be reasonably expected to supply? Nothing save the vaguest and most trivial generalizations come to mind, such as, economic necessity or social norm forced one to accept a poorer alternative. It is highly unlikely that anything more specific, much less quantitatively precise, can be had at the start, as in the case of the physicist or the chemist.

One interesting question for the historian of science was, Why was Mendel's theory ignored between 1866 and 1900? Garland Allen conjectures that there are "many reasons for Mendel's neglect. It may have been because Mendel himself was unknown; or because his work was published in a relatively obscure journal which, although it circulated widely, people may not have been in the habit of reading; or it may have been because the paper was highly mathematical, and seemingly inapplicable to living organisms."[38] Jean-Etienne Guettard after examining the sedimentary rocks in the Paris region conjectured that those were arranged in layers with the oldest layer lying lowest, and so on. He observed the change in the character of the fossils as one moved from one layer to the next, and guessed that an enormous span of time must have been required for the formation of layers; he also conjectured that various forms of life existed long before man. Guettard's theory so contradicted the literal interpretation of the Book of Genesis that he was forced by the theological professors of Sorbonne to publicly repudiate and recant his beliefs.[39] Between failing to read a paper for lack of mathematical knowledge and failing to please one's religious masters, there are literally thousands of disturbing factors that can account for why a scientist violated an ideal methodological law. Which factors can and ought to be listed at the start?

Perhaps it is because Koertge is after quantitative precision that she suspects introducing rational reconstructions in the history of science is not viable. Her suspicion is concealed in her questions: How can one measure the extent to which Galileo's acceptance of the Copernican system was due to the general ideological considerations and the extent to which his acceptance of the theory was based on a proper evaluation of the rival theories? What fraction of the rate of increase in scientific knowledge was due to the formation of scientific societies in the seventeenth century? How large was the influence of Protestant ethic?

Taking his cue from Allen, a historian of science might embark upon the testing of the hypothesis (*H*) that scientists in the late nineteenth century did not have an adequate background in mathematics to enable them to read Mendel's paper. The historian may draw up a roster of important, and some not-so-important, nineteenth-century scientists—morphologists, biologists, zoologists, and so on—and delve into their past. No records of schooling of individual scientists are found. What is discovered is a list of relevant courses in the mathematics department of a university or two, good relations between the members of the mathematics department and the members of the life science departments, membership lists of a few mathematical societies, together with the papers of very minor scientists in the same or similar field that showed the requisite mathematical background. One might reasonably conclude that (*H*) can be considered refuted.

At this point, Koertge might argue that all this is too general and vague (and so it is) and not quantitatively precise. We need, she might say, a fairly precise number of scientists and institutions who subscribed to the journal in which Mendel's paper was published; fairly precise data on the mathematical education of these scientists; a fairly precise number of scientists who could have read Mendel's paper; and so on. Furthermore, even when all that is in, she might say, as she does say in talking about Galileo, that we have no precise data that indicate the extent to which Mendel's paper was read and discarded for methodological reasons and the extent to which it was read and discarded for extraneous reasons, such as the notion that an outsider and an unknown could not possibly have anything important or interesting to say.

By contrast, a historian of science might investigate the hypothesis (*D*) that Darwin had not read Mendel's paper. He may conjecture, from certain unclear entries in Mendel's diary, that Mendel had sent Darwin his paper but that Darwin had not read it. The historian might make (*D*) more precise: an offprint of Mendel's paper will be found among Darwin's papers, but its pages will not have been cut. Such a conjecture would be corroborated![40] But in what sense is this conjecture quantitative although precise? How plausible is it to assume that such precise conjectures concerning external factors will be sufficiently frequently made?

Others have expressed a similar concern. We simply do not know enough about the history of science, they say, to judge rival methods. Of course, we do not. But would this concession force Lakatos to claim that our inability to answer questions precisely and quantitatively is reason enough to show that unlike the introduction of ideal laws in the physical sciences, introducing rational reconstructions in the history of science is not right? Is it not more reasonable to suppose that in all likelihood in this area one will have to settle for plausible, if vague, conjectures and answers?

What is more interesting is Koertge's claim that Lakatos has prejudged an issue between two *kinds* of approaches, the normative approach and the descriptive one. The first kind deals with norms and rational reconstructions in the way the second kind does not. Presumably, the first kind has under its rubric such methods as those of Popper, Carnap, Salmon, Lakatos, Laudan, and others, and under the second kind we have Marx's history, Hegel's history, psychoanalytical history, Harrissian history in terms of population pressures and ecological balance, and so on. In each of these accounts, the history of science would be but a single thread in the fabric.

A free Darwinian competition between *all* members of the two kinds of approaches is advocated in the hope that the fittest hypothesis will survive. Otherwise the competition will appear rigged in favor of normative methods inasmuch as entry to the competition is denied to descriptive theories. The aim is to give a more complete and total picture of the development of all of science rather than a mere account of "certain carefully selected episodes," in the history of science, episodes that are "preselected according to their rationality."[41]

These two kinds of approaches, perhaps complementing one another, are hardly on the same plane. The domain of discourse of these methods, their aims and goals, are different and not comparable. The situation in method, or in any other normative discipline, is analogous to that in ethics. It would be an odd criticism of John Rawls's view, encased in his book *A Theory of Justice*, that his original position, in which moral agents are trying to decide which normative principles of justice to select, was rigged in favor of normative ethical theories. Presumably, the argument would go as follows: the moral agents in the Rawlsian original position should be presented not only normative ethical theories—such as intuitionism, utilitarianism, moral egoism, teleological theories, and various variants of these—but also descriptive psychological and sociological theories, underpinned by economic factors, about how and why moral agents act the way they do. The descriptive theories are to be offered not as *constraints* on various principles of justice, but rather as *candidates* in direct competition with those principles. But can the task of normative ethics sensibly be set up in this way? Do moral agents qua moral agents choose *between* normative ethical theories and descriptive ethical theories? We have no hint as to how to evaluate the two approaches in method; and given the difference between norm and fact, it is not at all evident what complex and common criteria for evaluating these two radically different approaches one *can* have.

A philosopher might argue that there is no distinction between norm and fact and that if such a distinction does not exist, or the distinction is difficult to delineate, then distinguishing the two kinds of approaches is spurious.[42] He might claim that scientists do not act, although moral agents may, in accordance with normative principles, that their actions are best understood not in terms of principles of rationality but rather in social and economic terms. None of this would help Koertge. One of her examples of descriptive theories is Manuel's psychoanalytical account of Newton. Manuel himself, however, makes the Lakatosian distinction between rational (or internal) and irrational (or external) history of science, for he says that he hopes in his book "to grapple with the personality and non-scientific thought of Isaac Newton."[43] It is thus implied that there is room to grapple with the *scientific* thought of Newton. Far more importantly, counterobjections to Popper's well-known arguments against the possibility of a theoretical history of science, which Lakatos himself strongly supports,[44] need to be given. Until arguments for historicism and for abolishing the distinction between facts and norms have been found, the two kinds of approaches, the normative approach and the descriptive approach, represent well-worn distinctions worth preserving.

Finally, if one keeps in mind that methods are not predictive (in the sense of predicting the future development of science), then it is incorrect, too, to distinguish the normative and the descriptive approaches by viewing the former as guided by a narrower aim of accounting for a few, preselected cases in the history of science and the latter as guided by a much wider and all-encompassing aim. One begins with a few preselected cases because that is how a maturing discipline begins; there is no other reasonable alternative. But the hope of a methodologist can be expressed in terms of the ideal method, M^*, referred to earlier. An ideal method, no doubt a Galilean reconstruction, will explain all rational actions to be rational, all unscientific theories to be unscientific, and so on. Nor, in so picturing the ultimate aim or goal of a method, are we haunted by the specter of historicism.

So far, I have stated the problem as Lakatos conceived it; after important preliminaries, I scrutinized his proposed solution and his general approach and found several problems with them, while defending him against the criticisms of others. I now wish to show that there is an insuperable difficulty pervading Lakatos's solution which renders his solution unacceptable. This brings me to my paradox.

V. A PARADOX

The basic idea of the paradox is very simple. If a normative history of science is written from the standpoint of a certain method, and that method is then tested against that history, the method will be completely verified. We have argued in circles. If, however, one method is tested against a normative history of science written from the standpoint of another method, an evaluation of these two methods will show the first method as faring less well than the second, for an obvious reason: we have begged the question. Of course, the result can be easily generalized. Insofar as a normative history of science is indispensable (and it *is* indispensable in Lakatos's solution) the charges will remain.

Step 1

Let me begin an explanation of this argument by assuming that we have before us a history of ideas, and we will assume that there is a general agreement on what that history is. Our problem now is to delineate the history of science as a subplot of the history of ideas. On Lakatosian grounds we inevitably have to use some method to determine what this history of science is, a history that includes theories, and decisions related to these theories. Let us, therefore, assume that we use method M_1 to delineate the history of science. In accordance with our framework for methods, M_1 will have an objective component and a normative component. Its objective component will demarcate scientific theories from unscientific ones. The men who nurture, pursue, test, experiment with, criticize, and demarcate theories will be referred to as scientists. It is commonly accepted value judgments of *these* scientists that a methodologist will be interested in qua methodologist. The normative component of M_1 will distinguish the rational from the irrational decisions of these scientists; and so, we shall have data about these facts as well. Now that we have a proper subset of the history of ideas, which we shall refer to as the history of science, normatively constructed from the point of view of method M_1, we are ready to evaluate other competing methods in its light.

Step 2

We compare how these theories, scientists, and their decisions fare when looked at from the point of view of M_2. If, for instance, on M_2 most of the aforementioned scientific theories turn out to be unscientific, or most scientists turn out to be irrational, then M_2 would clearly be falsified and ought to be rejected. For clearly, in such a case it would be a very unsuccessful method, violating too many facts as determined by M_1. We repeat the above process with respect to methods, M_3, M_4, M_5, . . . , M_n. Finally, then, we shall have a method that least violates all the facts of normatively interpreted history of science (from the vantage point of M_1), and that will be the method we should accept as *(i)* a useful model for appraising scientific theories, *(ii)* a useful historiographical model, and *(iii)* perhaps (since this is a moot point in Lakatosian exegesis), a useful model of how scientific theories ought to be pursued.

When we have thus put the Lakatosian theory of method in terms of our framework, the paradox comes clearly home, for we are then wont to ask, What would happen if instead of using M_1 to write the normative history of science, we had used M_2? Surely, one is inclined to say, history seen in the light of M_2 would have rendered a different set of theories scientific, a different set of men scientists, and a different set of decisions rational—even allowing for some overlap in the resultant classification of theories, scientists, and decisions by the two methods.

If we had used M_2, instead of M_1, it is very likely—indeed, highly plausible—that M_1 would have fared rather poorly. This conclusion leads to two further questions: First, if M_1 is competing with others, what sense can it make to use the history of science constructed with the help of M_1 to test M_1? M_1 would of course be completely and conclusively verified, and in the strict sense of that phrase! Second, what arguments does Lakatos have, ***antecedent to any such comparison with the history of science***, that would justify our use of one method rather than another to write the normative history of science? We cannot invoke empirical success, since by hypothesis, we cannot determine it without comparing the method in question to normative history.

Step 3

The paradox, in the context of the foregoing statements, explanations, and queries, can be stated thus: If we use normatively interpreted history of science as a testing ground for competing methods, our attempt, at best, will be circular or question-begging. It will be circular against M_1, if we use M_1 to write normatively interpreted history of science, and then use that very history to see how well M_1 fares. It will be question-begging against other methods, if these other methods are tested against normative history written in the light of M_1.

VI. A MODEL OF THE PARADOX

In this extremely simplified model, each method, M_1, M_2, and M_3, considers a segment of the history of ideas in which three persons, fifteen theories, and five decisions of accepting or rejecting the relevant theory of each person (fifteen decisions in all) play central roles. The persons are Thomas Burnet (1635?–1715), Robert Hooke (1635–1703), and Nicolaus Steno (1638–1686). The theories or hypotheses, with exceedingly brief background, are primarily drawn from the history of geology so as to lend some unity to the model. They are:

1. Burnet's hypothesis, in his *The Sacred Theory of the Earth*, that there were two major events in the history of the earth up to the present: its origin from chaos and the universal Deluge; these are to be followed by two other events, the universal conflagration and the final end or consummation of all things.
2. Burnet's conjecture that the earth is very young; he thus regarded Aristotle's theory of the eternity of the world as false.
3. Burnet's conjecture of the shaping and lowering of mountains. He argued that the rivers were bringing mountain soil to the oceans, that the subterranean fires sometimes eat and weaken the roots of the mountains, and that earthquakes often bring about the collapse of mountains and molehills, not to mention the less perceptible actions of such agents as wind, rain, and storms. Burnet used this evidence to support his second conjecture (above), since if the earth's history was long enough there would have been no mountains, and the earth would have been everywhere flat.
4. Burnet's theory of the origin of the oceans. He argued that in the beginning water was pent up in the smooth surface of the earth. Subsequently, as a result of the action of the sun, the crust of the earth dried up and cracked, and the waters gushed out and oceans were formed.
5. The earth was created from chaos, and at the start it was a regular, smooth surface with no change of season; and it was the sin of man that brought upon the great Deluge, and ended the paradisical state.

Consider the diagram below using the key on the next page.

	S	*non-S*	*Sc*	*non-Sc*	*R*	*non-R*
M_1	T_1, T_2, T_3, T_4, T_5, T_6, T_7, T_8, T_9, T_{14}, and T_{15}	T_{10}, T_{11}, T_{12}, and T_{13}	P_1, P_2, and P_3	—	D_1, D_2, D_3, D_4, D_5, D_6, D_{10}, D_{11}, D_{14}, and D_{15}	D_7, D_8, D_9, D_{12}, and D_{13}
M_2	T_1, T_2, T_5, T_9, T_{11}, T_{13}, and T_{14}	T_3, T_4, T_6, T_7, T_8, T_{10}, T_{12}, and T_{15}	P_1 and P_3	P_2	D_1, D_2, and D_6	D_3, D_4, D_5, D_7, D_8, D_9, D_{10}, D_{11}, D_{12}, D_{13}, D_{14}, and D_{15}
M_3	T_1, T_3, T_{12}, T_{13}, T_{14}, and T_{15}	T_2, T_4, T_5, T_6, T_7, T_8, T_9, T_{10}, and T_{11}	P_2	P_1 and P_3	D_1, D_7, D_{11} D_{12}, D_{13}, D_{14}, and D_{15}	D_2, D_3, D_4, D_5, D_6, D_8 D_9, and D_{10}.

KEY

S	Scientific
non-S	Unscientific
Sc	Scientist
non-Sc	Pseudoscientist
R	Rational
non-R	Irrational
M_i	Method_i (i = 1, 2, and 3)
T_i	Theory_i (i = 1, 2, 3, . . . , 15)
P_i	Person_i (i = 1, 2, and 3)
D_i	Decision_i (i = 1, 2, 3, . . . , 15)

6. The hypothesis espoused by Robert Plot, Martin Lister, and Edward Lhuyd, that fossils were *lusus naturae*, sports of nature, and were produced by "plastic virtue." Hooke firmly rejected this theory.

7. Hooke's hypothesis concerning the origin and nature of fossils, stated in his "Lectures and Discourses of Earthquakes," in *Posthumous Works*. Hooke distinguished fossils into two categories: fossils of plants and animals, mostly marine organisms; and fossils of substances, such as salts and crystals. On the principle that nature does nothing in vain, that the fossils "owed their form and figure to the shells of the fishes they represent," and that these forms were not duplicated accidentally, the problem was, How could marine fossils be found on mountains, or deep within the earth, so far removed from their original habitat, the ocean? Hooke answered that the structural features of the earth were constantly changing so that, for instance, "many parts which have been Sea are now Land"; and thus it is that marine fossils are found on land far from the sea.

8. Hooke's hypothesis of the existence of a far more distinguished civilization than his own, "a preceding learned Age," before Noah's flood.

9. Hooke's theory about organic change. He conjectured the mutability of species as a result of the differences in the climate, soil, and nourishment on which the original members of a single species thrived.

10. Hooke's theory that the earthquake that sank Atlantis brought forth the British Isles from the sea, whence came the great banks of oysters and other marine life on this island. Hooke argued that the earth was more plastic and pliable in earlier times and the subterranean fires much stronger to enable the latter to wreak transformations on such a massive scale.

11. Steno's theory of the formation and alteration of the geological strata; it was the latter process that was the chief cause of the formation of mountains.

12. Steno's theory of how and why the content of each stratum told the story of the state of the earth during the time in which the stratum was being formed.

13. Steno's famous hypothesis in his *Prodromus* concerning the six stages of successive transformations that the surface of the earth had undergone in Tuscany.

14. Steno's hypothesis that fossils of plants and animals could survive for at least 4,000 years out of the 6,000 years of the earth's history.

15. Steno's theory that *glossopetrae* were teeth of fossil sharks, and were not, as was then generally believed, stones which grew in the earth like other minerals.[45]

Consider M_1. Its objective component renders T_1 through T_9, T_{14} and T_{15} scientific, and the rest unscientific. On this method, among the scientific theories are Steno's hypothesis concerning *glossopetrae* and Burnet's conjecture concerning the origin of the oceans; Steno's theory of the formation and alteration of geological strata is among the unscientific theories. Correspondingly, the normative component of M_1 renders certain decisions—such as Burnet's decision to accept the hypothesis concerning the geological history of the earth—rational, and certain others—such as Hooke's acceptance of the hypothesis of an ancient distinguished civilization—as irrational. A reasonable requirement that no demarcation criterion may make either the class of scientific theories or the class of unscientific theories empty is satisfied—indeed, this requirement is met by each of the three methods. The persons engaged in dealing with theories are deemed scientists. By "engaged in dealing with" is meant engaged in testing, experimenting, trying to deduce testable conclusions from the theory, attempting to reconcile a theory with other well-confirmed theories, and so on. On M_1, all three persons, P_1 (Burnet), P_2 (Hooke), and P_3 (Steno), are scientists, but notice that not all their decisions are deemed rational. Hooke is a scientist on this view, but his decision to accept his hypothesis concerning the origin and nature of fossils is irrational; similarly, Steno is also a scientist on this view, but his decision to accept his theory of how and why the content of each stratum mirrored the state of the earth during the time in which the stratum was being formed is irrational.

The other two methods, M_2 and M_3, are to be similarly understood as proposing rival evaluations and classifications.

If we use M_1 to write the history of science, we know which theories were scientific and which decisions were rational and which ones were not. If we judge M_1 against this normatively interpreted history, M_1 will be completely and conclusively verified. It cannot, *per impossible*, be the case that history normatively interpreted in the light of M_1 would classify the theory as unscientific while the objective component of that method renders that same theory scientific. Likewise for rational and irrational decisions. The charge of vicious circularity is fairly clear.

Let us suppose, however, that M_2 and M_3 are judged in the light of M_1. Consider M_2 first. According to M_2, T_{11} and T_{13} are among the theories classified as scientific, whereas they are unscientific in normative history. Therefore, M_2 is falsified since it does not square up with the "facts" in normative history. But M_2's failure is magnified: for while M_2 classifies Hooke as a pseudoscientist, he is regarded as a scientist in the normative history of science; also, decisions D_3, D_4, D_5, D_{10}, D_{11}, D_{14}, and D_{15} are classified as rational in the normative history, but M_2 classifies them as irrational. For instance, Burnet's acceptance of the hypothesis concerning the shaping and lowering of mountains and Hooke's acceptance of the theory that the earthquake that sank Atlantis heaved up the British Isles, were rational decisions which M_2 regards as irrational. In a similar fashion, it can be shown that M_3 is falsified as well.

M_1 emerges decisively victorious, while M_2 and M_3 are clear losers. *It is patently obvious that this victory is a sham because it is question-begging*. If M_2 or M_3 had been used to write normative history, M_1 would have been falsified. Thus—to take one example—if M_3 had been used to write a normative history, M_1 would have ended up classifying unscientific theories, such as T_2, T_4, and T_5, as scientific; it would have classified Burnet and Steno, both pseudoscientists in M_3's history, as scientists; and finally, it would have classified irrational decisions, such as D_2, D_3, D_5, and D_6, as rational, and rational decisions, such as D_7, D_{12}, and D_{13} as irrational. For instance, on M_1, Burnet's conjecture that the earth is very young is scientific, but it is not so in view of M_3; Steno's acceptance of the theory concerning the six stages of successive transformations which the surface of the earth had undergone in Tuscany is viewed as a rational decision on M_3, but not so on M_2. Hence, normative history of science, seen in the light of M_3, would falsify M_1 as well as M_2.

Aside from exhibiting the paradox, the model can be used to raise a few interesting questions. Ought a person be classified as a pseudoscientist when some of his decisions are rational? Does an astrologer, an alchemist, or a myth-maker do nothing rational? Is M_3 wrong in showing as rational Burnet's decision to accept the hypothesis concerning the major events in the earth's geological history, while classifying him as a pseudoscientist? At the extreme, can a pseudoscientist make decisions all of which are rational? Is M_3 wrong in portraying Steno as a pseudoscientist while rendering all of Steno's decisions rational? Alternatively, ought a person be classified as a scientist when some of his decisions are irrational? Is M_3 wrong in classifying Hooke's decision of accepting the hypothesis concerning the origin and nature of fossils as irrational, while classifying him as a scientist? At the other extreme, can a scientist make decisions all of which are irrational? Is M_2 wrong in classifying Steno as a scientist, while regarding *all* his decisions as irrational? Or is M_3 wrong in classifying Hooke as a scientist, while regarding *all* his theories as unscientific? Is it ever irrational to accept a scientific theory? Thus, can the case envisaged by M_1 ever be correct where Hooke's theory of organic change is regarded as scientific, but his acceptance of it is regarded as irrational? Is M_1 wrong in claiming that Hooke's hypothesis concerning the origin and nature of fossils was scientific but the decision to accept the hypothesis was irrational? Conversely, is it ever rational to accept an unscientific theory, as in the case exhibited by M_3 which regards Steno's hypothesis of the formation and alteration of geological strata as unscientific, but his acceptance of it as rational?

Given that Newton espoused alchemy, Lord Kelvin rejected the current estimate of the age of the earth, some believed in the weapon salve cure during the Renaissance, Pliny claimed that elephants lived 300 years, and so on, when does a scientist cease to be a scientist? How many irrational decisions is he allowed before he is scientifically defrocked, so to speak? How many rational decisions promotes a pseudoscientist to the status of a scientist? Perhaps a scientist is not a scientist by virtue of some isolated act of rationality. *What determines whether or not he is a scientist is a constant or near-constant appraisal of his scientific pursuit and product by appropriate methods.* At any rate, some answers have to be given to the above questions if we are to make headway with problems such as, What is a rational scientific agent? and, How is rational decision in the history of science to be explained?

To be sure, some of the problems and the paradox we have raised occur only insofar as we are using normatively interpreted history as a basis to test and support methods. If this view of Lakatos is replaced with the view that the basis of support and the testing ground should be concrete judgments of paradigm cases or descriptive history that reflects *no* methodological bias, then we may have an objective way of evaluating methods, and the paradox will disappear. Nothing contained in this chapter touches that view. Like Lakatos, I doubt that methodologically innocent history of science is possible. Here, at the end, I confine myself to a conjecture.

Early in the century, a cardinal doctrine was that observations were theory-neutral; theories of epistemology, language, scientific explanation, and scientific progress were premised on that view. Once that view was seriously challenged, however, it brought in its wake a powerful new tradition—especially in philosophy of language—with enormously interesting new problems. I suspect that when the problems of theory of method are as closely attended to, we will find (without being accused of weaving a myth of the methodological framework) that we can no longer innocently operate with the assumption that the history of science is a given or is methodology-neutral, either. We shall discover a new methodological tradition with a rich variety of problems, not least among them will be the ones Lakatos has already given us.

Appendix

I know no way of stating in a clean and picturesque fashion on the printed page the partial solution to the logical problem, under what conditions is one method, *M*, better than another method, *M′*? Hence the character of what follows.

In the solution, *internal history*$_t$ *of M** refers to the history of scientific theories according to *M**, and so by way of illustration will include such theories as the special theory of relativity, Maxwell's theory of electromagnetism, the theory of modern genetics, and so on. *External history*$_t$ *of M** refers to the history of nonscientific theories, which will include astrology and palmistry, among other things. The objective component of *M** will show, explain, or capture the scientific and nonscientific character of these theories, respectively. Likewise, *internal history*$_a$ *of M** refers to the history of rational decisions according to *M**, such as the rationality of accepting plate tectonics in 1970, while *external history*$_a$ *of M** refers to the history of irrational decisions, such as the irrationality of accepting scientific creationism in 1980. The normative component of *M** will show, explain, or capture the rationality or irrationality of these decisions, respectively. The objective and normative components of *M* and *M′* will chalk out their own respective internal and external histories of theories and decisions. Phrases like *internal history*$_t$ *of M* and *external history*$_a$ *of M′* are to be understood in a parallel fashion.

Partial Solution of the Logical Problem:

A method, M, *is better than another method*, M′, *relative to the best method*, M*, *if and only if:*

(I) Other things being equal, either (i) the internal history$_t$ *of* M* *captured by the objective components of* M *is greater than that captured by the objective components of* M′, *and the internal history*$_a$ *of* M* *captured by the normative*

components of M *is either greater than or equal to that captured by the normative components of* M′; *or (ii) the internal* $history_t$ *of* M* *captured by the objective components of* M *is equal to that captured by the objective components of* M′, *and the internal* $history_a$ *of* M* *captured by the normative components of* M′ *is less than that captured by the normative components of* M. *Or,*

(II) Other things being equal, either (i) the external $history_t$ *of* M* *captured by the objective components of* M *is greater than that captured by the objective components of* M′, *and the external* $history_a$ *of* M* *captured by the normative components of* M *is either greater than or equal to that captured by the normative components of* M′; *or, (ii) the external* $history_t$ *of* M* *captured by the objective components of* M *is equal to that captured by the objective components of* M′, *and the external* $history_a$ *of* M* *captured by the normative components of* M′ *is less than that captured by the normative components of* M. *Or,*

(III) Other things being equal, either (i) the internal $history_t$ *of* M* *depicted as the external* $history_t$ *of* M* *by the objective components of* M *is less than that depicted by the objective components of* M′, *and the internal* $history_a$ *of* M* *depicted as the external* $history_a$ *of* M* *by the normative components of* M *is zero, equal to, or less than that depicted by the normative components of* M′; *or, (ii) the internal* $history_t$ *of* M* *depicted as the external* $history_t$ *of* M* *by the objective components of* M *is zero or the same as that depicted by the objective components of* M′, *and the internal* $history_a$ *of* M* *depicted as the external* $history_a$ *of* M* *by the normative components of* M′ *is greater than that depicted by the normative components of* M. *Or,*

(IV) Other things being equal, either (i) the external $history_t$ *of* M* *depicted as the internal* $history_t$ *of* M* *by the objective components of* M *is less than that depicted by the objective components of* M′, *and the external* $history_a$ *of* M* *depicted as the internal* $history_a$ *of* M* *by the normative components of* M *is zero, equal to, or less than that depicted by the normative components of* M′; *or (ii) the external* $history_t$ *of* M* *depicted as the internal* $history_t$ *of* M* *by the objective components of* M *is zero or equal to that depicted by the objective components of* M′, *and the external* $history_a$ *of* M* *depicted as the internal* $history_a$ *of* M* *by the normative components of* M′ *is greater than that depicted by the normative components of* M.[46]

4

Laudan's Theory of Method

On the current scene in the philosophy of science, notions of truth, explanation, confirmation, corroboration, and such are on their way out; problem-solving is in. This is the view one gets from reading Larry Laudan's much discussed book, *Progress and Its Problems.*[1]

At first blush, it would appear that there is very little that is novel in focusing, especially in epistemology, on problems rather than on theories and facts. For although Collingwood first emphasized the role of problems,[2] it was Karl Popper who brought this idea to fruition in methodology. In *The Logic of Scientific Discovery*, of course, it was already dimly foreshadowed that problems would play a predominant role in Popper's later work.[3] More explicitly, in *Conjectures and Refutations* Popper claimed that a philosopher of science should spotlight the fact that science starts only with problems; that every worthwhile new theory raises new problems, problems of reconciliation and problems of devising novel tests; that one way to measure the fruitfulness of a theory is by the number of new and significant problems it raises; and that science is best seen as moving from problems to problems of ever-increasing depth.[4] In *Objective Knowledge*, Popper's historiography is informed by the thesis that problems and problem-situations are of primary importance. To explain why Galileo proposed his theory of tides based solely on the rotation and revolution of the earth, which gave no part to the gravitational pull of the moon, Popper reconstructed both the problem to which Galileo's theory of tides was meant as a solution and the problem-situation in which the problem arose for Galileo. His injunction to the historian of science was that "the history of science should be treated *not* as a history of theories, but as a history of problem-situations and their modifications (sometimes imperceptible, sometimes revolutionary) through the intervention of the attempts to solve problems."[5] Popper's historiography, of course, is only a special case of his theory of understanding.[6] Indeed, Popper's famous tetradic schema, $\text{Problem}_1 \rightarrow$Tentative Theory$\rightarrow$Error Elimination$\rightarrow \text{Problem}_2$, a broad generalization that accounts for a vast array of biological activity, begins and ends with a problem facing the subject.[7]

Now, although Laudan, more than anyone, has developed and extended the Popperian theme—namely, that problems are crucially important in the tasks of epistemology, theory of understanding, historiography, and the like—he radically breaks away not only from Popper but from most of the major alternatives to Popper's method. This break consists crucially in Laudan's claim, among other things, that *truth is irrelevant* when giving a philosophical account, for instance, of the nature of scientific activity, growth of knowledge, and rationality. Therein lies the significance and challenge and power of Laudan's "short book."

To understand how the issues are joined between Laudan and the other methodologists, consider the concepts of truth and explanation. Like Popper, Hilary Putnam posited as one of the aims of science the capture of interesting truth or approximate-truth and claims that a typical feature of science is that later theories "must imply *approximate truth of the theoretical laws of the earlier theories in certain circumstances.*"[8] In brief, science aims at truth and is to be seen as converging upon the true theory. Again, for Popper and Putnam, the concept of truth plays a central role in their accounts of explanation. Explanation consists of an argument whose premises are universal laws and initial conditions and whose conclusion is a statement describing the event to be explained. It is crucial that these universal laws be true, or approximately true, or corroborated, or confirmed, or at the very least, not known to be false.[9]

In order to appreciate Laudan's alternative theory of science, consider three central difficulties that face the Popper-Putnam view. First, as Popper has said all along, even if we hit upon the true theory, we can never know it. Laudan regards this consequence as showing the utopian character of the goal of seeking truth.[10] Second is the result of David Miller's and Pavel Tichy's theorem that shows that if two theories are false, one cannot compare them with respect to their verisimilitude.[11] Once the logical problem is declared insoluble, the hopelessness of the epistemic problem—namely, under what conditions can one know that one false theory is nearer to the truth than another—follows. Third, on behalf of Laudan, one might cite Miller's other result, which shows the difficulty of content-comparison between theories that are logically incompatible.[12]

In effect, what Laudan has done is to abandon the concept of truth and explanation. He has replaced those two concepts with the concept of problem-solving. The aim of science, then, is to solve problems and to come up with a theory that solves more important problems than does any other theory. According to Laudan, whether a theory solves a problem or not is independent of whether it is true or not. Laudan claims that by proceeding in this fashion not only does he avoid the logical problems that face Popper's theory of verisimilitude and content-comparison and Putnam's idea of approximate-truth but he is able to account for the history of science in a better way than can be done by any alternative method.[13] Clearly, the concept of problem-solving plays a crucial and indispensable role in Laudan's work, and this can also be shown as follows: Problems are divided into empirical and conceptual. There are three types of empirical problems: solved, unsolved, and anomalous. The success of a given theory is then determined by its problem-solving effectiveness, which is measured by the number of problems solved over ones that are anomalous. Both the rationality of acceptance and the rationality of pursuit are tied to problem-solving effectiveness. These are hardly all the instances where the concept of problem-solving is central, for it is also crucial in Laudan's account of the historiography of science, cognitive sociology of knowledge, intellectual history (broadly understood), and, finally, in his account of meta-method or the theory of the nature and evaluation of method.

In what follows, I shall argue, in light of an implicit theory of method that emphasizes matters logical and philosophical, that Laudan's concept of problem-solving, or his positing as the aim of science the discovery of a theory that has a maximum problem-solving effectiveness unrelated to the notions of truth and truth-seeking, encounters severe difficulties. In particular, I shall contend: problem talk can be translated into fact-explaining talk; Laudan's method faces the problem of making sense of the claim that theories entail problems; it also faces the charge of being utopian in the sense in which he condemns Popper's method; and it must contend with the highly unintuitive consequences of claiming truth as irrelevant to the question of whether a theory solves a problem or not. Also, Laudan's method suffers from similar difficulties that currently block the solution to the problems of verisimilitude and content-comparison. Furthermore, since the notions of truth and testing are closely related, Laudan's rejection of the notion of truth has unacceptable consequences for his theory of theory appraisal. Lastly, the rejection of the notion for truth also enables one to demonstrate that in several cases Laudan's method regards an inconsistent theory as at least as good as, or better than, its rivals. In the next section I present Laudan's historically oriented theory of method and his theory of explaining rational decisions in the history of science. The former theory could not be understood without the latter, and indeed squarely rests on it. I then offer a theory of explaining rational decisions, preceded by a paradigmatic example, and the next section defends the theory from possible objections. Next, I argue against Laudan's theory of method, and some of these criticisms in essential part rely on my constructive proposal. In essence, it claims that Laudan's position faces a dilemma: either his theory of explaining rational decisions in the history of science is false, or his theory of method is. The final section yields a rough sketch of how the growth of scientific knowledge and rationality in the history of science should be delineated. It is a generalization of the theory of explaining rational decisions.

I. TWO RIVAL METHODS: A LOGICAL COMPARISON

Laudan finds the classical model of explanation wanting and rejects the idea that to speak of solving a problem is just another way of talking about explaining a fact. His reasons are four: (*i*) Oftentimes presumed and not real states of affairs pose empirical problems; for instance, medieval natural philosophers, such as Oresme, took it to be the case that hot goat's blood could split diamonds, and physicist-astronomers assumed that the planets were carried by a crystalline sphere and wondered about the nature of the sphere and its distance from the earth. Facts, to be sure, cannot be counterfactuals. (*ii*) There are many unknown facts that could not possibly pose problems. Prior to the identification of a hitherto unknown ring around Saturn, the problem of determining its composition did not exist. (*iii*) Not all known facts pose problems. When the Iceland spar was first discovered, double-refraction posed no problem since there appeared to be no premium placed on explaining it. Finally, (*iv*) what are regarded as problems at one time may cease to be problems at a later date. What Aristotle regarded as the problem posed by free-falling objects in his *Physics* was by no means the same problem that was later the concern of the medievalists and Galileo. This can hardly be true of facts, for facts do not alter with time.[14]

I propose to save the classical view by making a very simple and obvious distinction: the distinction I have in mind is one between a *fact* and an *alleged fact*. I shall argue that there is a corresponding distinction between a *problem* and an *alleged problem*. Let me begin with the latter distinction first. Once the real numbers were created and we were in possession of the notion of cardinality, there was an objective problem (Popper would say a World 3 problem), namely, Is the cardinality of the set of reals greater than the cardinality of the set of natural numbers?[15] As we all know, Cantor solved the problem in the affirmative. But when Gerolamo Saccheri was trying in the eighteenth century to derive the parallel postulate from the other Euclidean axioms, he was trying to solve an alleged problem since the so-called parallel postulate is an independent axiom. The distinction between a problem and an alleged problem in the natural sciences can be analogously explained.

In a similar fashion, the classical view might claim that there is a distinction between facts and alleged facts. Copernicans were trying to explain the fact that the planets revolve around the sun, but the Ptolemaists were trying to explain the alleged fact that the sun and the other planets revolve around the earth. Indeed, contra Laudan, it can be shown that all talk of problems can be simply and easily translated into talk of facts and all talk of alleged problems can be simply and easily translated into talk of alleged facts; and *vice versa*. Laudan's criticisms can be met by saying that what he took to be an explanation of a fact in his point (*i*) was simply an explanation of an alleged fact. His argument in (*ii*) can be met by saying that insofar as there is no talk of facts (the facts are unknown), there is no need or occasion to translate them into talk of problems. The charge leveled in (*iii*) can be answered because problems, like facts, are shelved for a variety of reasons: they are too difficult to solve, they are not interesting enough, and so forth. The fact that trees generally have green leaves, says Laudan, was never explained. But one might equally well say that the problem, Why do most trees have green leaves?, was left unsolved. What Laudan says of articulated problems is true of known facts: there is a premium on explaining some facts but none on explaining others.[16] Finally, his objection in (*iv*) can also be met. What changes, or what is seen to change or alter, are not facts but rather alleged facts. Thus—to defuse one of Laudan's counterinstances—early geologists assumed that the earth had evolved in less than 6,000 to 8,000 years and what they set about explaining was an alleged fact.

Laudan, I suggest, needs my distinction most. For with it, he is able to state clearly what he conceives to be the ultimate goal of science. He is able to express what the best and ideal scientific theory should be able to do: namely, *the best and ideal scientific theory should be able to solve every possible problem in a given domain*. By implication, the best scientific theory is not one that we think solves problems in a given domain, but where, in fact, the problems are only alleged problems. Without that distinction, how can the ultimate goal or aim of science be formulated within the framework of Laudan's method?

Let us suppose, for the sake of argument, that there is a radical, nontranslatable difference between facts and problems. We still need to ask, Under what conditions is a problem to be regarded as solved? This question is clearly analogous to our asking, Under what conditions is a fact to be regarded as explained? Now whatever the deficiency of the classical view, and it is deficient, we at least have a theory of explanation. But Laudan has provided us with no theory for his central concept of solves-a-problem. Even so, let me draw attention to at least three crucial issues.

Laudan claims that "a theory may solve a problem so long as it entails even an *approximate* statement of the problem; in determining if a theory solves a problem, *it is irrelevant whether the theory is true or false, well or poorly confirmed*; what counts as a solution to a problem at one time will not necessarily be regarded as such at all times."[17] Again, "Generally, *any theory, T, can be regarded as having solved an empirical problem, if T functions (significantly) in any schema of inference whose conclusion is a statement of the problem*."[18]

Unfortunately, there is no formal model in which theories entail problems. Alternatively, we do not have a formal theory in which declarative sentences entail interrogative ones—not even in erotetic logic. The principle of charity does not apply here. One cannot say Laudan made an inadvertent slip, he did not mean to say that a theory entails a problem but rather—what? A statement or a description of a fact or an alleged fact? One might add, following Michael Dummett, that insofar as Laudan speaks of entailment, he can hardly do without the notion of truth. For the only viable analysis of entailment is in terms of logical consequence which in turn essentially rests on the notion of truth. Indeed, it is unclear that even granting the notion of truth is sufficient, since a statement of a problem is neither true nor false, and on Laudan's view what theories entail are such statements.

Let us assume that Laudan has given us a philosophical theory that is an answer to the question, Under what conditions is an empirical problem to be regarded as solved? Let us call this hypothetical theory, *L*. We need to distinguish two issues: (*i*) the *logical issue* that we raised above, and (*ii*) the *epistemological issue*, namely, Under what conditions can we know that a theory designed to solve an empirical problem in fact meets the condition stipulated by *L*? Now *L* answers (*i*) when, among other things, it lays down the conditions under which *T* functions significantly in an inference schema whose conclusion is a statement of the problem. With respect to (*ii*) it is clear that Laudan's theory, *L*, whatever it is, is as utopian, to use his phrase, as any fallibilistic epistemological theory, such as Popper's. In principle, problem-solvers are like fallibilist truth-seekers in at least one important respect: they can never know anything for certain. For, unbeknownst to them, a scientific theory, *T*, may violate the conditions of significance of *L* so that even though the scientist thought he had solved a problem, he could always be mistaken in principle.

Nor could the following defense be urged either. The classical theory of explanation is idealistic and mistaken inasmuch as it attempts to lay down all-purpose and all-time conditions for a theory to explain a fact; it would be erroneous to try to state similar conditions for the concept of solves-a-problem. On the contrary, so the argument goes, "the criteria for what counts as solving a problem have evolved so much that what was once regarded as an adequate solution ceases to be regarded as such."[19] But relative to *any* proposed criterion, there is always the corresponding epistemic issue, namely, Under what conditions can one know whether a theory has met *that* criterion? It is unlikely that every epistemic theory provides a success guarantee. Parenthetically, insofar as Laudan's theory of science is primarily *descriptive*,[20] one might also well ask how adequate (true?) it is in its presumably historical claim that truth was never an important ingredient in what counted as a criterion for solving a problem.

By far the most counterintuitive consequence of Laudan's view that truth is irrelevant to problem-solving is that it allows for the possibility of claiming that *any false theory, and one known to be false, may be regarded as a problem-solver*. Now it is one thing to say that Galen, armed with his humoral theory of medicine, regarded certain pathological problems as solved; it is something quite different for *us* to claim this when we know the theory to be false. But if truth is not even a necessary condition that a theory must satisfy, why would it be wrong for us to make such a claim? It is possible that when the aforementioned hypothetical theory, *L*, is supplied, it may as a matter of fact rule out theories that are false or known to be false. Will the latter function as a desideratum *L* must satisfy? Or, will this just be a happy coincidence?

Let me turn to a different set of issues. According to Popper, once a theory has been initially protected so that it is developed in full, it must then be put to a severe test. A test is severe if, given what we know, it is unlikely that the theory will pass the test. The experimental test will generally be based on novel predictions made by the theory, predictions not made by any competing theory in the field. If the theory does fail the test, one can say that the theory or complex of theories is false. Such a test functions crucially in appraising the work of a theory, and Popper's notion of corroboration is based on such significant tests.

Laudan's view is different. He distinguishes between three kinds of empirical problems: unsolved problems, solved problems, and anomalous problems. A problem is unsolved if it is not solved by any extant theory in the field; a problem is deemed to be solved if it is solved by at least one theory in the field; and, finally, a problem is anomalous for a theory *T* if it is not solved by *T* but is solved by some other theory, *T′*.[21] Now Laudan claims that for *theory appraisal* what is most significant are solved problems and anomalous problems. Because of the difficulty of reproducing many experimental results and because of the uncertainty about the domain to which they belong,[22] unsolved problems do not enter into the appraisal picture at all. As Laudan puts it, "In appraising the relative merits of theories, the class of unsolved problems is altogether irrelevant."[23] How is merit to be measured? "We could define an appraisal measure for a theory," says Laudan, "in the following way: the overall problem-solving effectiveness of a theory is determined by assessing the number and importance of the empirical problems which the theory solves and deducting therefrom the number and importance of the anomalies and conceptual problems which the theory guarantees."[24]

Finally, "Progress can occur if and only if the succession of scientific theories in any domain shows an increasing degree of problem-solving effectiveness."[25]

Since much of what follows is crucially dependent on a clear understanding of Laudan's definitions, I will illustrate. Consider

Case 1

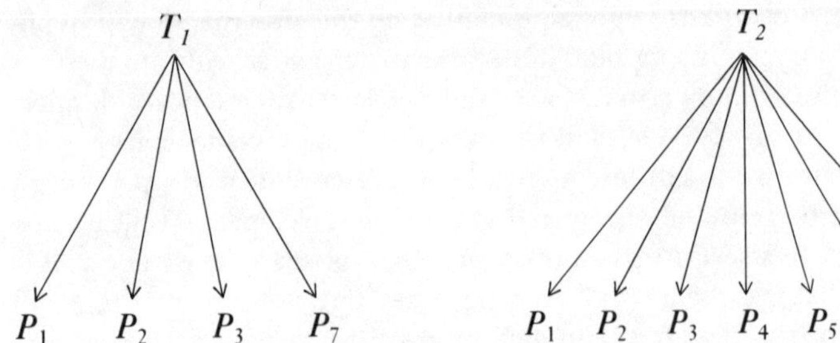

For the sake of simplicity, I will assume that T_1 and T_2 are the only competing theories in the field. P_i is a statement of a problem that a theory entails.[26] P_1 through P_7 are solved problems; P_4, P_5, and P_6 are anomalous problems for T_1 in view of the fact that they are solved or entailed by T_2; similarly, P_7 is an anomalous problem for T_2. Let us assume that ~ 0 is the state of affairs. If 0 were the state of affairs then T_2 could have been regarded as having solved the problem, P_0. $P_{\sim 0}$ is at best an unsolved problem, but it is not an anomaly for T_2 since T_1 does not entail it. To quote Laudan, "In stressing that a problem can only count as *anomalous* for one theory if it is *solved* by another, the analysis seems to run against the common view that one sort of anomaly, *the refuting instance, poses a direct cognitive threat to a theory*, even if it is unsolved by any competitor. If a theory predicts a certain experimental outcome (say 0) and experiment reveals that ~ 0 is the case, then surely, ~ 0 constitutes an anomaly for the theory even if no other theory can solve ~ 0? As paradoxical as it may seem, this is generally unsound."[27]

Let us begin with two theories, T_1 and T_2, such that T_2 entails the statement of every problem solved by T_1 but T_1 does not entail the statement of every problem solved by T_2; and, T_1 and T_2 have no refuting instances. If both theories are true, Popper would say that T_2 is nearer to the truth than T_1. Laudan would correspondingly say that T_2 is a better problem-solver than T_1; T_2 solves all the problems that T_1 does, and hence it has no anomalous problems, whereas T_1 does have anomalous problems. So far, both methods are adequate.

But consider a theory T and a set of other theories in the same domain, $T_1, T_2, T_3, \ldots, T_n$. Let us suppose we begin with a situation in which T has only marginally better problem-solving effectiveness than a T_i. T makes a set of novel predictions, $P_1, P_2, P_3, \ldots, P_n$. Every novel prediction turns out to be false. Assume that P_1 through P_n pose unsolved problems, namely, no theory in the set $T_1, T_2, T_3, \ldots, T_n$ can solve the problems posed by the false novel predictions of T. On Laudan's view, T's status remains unshaken as the leader in the field since it has only succeeded in generating a sequence of unsolved problems, which is irrelevant in appraising theories. This lends added significance to the claim that only if we are interested in truth does the testing of novel predictions make sense.[28]

Next, suppose that both T_1 and T_2 have as consequences statements of anomalous as well as solved problems (Case 1). If a comparison of transfinite consequences of the respective theories is to be made in order to determine which theory has a greater degree of problem-solving effectiveness, then it is no longer obvious that T_2 is a better problem-solver than T_1. T_2 may entail more statements of anomalous problems than T_1 does. But this case is analogous to the one in which both T_1 and T_2 have as consequences false statements as well as true statements; and we know that in that case we cannot determine which theory has a greater degree of verisimilitude. Consequently, there are good grounds for believing that, on a similar score, Laudan's method is at least as inadequate as Popper's.

Suspecting this difficulty, Laudan decided to propose a theory of theory appraisal that would deal only with appropriately restricted finite classes of consequences. He now claims that the virtue of his theory of appraisal measure, against one such as Popper's, is that "it involves the comparison of finite sets of sentences whose members can be judged utilizing the rule 'prefer theories which solve the larger number of problems.' Why is the number of solved problems finite? To speak of those problems whose solutions can be credited to a theory is to refer to those *already observed* states of affairs which the theory entails. The membership of this set will always be finite, even though theories entail an infinite number of consequences, since only a finite number of the consequences can be examined."[29]

First, this artificial restriction to solutions of problems posed only by observed states of affairs, when discussing the logical problem, offers no relative advantage to Laudan. If Popper and Lakatos, like Laudan, were to restrict the content of theories to *observed* states of affairs, they would no longer be faced by the problem Laudan charges them with. Here would be Popper's solution: prefer the theory that is best corroborated, where corroboration is defined in terms of severe tests, and where severe tests can only be finite.[30] Second, Laudan never explains how problems are to be individuated; and a theory of individuating problems is crucial since theory appraisal in Laudan's method essentially relies on *counting* problems.[31]

Now consider two consistent but incomplete theories, T and T', such that T entails the statement of a solved problem, P (Why is the sky blue?)[32] and T' entails the corresponding statement of the problem *not-P* (Why is the sky not blue?). Let K be some solvable problem not solved by T. Then (not-P or K) is a statement of a solvable problem entailed by T' but not by T. In brief, any claim about the possibility of comparing the problem-content of two theories that together are logically incompatible remains unsupported. Indeed, it is not at all obvious that even being restricted only to observed states of affairs helps in such a case.

Some philosophers have correctly claimed that only if truth is our aim can we have any objection to theories that are logically inconsistent.[33] Here is Laudan's response: "I have a straightforward explanation of the demand for consistency: because inconsistent theories entail every statement, they will always be confronted by as many anomalies as solved problems. Replacement of one inconsistent theory by another could thus never count as progress with respect to problem-solving effectiveness."[34] In what follows, I defend the position that our desire to get rid of contradictions can only be explained by invoking the notion of truth by trading on the assumptions Laudan allows himself: namely, deal solely with problems that are clearly related only to already observed states of affairs; this will ensure that the class of such problems is finite.

To repeat, on Laudan's view the problem-solving effectiveness of a theory is determined by the number of problems solved *minus* the number of anomalies. Unsolved problems and refuted instances are irrelevant. Distinguishing carefully between the *context of acceptance* and the *context of pursuit*, Laudan claims that his theory of appraising theories, or research traditions, as he calls them, has three virtues. It is workable; it proposes a novel way of relating rational acceptance with scientific progress; and it squares with scientific practice more than does any other extant model of rationality.[35] I shall consider only the context of acceptance; my arguments can easily be transferred to the context of pursuit.

Consider

Case 2

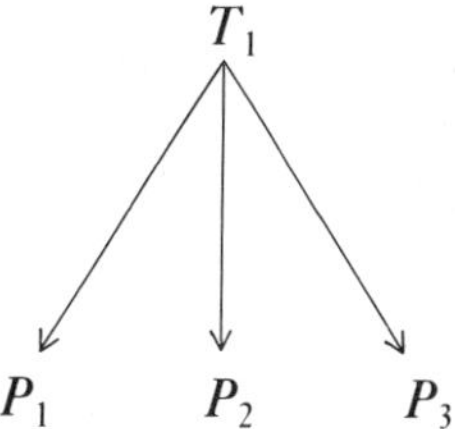

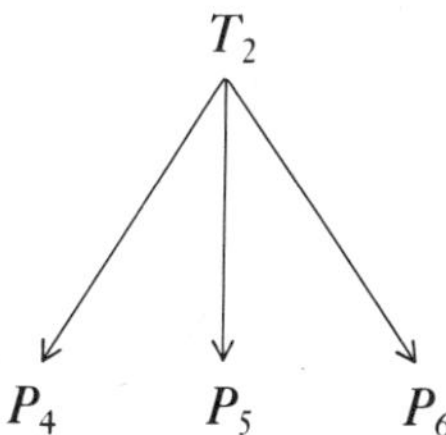

T_1 and T_2 are consistent theories. Clearly, the problem-solving effectiveness of T_2 is the same as the problem-solving effectiveness of T_1; for the problem-solving effectiveness of T_2 is $3 - 3 = 0$, while the problem-solving effectiveness of T_1 is $3 - 3 = 0$, too. Now later, I propose an inconsistent theory, T^*, thus enabling me to solve all the problems P_1 through P_6, and of course, my theory would entail the negation of each P_1 as well. As Laudan would put it, T^* "will always be confronted by as many anomalies as solved problems." The problem-solving effectiveness of my theory would be $6 - 6 = 0$. On Laudan's view, it is as rational to accept T^* as it is to accept T_1 or T_2.

Case 3

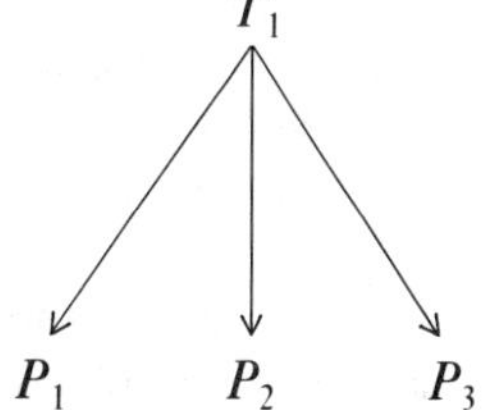

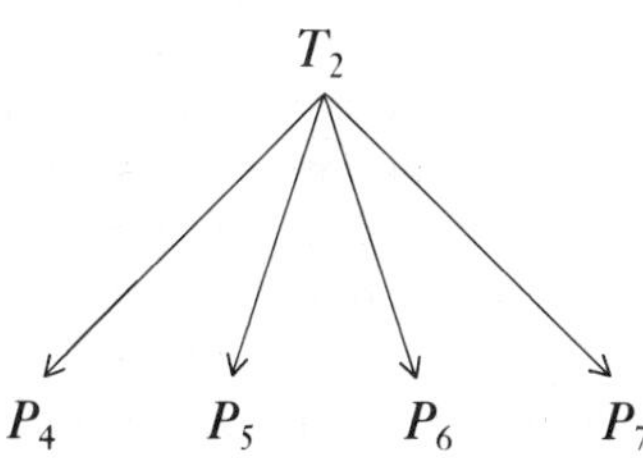

There are unsolved problems, P_8 through P_{100}.

The problem-solving effectiveness of T_2 is greater than the problem-solving effectiveness of T_1; for the problem-solving effectiveness of T_2 is $4 - 3 = 1$, while the problem-solving effectiveness of T_1 is

3 − 4 = -1. Unsolved problems do not count. Later, I propose an inconsistent theory, T^*. T^* will entail not only every solved problem entailed by T_1 and T_2, respectively, but it will obviously entail hitherto unsolved problems, P_8 through P_{100}, as well. To be sure, T^* will also entail the negation of each P_i. Evidently, on Laudan's view, progress has occurred, and I should rationally accept my inconsistent theory, T^*, rather than T_1 or T_2 since the problem-solving effectiveness of T^* is demonstrably greater than either of the two consistent theories, T_1 and T_2. Thus, the problem-solving effectiveness

of T^* is $100 - 100 = 0$,

of T_2 is $4 - 96 = -92$,

and of T_1 is $3 - 97 = -94$.

Indeed, there is a very strong prima facie assumption that the number of solved problems, in any given field at any given time, is likely to be far fewer than the ones that remain unsolved. It follows that while the problem-solving effectiveness of T^* will be zero, that of the other competing and consistent theories in the domain will nearly always remain *less* than zero.[36]

Last, without a formal proof, and relating to the class of competing and consistent theories, I state a highly plausible conjecture concerning Laudan's notion of anomalous problems which apparently plays an essential role in his theory of theory appraisal. Conjecture: If, in a given domain, a theory solves more problems than does any other competing theory, then the number of anomalies facing it, if any, can never reduce its problem-solving effectiveness to second place. More generally, in a given domain, the ranking of any group of theories according to the number of problems solved is identical to the ranking of those theories according to their problem-solving effectiveness (solved problems minus anomalous problems). If this conjecture is correct, it shows that Laudan's notion of anomalous problems is superfluous.[37]

Laudan's alternative method or theory of science, in which the concept of problem-solving holds a central place, has enough problems of its own. Consequently, there is ample reason not to discard the notion of truth—yet. Or so at least I have tried to argue so far.

"As natural as the proposal to utilize history of science as a testing ground for philosophical models of rational choice might seem," avers Laudan, "there are probably those purists who regard it as unseemly that philosophy should have to look beyond itself and its own argumentative strategies for legitimation. But where, *within* philosophy, can one find the appropriate decision criteria?"[38] This section is my answer to Laudan's question. At any rate, it is clear that history of science was not invoked, or used as a testing ground, for comparing and evaluating Popper's method and Laudan's.[39]

Let me turn from the side of logic, however, to the side of Laudan's historically oriented approach to method evaluation. I am less interested in showing that there is a cluster of cases in the history of science for which the methodology of research traditions does not provide the best explanation, than I am in showing that Laudan's entire approach toward evaluating methods rests on a mistake. But, first, Laudan's theory of method.

II. LAUDAN'S THEORY OF METHOD

Laudan makes a distinction between what he calls HOS_1 and HOS_2. HOS_1 refers to the actual past of the science, which "at a first approximation, can be regarded as the chronologically ordered class of beliefs of former scientists." HOS_2 refers to the writings of the historians of science about that past, namely, HOS_1.[40] Laudan then argues that since within philosophy no answer to the question, Which of the competing methods should be accepted? can be found, one is compelled to turn to something objective, independent, and outside of philosophy, namely, the history of science (in either sense). Ronald Giere had argued that any such proposal leads to a standard objection. The major task of a method is to propose norms for determining what is scientific, what theory is progressing, what appraisals ought to be made, which theory should be accepted (or rejected), and so on, whereas history of science is a mere fact, a chronicle of appropriately related events from which no such sought-after norms can be derived.

In answer to that problem, Laudan claims that there is a widely held set of normative judgments—he gives seven examples—which he refers to as "*our preferred pre-analytic intuitions about scientific rationality (PIs)*."[41] For instance, (1) it was rational to accept Newtonian mechanics and to reject Aristotelian mechanics by 1800; (2) it was rational for physicians to accept the tradition of pharmacological medicine over the homeopathic tradition by 1900; (3) it was rational to reject the hypothesis that heat was a fluid by 1890; (4) it was irrational not to believe that the chemical atom had parts after 1920; (5) it was irrational to believe that light moved with infinite velocity after 1750; (6) it was rational to accept the general theory of relativity after 1925; and (7) it was irrational to accept the biblical chronology as a correct hypothesis about the earth's history after 1830.[42] Any model of rationality that can explicate the underlying rationality behind these preanalytic intuitions ought to be initially acceptable.[43] In effect, two conditions are proposed for a methodology to satisfy: "(1) that at least certain specified developments in the history of science were rational; and (2) that the test of any putative model of rational choice is whether it can explicate the rationality assumed to be inherent in these developments."[44] Finally, "the degree of adequacy of any theory of scientific appraisal is proportional to how many of the PIs it can do justice to."[45]

Laudan thinks that the procedure for testing a putative model of rationality is a very simple one. The model to be tested will specify parameters and norms and determine what the scientific agent, in the light of those parameters and norms, ought to have done. We then check the history of science to see if the scientific agent did what the putative model of rationality claims he ought to have done. The model is then confirmed or disconfirmed in the usual way. The following, by way of an example, is a very rough sketch of what Laudan means: Popper's method has among its injunctions that one ought not to propose a nontestable theory and that one ought not to use ad hoc moves in saving one's theory from criticisms. Let us suppose that our preanalytic intuitions suggest that Lamarck was irrational and that his theory of descent was nonscientific.[46] On the basis of its parameters and norms, can Popper's method account satisfactorily for those intuitions?

We may claim that Lamarck's basic work *Philosophie zoologique* (1809) was indeed not testable and that Lamarck offered very many ad hoc explanations. For instance, to account for the origin of a new organ, he invented two ad hoc factors: a tendency for improvement, and the effects of the environment (a criticism voiced by Charles Lyell in *Principles of Geology*). Oftentimes Lamarck used these two factors separately to account for the same kind of phenomena, as when he tried to explain the absence of a head in shells and in lower animals of less complex organization such as the infusorians. In vertebrates, according to Lamarck, the number of ventricles of the heart is due to the tendency for improvement, whereas the number of auricles is due to the effects of the environment. According to Lamarck, a specified environment induces similar needs even in dissimilar animals. "Here was an opportunity," says Ernst Mayr, "for Lamarck, the experienced zoologist, to test his theory," but he did not. For instance, Lamarck cited the sloth (Bradypus) as an animal that lived among the trees, ate leaves, and existed in the hot tropics; consequently, it had acquired adaptations that included extreme slowness of movement. Had he tried to test his theory, however, Lamarck would have found, that the monkeys in the same environment, place, and climate had acquired different adaptations.[47]

Lamarck's theory of 'requirements' is well known. The requirements or habits of an organism determine the form of the organism rather than the form determining the habits. The habits cause or control the use of organs, which leads to the organs' strengthening or modification. As instances of organs atrophying through disuse until they eventually disappear, Lamarck cites the absence of teeth in whales and anteaters; the absence of eyes in the acephalous mollusks; the absence of legs in snakes; and the absence of wings among several insects. To show that use strengthens an organ, he cited the long necks of shore birds, swans, and geese; the long and forked tongues of anteaters and woodpeckers; the forked tongues of flycatchers, lizards, and snakes; and the large hind legs and tail of kangaroos. But the idea of "requirements" or "habits" could not be experimentally tested, and his explanations often smacked of ad hocery, as when he explained that the shore bird acquired the disposition to stretch and elongate its legs because it "wished" to prevent its body from getting wet. When his theory of requirements failed, he invoked his theory of "fluida." He thought he solved the problem of why the starfish was radial by claiming that "the fine fluida are continuously displaced from the center towards all points of the circumference." Occasionally, he even invoked the notion of fluida to explain the origin of a new organ, such as the horns on the once-hornless cattle. In this theory, too, however, fluida performed only an ad hoc task.[48]

Alternatively, if our PI was that Lamarck was rational[49] and that his theory of descent was scientific, then the history of science would show Popper's theory to be in serious jeopardy. Another method would have to be found that would place the old facts in a new light and show the reasonableness both of the doctrine and the moves Lamarck made with his theory of descent. When two or more models of rationality are being evaluated, the model of rationality that most captures our PIs is to be preferred over the rest.

From what has been said so far, Laudan's historiographical suggestions are not difficult to fathom. He claims that "the task of the historian of science is to write an account (HOS_2) of the episodes in the history of science (HOS_1) utilizing as his criteria of narrative selection and weighing those norms contained in that philosophical model which is most nearly adequate to representing"[50] our PIs.

The historian, qua historian of science, makes a selection of figures and facts that will go into the making of a historical narrative. Such a selection will call for criteria, and such criteria are best supplied by the best model of rationality available to the historian of science. A historical explanation of why Kepler believed the universe was constructed according to geometrical principles or why he was involved in solving the problem posed by the motion of Mars constitutes more than a historical chronicle that merely relates that Kepler believed such and such, or that he was engaged in such and such an enterprise. A historical explanation tries to explain not only where, when, and by whom experiments were performed and theories accepted or rejected, but also why experiments were performed, why their results were interpreted in one way rather than another, and why theories were accepted, rejected, or modified in certain ways. For both the historian's narrative and the historian's explanation of rational beliefs, the best model of rationality, claims Laudan, is an indispensable tool. What, then, is Laudan's schema for explaining rational beliefs?

This is what Laudan proposes:

> "(1) All rational agents in situation type, *a*, will accept (or reject, or modify) belief type, *b*.
> (2) Smith was a rational agent.
> (3) Smith was in situation a_1 (i.e., an *a* type situation).
>
> ---
>
> (4) ∴ Smith accepted (or rejected, or modified) belief b_1" (i.e., a *b* type belief).[51]

Laudan remarks that (3) and (4) are unproblematic. He regards the truth of (2) as being quickly settled by careful biographical studies whether a given agent was (or was not) rational in his appraisal of beliefs. He thinks that the most problematic premise in the schema is (1) for he says, "how do we discover laws or principles of type (1)? The question cannot be avoided or postponed, for a plausible answer to it is a necessary pre-requisite to any history (as opposed to a chronology) of ideas."[52]

Laudan claims that it is the task of the theories of rational beliefs to provide statements of the type in Premise (1). Not surprisingly, he finds various extant theories of rationality, such as inductivists' and deductivists', deficient in various degrees. Since the historian of science was enjoined to use the best model of rationality,[53] Laudan advocates that the historian use the methodology of research traditions, which, in Laudan's view, is the best model.

How does this model help in specific cases? Laudan says—and this is quite crucial for later—"The method of application of the model is relatively straightforward. One begins by identifying the pool of available explanatory systems (i.e., research traditions) in any given epoch and intellectual community. One then determines for each of these research traditions how progressive they were (i.e., how effective they were at maximizing solved problems and at minimizing anomalous and conceptual ones). The analysis will allow the historian to construct a profile on the progress of each of the available options."[54]

Certain general principles—such as, all rational agents will prefer a more effective research tradition to a less effective one—together with the profiles of progress of the available research traditions drawn on the basis of Laudan's methodology of research traditions "will allow one to *explain* many developments within the history of thought."[55] It follows, according to Laudan, that "*when a thinker does what it is rational to do, we need inquire no further into the causes of his action*."[56] Thus, the intellectual historian of scientific knowledge seeks *reasons* to explain why a particular belief was accepted, rejected, or modified, whereas the cognitive sociologist of knowledge seeks *causes* to explain why a particular irrational belief was accepted or rejected in terms of social, political, and economic features and forces.[57] Consequently, even a cognitive sociologist of knowledge will need the best model of rationality to answer the question, "*What sorts of beliefs are candidates for a sociological analysis and which are not?*"[58] In brief, the first presents us with the internal history of science, the second with the external history of science.

This is Laudan's theory of how to explain rational actions or decisions in the history of science, especially as it pertains to the acceptance or rejection of theories and hypotheses. His theory of method claims that any method that explains more rational actions or decisions than any other extant method is the best one.

III. A THEORY OF EXPLAINING RATIONAL DECISIONS

A paradigmatic example of rational decision precedes the general theory.[59] Suppose, in trying to determine which gravitational theory to accept as the best among the various competing and contemporary theories, we proceed as follows. We begin by listing all the recent theories of gravity, such as Einstein's general theory of relativity, the Brans-Dicke theory, and the Lee-Lightmen theory. Next, we list the various methods that are currently available: inductivists', Popper's method, Kuhn's method, Lakatos's methodology of research programs, Laudan's methodology of research traditions, and so on. Finally, we espouse the best theory of method (however determined) which will enable us to decide on the best method. Let us say that that method is *M*.

Then, we use *M* to enable us to appraise the best current gravitational theory. Assume that *M* has the following injunctions (normative components) made specifically to deal with the problem at hand. (1) Prefer a theory that does not conflict with the gravitational red-shift and Eötvös experiment (or the more refined experiments of Dicke and Braginsky). (2) Prefer a theory that can explain newly discovered phenomena such as quasars, pulsars, neutron stars, cosmic background radiation, compact celestial X-ray sources, and perhaps even gravitational radiation. (3) Prefer a theory that arrives at the same result or prediction calculated by different methods or techniques. (4) Prefer a theory whose laws mesh with the nongravitational laws of physics, such as the laws of electromagnetism, quantum mechanics, and elementary particle theory. (5) Prefer a theory that is relativistic, namely, one whose nongravitational laws agree with the laws of standard special theory of relativity. (6) Prefer a theory that agrees with the standard Newtonian theory so that its prediction squares with the observed properties of gross matter as accounted for by Newton's theory (that is, it must have the correct Newtonian limit). (7) Prefer a theory that makes correct predictions about the phenomena of light and atomic clocks. Of course, appropriate weights to the injunctions (1) through (7) are assigned by *M*.

As a next step in the process of determining the best theory, we go through the list of gravitational theories and determine which theory satisfies all or most of the criteria laid out by our chosen model of rationality.

We check to see if any theory violates criteria (7), (3), (5) and (6) since these are heavily weighted by *M*. Any theory that fails to meet these criteria will be regarded as fundamentally nonviable. Thus we find E. A. Milne's kinematical relativity theory lacks the necessary mathematical paraphernalia for predicting gravitational red-shift; it violates norm (7). Kustaanheimo's theory of gravitation predicts one result for the red-shift when light is considered as a photon, and a different result when light is considered as a wave. It violates norm (3). Newton's theory clearly violates (5), and Birkhoff's theory is in sharp disagreement with the correct Newtonian limit since it claims that the speed of sound is equal to the speed of light. We regard these gravitational theories as seriously deficient, and so we turn to the viable gravitational theories remaining.

We divide viable theories into two: metric and nonmetric. Essentially, a metric theory claims that gravity is curved space-time, whereas nonmetric theories explain gravity differently. We find now that nonmetric theories violate certain requirements of *M* that nearly all metric theories satisfy. Thus, all nonmetric theories violate the weak equivalence principle, which states in effect that the trajectory of a small noncharged body is independent of the composition of its mass. In brief, they conflict with the Eötvös experiment and hence violate criterion (1). Finally, nearly all nonmetric theories fail to predict the correct gravitational red-shift, thus failing to satisfy criterion (1) again.

We are now left only with metric theories. We find that there are considerable differences among metric theories. There are some that predict a different post-Newtonian limit, although they yield the same result for weak gravitational fields; some theories claim that conservation laws will be violated under certain circumstances, while others make no such claim; some claim that there is a preferred frame of reference, others deny it; some claim that gravitation is nonlinear, that is, the combined gravitational potential energy of two bodies is not simply the sum of individual gravitational potentials; other theories argue that gravitation is linear; metric theories differ in the degree of curvature assigned to space; and finally, some claim that there must be observable gravitational effects from nearby matter, which other theories deny. Consequently, we proceed next to evaluate metric theories.

Those metric theories that claim there is a preferred frame of reference predict an anomaly in the tides of the solid earth, anomalous variations in the earth's rotation rate, and anomalous shifts in the perihelion of Mercury (over and above the ones discussed later) and other planets. However, geophysical data and measurements of perihelion of various planets show no such predicted effects. Rosen's theory, for instance, is therefore eliminated. Likewise, theories that claim that matter from a nearby galaxy should give rise to similar effects are faulted, and hence a theory such as Whitehead's is eliminated. Indeed, such theory, classified as stratified theory of Type A, which predicts sizable effects of this type, is in sharp disagreement with experiment. We infer, then, that there are only two viable metric theories that are serious contenders for first place: the general theory of relativity, and the Brans-Dicke theory.

As is well known, the anomalous shift of 43 seconds of arc in the perihelion of Mercury can be accounted for by the general theory of relativity. The Brans-Dicke theory can only account for 39 seconds and tries to propose an independent test for the remaining 4 seconds of arc. It claims that this discrepancy can be accounted for if the sun were oblated. However, let us say it is proposed that the sun's apparent visual oblateness is explainable as an equatorial temperature excess of 30°K that is located in the high photosphere and low chromosphere and thus does not oblate mass distribution. An experiment is conducted that overwhelmingly supports the temperature effect. Einstein's theory predicts that light will bend 1.75 seconds of arc when passing through the gravitational field of the sun, whereas the Brans-Dicke theory predicts it will bend only 1.62 seconds of arc. Experiments show that by a margin of error of less than 1 percent, the Brans-Dicke theory is correct and hence has an edge over the general theory of relativity in this respect. However, gravitational waves are detected, and experiments with a high degree of accuracy reveal that the gravitational waves have two polarized states, in accordance with the general theory and in opposition to the Brans-Dicke theory, which predicts three polarized states. We finally conclude, after due weighing of the relative merits of the general theory and the Brans-Dicke theory, that in accordance with M, Einstein's theory is to be accepted as the best current gravitational theory. If this example does not illustrate a rational decision on our part, then nothing does.

Three points can be made about this example. First, historical accuracy or the correctness of the physical facts or theories reported here is not at issue. Nor is the issue, what is M?

Second, we have focused on which is the best current theory to accept rather than on the more interesting problem, namely, Which theory ought we to pursue actively for further theoretical and experimental research and investigation? To answer the latter question, however, our strategy would not have been markedly different. We would have used norms of *M* leading to theories worthy of further pursuit.

Third, to draw out the central historiographical claim, it can be said that any future historian of science trying to explain our acceptance of the general theory of relativity among its other rivals will have done everything that needs to be done once he has reconstructed our problem-situation and the manner of our arriving at our decision. Such a historian will not only array the various theories and experimental results known to us, he will seek out, and perhaps conjecture, the method, *M*, we used in evaluating various competing gravitational theories.

What a future historian will not do is to judge the relative merits of the theories confronting us by *his* best model of rationality (which, let us assume for the sake of argument, is better than ours). If *M* was Laudan's methodology of research traditions in the above illustration, the future historian ought not to say, "They adopted a poor method, a method that ignored truth and verisimilitude; the criteria proposed by such a method led to quaint appraisals since it allowed the acceptance and pursuit of inconsistent theories. By their method a false prediction of a theory often pointed only to an unsolved problem but never reflected on the theory, no matter how numerous such predictions were. Therefore, I should judge them and explain and understand their actions, decisions, and beliefs on the basis of the best model of rationality *I* hold." To do so would be plainly anachronistic.

Consequently and significantly, we are led to adopt the *principle of parity*. *As future historians to scientists in the past, we should do for them what we would have future historians of our scientific beliefs and decisions do for us.*

As a general schema for explaining rational decisions in the history of science, I propose the following:

Factual Premises:

1. *S* was seeking to accept the best theory (to a practical problem, heuristic problem, etc.) from rival theories, T_1, T_2, T_3, . . . , T_n, available to him.

	2. T_1, T_2, T_3, . . . , T_n were relevant to the problem-situation.
	3. *S* was committed to *M*.
Objective Component$_M$ Premise:	4. T_1 is (________). (An example of what goes into the blank would be "better corroborated than its rivals.").
Normative Component$_M$ Premise:	5. One ought to accept as the best theory one that is (________).
Conclusion:	6. *S* accepted T_1 as the best theory (to solve a practical problem, heuristic problem, etc.).

Armed with the general schema, anyone would be able to explain our decision to accept Einstein's general theory of relativity as the best gravitational theory. Furthermore, one should be able to explain the rational decisions of scientists in the past with its aid, too. It is worth noting that the schema is sufficiently general and is not designed for a highly specific purpose or problem. It can accommodate the explanation of anything from choosing theories for practical purposes, such as determining constants, densities of materials, boiling points, Curie temperatures, and so forth, to choosing theories for research purposes, such as developing better theories about cosmology, cancer, the binary star system, or the physical structure and composition of the outer core of the earth.

Three problems must be distinguished. First is the scientific problem facing *S*, such as, What is the cause of craters on the moon?, What is the genetic structure? or, What relationship existed between the continental drift and the biological diversity in the post-Jurassic period? Second is *S*'s problem of selecting a theory. Third is the problem of explaining the choice *S* made in that historical situation. In the second case, *S* (say, Louis Agassiz) probably asked himself some such question as, Which theory of earth, uniformitarianism or catastrophic theory, shall I choose? In the third case, a historian of science (say, L. Pearce Williams) may ask, Why did Faraday reject Ampère's electrodynamic theory? Rheticus preferred Copernicus's heliocentric theory, even though it grossly violated the then-accepted Aristotelian physics, over the various geocentric theories. Rheticus probably asked, or at least tried to avail himself of an argument, why he should accept the heliocentric theory as either true, or nearer to the truth, or worthy of further theoretical development, rather than accept one of the geocentric theories. A significant part of that theoretical development, as he and Copernicus both knew, consisted in answering the Aristotelian objections. The historian of science, unlike Rheticus, does not have a real problem as to which astronomical theory to pick. His problem is to determine what considerations went into *Rheticus's* picking of the heliocentric theory and to ascertain whether or not that choice was rational. Popper would refer to the historian's problem as the *problem of understanding*.[60] It is with this problem, of understanding how theories are chosen in science, that I am presently concerned.

In Premise 1, perhaps it is necessary to add the clause that *S* knew of the alternatives available to him; otherwise, his decision could incorrectly turn out to be irrational. The most enterprising and dynamic teacher in the Middle Ages, at a time that coincides with the beginning of the Age of Translation, was Gerbert of Aurillac (later Pope Sylvester II [999–1003]). Using Church influence Aurillac obtained Latin translations of Arabic works, primarily on astronomy and geometry. At the cathedral school of Reims, he taught elementary mathematics, astronomy, and as an incredibly effective pedagogical device constructed a sphere to represent the heavens and simulate the motions of the constellations.

Emerging from such an environment, students went abroad and engaged in philosophical bouts through correspondence. One such "scientific tournament" took place between Ragimbold of Cologne and Radolf of Liège. It revolved around the problem of calculating the side of a square that was twice the side of a given square. Both parties knew that the side of the larger square was equal to the diagonal of the given square. Ragimbold suggested that the ratio of the sides of the two squares was 17/12 whereas Radolf suggested it was 7/5. Their knowledge of geometry was extremely meager, and they did not know that the ratios could not be related by whole numbers.[61]

A historian who knows that the ratios are incommensurable might ask, Why is it that the contestants ignored the geometry of the Greeks translated into Latin? He may find out various things. Perhaps the geometry taught by Aurillac from the translations obtained through Church influence did not deal with that problem. The participants thus would have had very little understanding of the nature of geometry, the nature of proofs, and the like, as is attested by the fact that they decided to settle their claims experimentally. Oftentimes a scientist will be unaware of the various alternatives that may objectively solve the problem better than the rival he is familiar with. This lack does not automatically cast doubt on the rationality of the scientific agent. The historian, in this instance, can independently confirm his conjecture by finding out if the Latin translations, with which the participants were or could have been familiar, carried the solution to the problem. Obviously, such conjectures may not easily be confirmed or refuted.

Premise 2 is clearly in need of a similar qualification. Premises 4 and 5 are relatively unproblematic, given the discussion in chapter 1. Premise 3 is the controversial one.

Just as espousing a true theory in science is not a necessary condition for rational decision, so also espousing the best model of rationality should not be a necessary condition for rationality—certainly not the espousing of the best model of rationality a later historian of science is familiar with. *One should not dislodge a scientist's claim to have acted rationally from the specific reasons he gives.* We must distinguish between the two questions of why a given decision was considered rational *then* and why it is considered rational *now*. It is by no means obvious that the answers to these two questions will be the same. Thus it becomes clear why *M*, the method espoused by the scientist whose decisions we are trying to explain, is so important. The normative components of his method, both those that help in the appraisal and those that yield heuristic advice, *were the scientist's reasons for making the choice in the way he did.* Copernicus's reason for rejecting the Ptolemaic program sprang from his commitment to a method. That method forbade the use of equants; it favored the Pythagorean tradition, which made it more attractive to put the sun at the center; it permitted the heliocentric idea to be further used and explored since it had been espoused by some of the ancient astronomers; and so on. In short, on my view, to say that *S* is committed to *M* is in effect to say that *S* does what he ought to do in accordance with *M*. So a general premise in my schema might be, "If *S* was committed to *M*, then if he ought to have done *X* according to *M*, *S* did *X*." (This statement is essential to the validity of the argument; it is not stated separately in the schema since, as I have argued, it follows from Premise 3.)

In discussing his Premise 2, "Smith was a rational agent," Laudan supposes that the question can be settled simply by looking up the relevant biographical details. But what details are relevant, and as a general philosophical theory, what makes an agent rational? I make a distinction between the rationality of a single decision and the rationality of the agent. To say that a single decision of a scientist is rational is to say that it was carried out in conformity with the normative components of the method to which the scientist was committed. However, to say that the scientist is a rational agent is to say that *he generally acts in conformity with the normative components of that method*. This distinction enables us to claim that a scientist can be rational although he sometimes fails to be rational in particular cases—a significant gain. Einstein's decision to reject quantum theory was irrational, as was Lord Kelvin's decision to reject the contemporary age of the earth. Neither one was an irrational individual. However, if a scientist continuously infringes on the norms of a method he could sensibly be said to have ascribed to, or Feyerabend-like he adheres to no norms at all, then he is irrational, and we need not bother about the rationality of his individual decisions. This has enormous implications for the historically minded methodologists who argue that methods must explicate the rational decisions in the history of science. Clearly, explicating individual decisions are of little value if the scientist is not a rational agent. Of course, the only way in which a historian can determine whether a scientist acts in conformity with a method or not is by paying attention to the particular decisions. Finally, however, it is the general claim about the rationality of the scientific agent that is important.

The plausibility of this premise will be strengthened in the last section when I outline a general theory of the growth of scientific knowledge; and then again in section V when I argue against Laudan's theory of explaining rational decisions in the history of science, and hence against his theory of method, in the light of my alternative proposal.

IV. OBJECTIONS ANTICIPATED AND ANSWERED

First, it is frequently claimed that scientists do not or cannot practice what they methodologically preach. For instance, Popper might argue that although Newton said that he was "inducting" from the phenomena and "proving" his laws from them, there is no such thing as induction or any such thing as proving conjectured laws. Hence, Newton could not have followed what he regarded as his methodological precepts. Or, as

Lakatos says, scientists "even when they act rationally may have a false theory of their own rational actions."[62] Lakatos clearly implies that his methodology of research programs, or any best theory of rationality, could successfully explain why such scientists' decisions were rational when the scientists' own overtly held theory could not.

However, *M* in Premise 3 is not necessarily the method the scientist *says* he is espousing. The fact that a scientist may not have been, as he claimed, an inductivist, or that he was mistaken in what he believed were his methodological norms, does not imply that either (i) he had no method at all, or (ii) he espoused the best model of rationality. It is quite possible, for instance, that Newton drew unsuspectingly on a methodological tradition in which he was historically placed and which can be used to explain his rational decisions—a methodological tradition, moreover, that we with our hindsight may find quite implausible.

Second, it might be objected that in some cases the task of uncovering general methodological commitments is virtually impossible, to say nothing about being able to detect specific objective and normative components of that method. For instance, if we take those first few centuries before the dawn of Christianity, a period that helped in establishing "the handbook and encyclopedic tradition of learning" and whose later and better-known practitioner was Pliny, we would find it very difficult to uncover a methodological tradition if only because several works have been lost (for instance, the works of Posidonius). In this tradition, I am thinking primarily of Eratosthenes, Crates, Geminus, and the like, who together supplied much knowledge of geography, meteorology, astronomy, and so on. However, the difficulty of uncovering their specific methodological commitments is not specifically related to the problems and issues under discussion; it is a general historical worry. Often on slim historical evidence, historians make guesses of all sorts—and not only ones pertaining to methods—to make their narratives plausible.

Third, it might be pointed out that scientists do not commit themselves to a single method; often they espouse many. Assuming that scientists do not adopt two or more conflicting methods *simultaneously*, this objection is not damaging at all. One historian has argued that the methodological controversy between instrumentalists and realists was settled in favor of the realists once a younger generation, after Maestlin, teacher of Kepler, had come to look "at the cosmological arguments of *De Revolutionibus* with a fresh gaze."[63] I extrapolate. Not only was there a change in the scientific theory adopted—geostatic theory being replaced by the heliostatic theory—but there was a change in the methodological commitment as well, from an instrumentalist method to a realist one.

For Praetorius and Maestlin, a theory was an instrument for making predictions, and so mathematical simplicity and tallying with observations were enough. "The astronomer," said Praetorius, "is free to devise or imagine circles, epicycles and similar devices although they might not exist in nature."[64] Not so for other astronomers. A theory was not merely a useful fiction, it was a depicter of the world. If astronomers accepted the "Axioma Astronomicum," which enjoined them to reject the equant, which sometimes occasioned a wobbling epicycle,[65] it was for physical, rather than mathematical reasons.

Of course, the methodological transition could not have been abrupt, yet at least in some individual cases there must have been a transfer of methodological allegiance. It is possible, for instance, that Rheticus's choice of an astronomical system can be explained as being within the instrumentalist methodological tradition previous to his meeting Copernicus, and as being in the realist methodological tradition thereafter.[66] It might be mentioned in passing that the transition of commitments from one method to the next will call for interesting answers to problems, such as, How precisely do scientific theories change and influence methods, and vice versa?

Finally, it might be argued that since I have placed no constraints on the acceptance of a method at all, an action or decision consistently carried out in accordance with *any* method is rational. A scientist, such as Mach, who closely studies the history of his subject—mechanics, optics, thermodynamics, and so on—and who has well-articulated philosophical and methodological views on it, and who furthermore accepts or rejects scientific theories in conformity with the norms of his method is on par, so the argument goes, with astrologers, palmists, or chiropractors who carry out their decisions consistently with *their* methodological commitments. Surely this is absurd.

Let us return to our paradigm case of rational decision. Could *we* have picked any method at all to decide which was the best gravitational theory? Clearly not. What was brought to bear was an implicit, assumed-to-be-plausible theory of method, in the light of which the best method was picked. Analogously, in attempting to judge whether a scientist picked a reasonable method we have to plausibly reconstruct in a Collingwoodian fashion (I speak very loosely) the scientist's theory of method. We will have to understand what the previous and contemporary methods were, what then-current methodological problems were facing the scientists, and so on. Such an analysis may show that certain scientists did espouse a wrong or incorrect method and hence acted irrationally. For instance, someone holding to Eudoxus's planetary model in the early seventeenth century was probably holding onto a nonviable method, and not just to a poor scientific theory. However consistently he held to his method, that would not in and of itself make him a rational agent, or make some particular act or decision of his a rational one.

True, I did not place any constraints on acceptable methods, but this is not because I think that in method anything goes, but rather because the problem of proposing constraints is an exceedingly difficult one for which I have as yet no solution save to recommend a case-by-case approach. In any event, I am not as sanguine as Laudan is when he says, "The model of research traditions argues that there are certain very general characteristics of a theory of rationality which are *trans-temporal* and *trans-cultural*, which are as applicable to pre-Socratic thought, or the development of ideas in the Middle Ages, as they are to the more recent history of science."[67]

V. CRITICISMS OF LAUDAN'S THEORY OF METHOD

Let us consider the problem of explaining why Newton rejected Descartes's vortex theory of planetary motion. A historian of science proceeds in the manner Laudan suggests and, indeed, uses the methodology of research traditions as his model of rationality to sift among the facts, so that he knows what to weave into his historical narrative. The historian will analyze two research traditions, Descartes's and Newton's (for the sake of simplicity, we shall ignore other rival traditions, if any). He will cull out the various empirical and conceptual problems the scientists were then faced with. He will proceed to classify the empirical problems into those that are solved, unsolved, and anomalous, respectively. He will do likewise for conceptual problems. Finally, he will chalk up the number of solved and anomalous problems that belong to these two rival traditions. If, on the basis Laudan recommends, the historian determines that Newton's research tradition has a greater degree of problem-solving effectiveness, then he will pronounce that Newton's theory is better than Descartes's.

The historian, using Laudan's schema, will present his explanation of Newton's rational decision in rejecting the Cartesian vortical theory as follows:

(1′) All rational agents in situations where they are confronted with two research traditions, one of which is a better problem-solver than the other, will reject the poorer problem-solver.

(2′) Newton was a rational agent.

(3′) Newton was in a situation where he was confronted with two research traditions (Descartes's and his own), one of which (Descartes's) was a poorer problem-solver than the other (his own).

(4′) ∴ Newton rejected the theory (Descartes's) that was the poorer problem-solver.

Since Newton did what was rational, according to the methodology of research traditions we need inquire no further into the causes of his actions.

Put boldly thus, difficulties quickly sprout. Unless such reasoning—that is, reasoning in terms of problems, problem-solving, and problem-solving effectiveness—was part and parcel of Newton's reasoning for accepting or rejecting Descartes's vortex theory, this is no historical explanation at all; and thus the methodology of research traditions is not to be credited with having successfully explained an episode in the history of science. What Feyerabend said, when Imre Lakatos and Elie Zahar tried to explain the rationality of the acceptance of the Copernican theory over the Ptolemaic theory in terms of Lakatos's methodology of research programs, is pertinent here. He said, "We hardly shall call people rational who act rationally in *our* sense but achieve this by bungling standards they regard as important."[68] Perhaps Newton bungled his standards when he evaluated the vortex theory touted on the Continent; perhaps he did not. The point, of course, is that Newton's method must play a significant role in our explanation of his rational decision, while our method should play no role at all.

One might propose a contrafactual account: *Had* Newton accepted the best model of rationality, namely, the methodology of research traditions, he would have rejected the Cartesian vortex theory as being not as effective a problem-solver as his own theory. I use and explore this point more fully, and to good purpose, in the last chapter; but for now, it is unclear what sort of explaining of a rational decision this is, *even if the contrafactual is true*. Or, whether any methodologist who seeks history of science—and not some possible course that history could have taken—to arbitrate between competing methods can accept the methodology of research traditions as having successfully explained Newton's rejection of the vortex theory.

Since Laudan makes no distinction between distant and more recent science history for purposes of evaluating methods,[69] we could also argue as follows: Let the best model of rationality be Laudan's methodology of research traditions, *L*, and the model of rationality espoused by a scientist, *x* (say, John Eccles or Peter Medawar), who is the subject of the historian's investigation, be Popper's method, *P*. *x* believes *B*. *x* also believes *Q*, *R*, *S*, . . . , *Z*. From Laudan's vantage point, the historian of science, then, "looks for, and finds, a way of showing that *x*'s belief is rationally well founded, given *x*'s other beliefs."[70] Further, let us grant for the sake of argument that given *x*'s beliefs *Q*, *R*, *S*, . . . , *Z*, we can show that the belief *B* was the most effective problem-solver of the various theories available. It is consistent with everything said so far, however, that the following hypothesis is also true: *x* espoused his belief in *B* because he thought *B* had a greater degree of verisimilitude than the other theories available to him. His reasoning, in his acceptance of *B*, involved the concepts of truth, verisimilitude, explanation of facts, severe tests, degree of corroboration, and so on—that is *x*'s reasoning involved *concepts and suppositions that L rejects*. To put the matter differently, the model of rationality the scientific agent *x* adopted to evaluate his beliefs was in direct conflict and opposition to the method or model of rationality espoused by the intellectual historian of science to account for *x*'s belief. In this case, why should the historian's account be accepted as historical rather than imaginary? Indeed, how could the best model of rationality let another method with which it competes and conflicts enter into the explanation essentially? How could this case in the history of science allow us to arbitrate between the methodology of falsificationism and the methodology of research traditions? To be sure, the method of Newton (its objective and normative components) is different from the method of Popper, *P*, but that is of less significance here. What is crucial is that Newton's method is also different from *L*. As a result, if one finds the first case a problem for Laudan's theory of method, so will one find the second case.

Laudan might claim that this argument overlooks a crucial element in his theory. Thus, he had repeatedly argued that one of the vices of other models of rationality such as the deductivist and the inductivist was their insensitivity to the degree to which "*specific canons of rationality are time-dependent*."[71] As he claims more explicitly, "Unlike (the other methodologists), I argue that the actual beliefs of historical agents, *and* the canons of rational beliefs of their epoch, must be scrupulously attended to."[72]

But it is crucial *not* to argue as does Laudan. No model of rationality can be regarded as the best one if it considers the acceptance of a theory irrational even though it was rational to accept that theory in the light of the method espoused by the agent x, whose belief the intellectual historian of knowledge is trying to explain. For, *if the evaluation by a contemporary method must square up with the evaluation made by the method used by a scientist in the past, then strictly speaking L or any contemporary method is quite dispensable*!

Laudan's theory of method evaluation, accompanied by his theory of explanation of rational decisions in the history of science, is impaled on the horns of a dilemma. Either a current competing method or model of rationality should be used in the explanation of rational decisions in the history of science or it should not be used. If such a method is used, then our own decision, as in the paradigm case (Section IV), will have to be explained differently than by using our best model of rationality. Presumably, it will be explained by the best model of rationality held by some future historian of science. This is absurd. However, if a competing contemporary method is not used, then while we do not violate the principle of parity, the history of science clearly can neither confirm nor confute such a method.

But, I must be cautious. Take Gerd Buchdahl's important and delicately argued paper, "History of Science and Criteria of Choice,"[73] for instance. Buchdahl delves into the history of science to discover the basic criteria or components that actually went into the making of a decision to accept or reject a hypothesis or concept. He finds that neither confirmation, nor falsification, nor predictive power, singly or together, constitute sufficient conditions for making such a decision; he refrains from charting a stronger view that they are not even, singly or jointly, necessary conditions.

What Buchdahl finds playing a crucial role is a trio of factors, which he christens the *architectonic* component, the *conceptual* component, and the *constitutive* component. He illustrates the first thus: justifying a concept such as 'field,' or justifying a law such as the gravitational law, by invoking the architectonic component involves invoking such ideas as rules of simplicity and economy, aesthetic considerations, teleological, and even theological, notions, principles of continuity or discontinuity, prevailing metaphysical maxims, and so on. Newton worried about the cause of gravitation and found solutions of a teleological nature less objectionable than others, even if he did not actually welcome them. Maupertuis regarded his concept of action-at-a-distance as well entrenched by noting that the concept satisfied the requirements of uniformity and analogy and that the effects of such gravitational attraction seemed subject to the law of least action, a favored notion.

To make a concept intelligible, one provides semantic or conceptual criteria. So, Galileo is seen to have begun his study of mechanics by articulating the proper meaning of velocity, acceleration, and so on, while Descartes's theory of cosmology is seen as preceded by his study of dynamics, which he in turn built on answers to such questions as, What is the meaning of space and motion? The meaning of the terms in question may be more tightly defined than the meaning of other terms. What turn the meaning of a term takes depends upon the individual historical context. It may evolve slowly, or it may change radically—as did the concept of matter in the hands of Stallo—under the pressure of theoretical and experimental findings or for more general or metaphysical reasons.

Finally, the constitutive component is one that invokes the notion of empirical adequacy, simplicity (defined in empirical terms), testability, and the manner in which the proposed hypothesis dovetails with the other prevailing hypotheses of the time. To be sure, these components were not clearly and explicitly defined by the practitioners of a science, and their scientific decisions were not consciously based on such components or criteria. Nor did the components in the decision-making process of the practitioners precede each other in a proper sequence, with the architectonic component bearing first upon the concept, followed by the semantic component, and finally the constitutive component. Nor, it must be emphasized, were these three components in neat and tightly sealed boxes; rather, they were interrelated and deeply influenced one another. What is more, the degree of importance attached to each component varied a great deal. For instance, in the discussion of the concept of action-at-a-distance during much of the eighteenth and nineteenth centuries, the conceptual component played a very major role, while the constitutive component amounted to little; in other periods and for other concepts and theories, the roles may well have been reversed.

What, then, am I being cautious about? Unlike Lakatos, Laudan, and Popperians (if not Popper himself, even occasionally), Buchdahl does not argue for certain methodological concepts, such as falsification, problem-solving, or the methodology of research programs, with which to look backward and read the history of science. He does not say that whenever the problem-solving effectiveness of a theory was greater than its rivals, that theory was always accepted; or that scientists always accepted the best-corroborated theory. Buchdahl does not recommend any such time-independent methodological strictures for understanding the history of science or the manner of decision-making in the past, so I cannot use my arsenal against his moderate and measured arguments. He is certainly not guilty of transgressing the principle of parity. Indeed, one can see that the history of science *can* be used to judge Buchdahl's methodological conjectures. Perhaps a historian of science might find certain episodes in which the architectonic component or the semantic component played no significant role and thus may conclude that Buchdahl's method is false (assuming, of course, that Buchdahl maintains that all three components, together and always, played significant parts in the making of a decision to accept or reject a theory or a concept).

This is the quasi-empirical approach—in the best sense of that abused phrase—that Lakatos makes so much of (but without avoiding the pitfalls attendant to it). However, useful questions can be raised. One might argue that granting the empirical adequacy of Buchdahl's conjecture, why should a methodologist be interested in it? A contemporary scientist reading and studying Buchdahl might ask, How will this assist me in my scientific practice? What invites these questions, of course, is the divide between the historical-is and the methodological-ought. Granted, a scientist might say, that for Faraday the concept of action-at-a-distance was unintelligible and that the conceptual component played a stronger role in his decision than did the constitutive component. Granted also that Kepler's scientific practice was marked by his stronger adherence to the architectonic components than to the constitutive components. However, the historical and intellectual background and beliefs that provided the medium in which a Faraday or a Kepler made decisions are not the contemporary scientist's, and the latter may well seek to know what components *ought* to play a decisive factor for *him*.

The scientist would not ask merely how to weigh these various criteria or components but rather what are, and ought to be, the substantive components in terms of which he should make his decisions concerning the acceptance or rejection of scientific theories. In other words, even if, let us say, he were told that the architectonic should weigh the most, he would ask, What are the components? What ought they be? He may no longer accept the maxims and principles once espoused by Brahe or Boscovich, by Mach or Maupertuis. Buchdahl, however, does not supply these specific, and detailed methodological maxims with which a scientist today could evaluate his theories. (Let me hastily add that it is not his aim to do so in the paper under discussion.)

In short, Buchdahl's views are open to confirmation or confutation by the history of science, and so my arguments are inapplicable to them, but they leave some questions of a normative nature unanswered. Laudan's thesis, as well as those of other philosophers of science, supplies rival answers to normative questions, but then they are not open to arbitration by the history of science. If Laudan's view appears to have any degree of plausibility, it earns it by fusing three distinct theories: a theory of science or method, a theory of method, and a theory of explaining rational decision in the history of science. A correct theory of the one sort may have a tenuous link with the correct theory of another sort. For instance, the implicit theory of method used in section I to evaluate the methods of Popper and Laudan has minimal bearing on my theory of explaining rational decision in the history of science sketched in section III, and vice versa. Thus, by a different route, I arrive at a conclusion similar to the one reached in the chapter on Lakatos: history of science cannot be used as an arbitrator between methods.

VI. GROWTH OF SCIENTIFIC KNOWLEDGE AND RATIONALITY

In this section I paint in broad strokes.

The problem I am concerned with here is, How are we to explain the rational development of the history of science? To begin with, let me draw some crucial distinctions. There is first what I shall call the *scientific tradition*, the tradition of scientific theories, problem-solving, attempts at explaining facts, resolving inconsistencies, deriving testable consequences, and so on. Second is the ***methodological tradition***, the tradition of appraising the status of competing theories, giving heuristic advice, sharing a common understanding of the nature of science and its goals, and so forth.[74] Finally, there is the ***meta-methodological tradition***, which appraises and evaluates the methods one has espoused or those espoused by others. No one seems to dispute the scientific tradition or even the methodological tradition. Certainly Laudan has done much to enhance our appreciation of these two traditions, but few notice, much less emphasize, the importance and significance of the meta-methodological tradition. On my view, it is imperative that the history of science be seen as a carrier of these three traditions, although admittedly the meta-methodological tradition is far in the background. Perhaps it emerges to the fore only in times of crisis.

To explain the rational development of science or the growth of scientific knowledge, we begin with the three traditions early scientists were placed in. The norms or aims of methods changed in the light of the meta-methodological tradition, while the change and succession of scientific theories was wrought by the consistent adoption of the methodological norms. The changes in the scientific tradition—unintended consequences, no doubt—probably reflected on the methods, which in turn affected the theory of method. What is more conspicuous is the following dual interaction: the scientific tradition slowly changing and molding the methodological tradition, and the latter ringing in a sequence of scientific theories over a fairly long interval of time.

Precisely what is meant by saying that the methodological tradition rings in a sequence of scientific theories? After the publication of Alfred Wegener's *The Origin of Continents and Oceans* in 1915, no other problem was in greater limelight than the problem of the distribution of faunal and floral life forms having a geographically disjunctive distribution. For instance, an apparently high percentage of identical reptiles and mammals was found on both sides of the Atlantic; the distribution of earthworms, *Lumbricidae*, pearl-mussels, garden snails, perch, and other freshwater fish were similarly disjunctively distributed; the reptile Mesosaurus was found both in Brazil and in Africa; *glossopetris* flora was discovered in India, South America, Africa, and Australia (and as such was to play a major role in the ensuing debate and to attract the attention of paleontologist and paleoclimatologist alike); and, finally, the sea cow *Manatus* was found in West Africa and Central America. How could similar things be found in such vastly different places?

Several hypotheses were proposed to explain this rather intriguing phenomenon, including the theory of sunken landbridges (Eduard Suess, T. Arldt, J. W. Gregory. H. von Ihering), the theory of permanentism (G. G. Simpson, Charles Schuchert, Bailey Willis), and the theory of drifting continents (Alfred Wegener, Alex du Toit). The theory of sunken landbridges argued that landbridges once existed (often as many as eight were postulated) across oceans, and these landbridges provided means for the migration of life forms. The theory of permanentism argued (in Simpson's version) that there were permanent landbridges, such as the Bering landbridge extending from Siberia to Alaska, and Central America which provided a bridge between North and South America. The bridges were of three types: corridors, where no barriers existed, as between New Mexico and Florida; filter bridges, which allowed only some mammals to pass but not others; and sweepstakes routes, the adventitious migration across which was based purely on chance. Finally, the theory of drifting continents argued that landmasses were once contiguous, hence making similarities between flora and fauna easily accounted for. For instance, it was said that because Australia and India (not to mention Ceylon, Madagascar, and South Africa) were once linked together, the oldest Australian fauna are quite similar to those prevailing in India.

No theory was without objections from the rivals, of course. Wegener's theory was open to the charge, leveled by Sir Harold Jeffreys in *The Earth*, that not enough energy was stored within the earth to make continents move laterally through the seafloor; the theory of permanentism was met with the objection that Simpson had relied too heavily on paleontological arguments, that focusing on mammalian distribution was too inconsequential since mammals were relatively insignificant until the continents had completed their drifting; and the theory of sunken landbridges was subject to the criticism that no geophysical mechanism was provided to show how an overloading process had occurred by virtue of which the density of the landbridge increased sufficiently for it to crack and sink into the seafloor; also, such a notion flagrantly flew in the face of the principle of isostasy.[75]

What deeply influenced the development of this field of science must have depended much more markedly on the theories adopted for further theoretical and experimental research than it will *ever* have depended on what was adopted or regarded as the best theory in the field to date. Confronted with the advantages and the disadvantages of the several competing theories, a scientist must have asked at least two questions, one far more significant than the other: Which is the best hypothesis among the current competing ones? And, more importantly, which hypothesis has a greater potential for being developed into a better theory than the rest? The answers to these two questions will hardly ever coincide; at any rate, they need not. It is the methodological tradition that dictates which theories should be rejected for further development and which ones should be pursued. It is this part of the method that has, in my judgment, a greater claim as the principal explainer of the development and growth of scientific knowledge than anything else. In general, before as now, it is the methodological commitments of the scientists, and especially the heuristic advice such a method gives, that will ring in, or profoundly affect, the scientific tradition.

If a methodological tradition can affect theories, however, the theories can affect the methodological tradition, too, particularly if the theories the method brings forth are not fruitful. Nicholas Stensen started out as a Cartesian, and in accordance with the method of Descartes he sought certainty and quantitative knowledge. In the 1660s, Stensen embarked on the study of the structure and function of the heart. His studies led him to conclude that Aristotle, Galen, and a reluctant Harvey were wrong in thinking that the heart was the seat of the soul, the source of life, the central organ of all motion and sensation, and the source of blood or of the *spiritus vitales*. The heart was merely a muscle. He noticed that the vena cava moved independently even after the heart had stopped beating; so he experimented with muscles and then returned to the study of the heart. He discovered that the latter had arteries, veins, fibers and fibrils, nerves and membranes, as did the muscles. He concluded that there was nothing in the heart that was not in the muscle, nor anything in the muscle that was not in the heart. But that was not all: he concluded that his discovery of the muscular structure of the heart showed the Cartesian view of the heart to be hopelessly wrong, which was reason enough, he felt, to reject the Cartesian method as well. (He confided to Leibniz: "If these (Cartesian) gentlemen have been so mistaken with material things which are accessible to the senses, what warranty can they offer that they are not mistaken when they talk about God and the soul?")[76]

The meta-methodological tradition will have contributed indirectly to this process of the growth of knowledge by impinging on the methodological tradition. Over a long interval of time, however, it will have been impinged upon, too, by the methodological and the scientific traditions.

Unlike Lakatos and other methodologists, Laudan does not ignore the issue of heuristics. He makes the earlier-noted distinction between the context of acceptance and the context of pursuit. A research tradition or a theory is acceptable if it is a better problem-solver than its rivals. By contrast, a research tradition or a theory can be pursued even if it has a very low problem-solving effectiveness, so long as its rate of problem-solving effectiveness, that is, its progress, is higher than its rivals.

Laudan would advocate, in the example described earlier, that it would be rational to pursue the hypothesis of the drifting continents provided its rate of progress was higher than that of its rivals. Laudan believes that his twin notions of progress and pursuit happily enable one to straddle the two extremes: namely, it is irrational to pursue any but the best theory, and it is rational to pursue any theory.[77] The Galilean research tradition was initially a poorer problem-solver than its Aristotelian counterpart; and, Dalton's atomic theory at the start did not fare as well as the chemical theory centered upon the idea of elective affinities. Both inferior theories were pursued, according to Laudan, because their rate of progress was greater than that of their respective rivals.[78]

This account is inadequate, however, not merely because it is ill-defined or because the examples have not been fully and carefully worked out. First, it is not clear which unit of appraisal must exhibit the highest rate of progress, a theory constitutive of a research tradition or the research tradition itself? When Laudan speaks of the context of acceptance, he says, "*Choose the theory or (research tradition) with the highest problem-solving adequacy*."[79] It is therefore reasonable to assume, so that his claims are parallel in the two contexts, that it is always rational to pursue not only any research tradition that has a higher rate of progress than its rivals but *any theory* in a research tradition that exhibits a similar characteristic. It is significant to notice that the problem-solving effectiveness of a research tradition is parasitically dependent upon the problem-solving effectiveness of its constitutive theories.[80] But here difficulties arise.

Laudan *defends* the highly unintuitive idea that even a much poorer theory can be pursued if the research tradition in which it is embedded is showing signs of progress. Although, says Laudan, the physiological theories of Borelli and Pitcairn "were significantly inferior" to theories embedded in less successful research traditions than the mechanistic traditions in which the just-mentioned physiological theories were placed, they were and should have been pursued.[81] By the criteria Laudan recommends, however, they should have been neither accepted nor pursued. Again, by Laudan's own appraisal, from 1800 to 1815 Rumford's theories of conduction and convection of heat "were far superior" to the alternatives in the domain. Nonetheless, Laudan agrees that scientists should not have taken seriously (as, indeed, they did not) Rumford's theories of thermal flow in fluids because the research tradition in which Rumford worked had been discredited by the emergence of a chemical tradition—partly owing to Joseph Black—that suggested that heat was a substance rather than the random motion of atoms, as Rumford held.[82]

This is a curious justification for rejecting Rumford's theories of heat transfer. A rival tradition is bound to propose and conflict with the ontological commitments of other theories in the domain. If the problem-solving effectiveness of a research tradition is parasitically dependent upon the problem-solving effectiveness of its constitutive theories, why should the admitted success of Rumford's theories not redound to the credit of the research tradition in which they were placed? If this were not permitted in principle, then Laudan's example of the pursuit of Galileo's research tradition would fail to make his point. For the Galilean tradition rested on the Copernican world view, which conflicted with the then generally accepted Aristotelian idea of the earth-centered universe.

Second, is it irrational to pursue a theory in a research tradition whose rate of progress is *not* the highest among its rivals? If it is rational, then it is unclear how Laudan has avoided the one extreme view he attributes to Lakatos, namely, that any theory can be pursued as rational. If it is irrational, then Laudan is in an odd situation of having to explain why Aristotelianism or the theory of elective affinities had a substantial following when their rate of progress was not, by Laudan's own hypothesis, the highest.

Third, an old difficulty that Feyerabend raised for Lakatos's method crops up again. Feyerabend had argued that without a specified time limit, it is unclear why a scientist should abandon work on a theory that is in a degenerating problem-shift and pursue a theory that shows an empirically progressive problem-shift.[83] Feyerabend may well argue that for Laudan, with his talk about the *rate* of progress, specifying such a limit is even more imperative on pain of being unable to determine that rate. What time span may be allowed in terms of which the rate of progress is to be determined? *Any* time span. "The rate of progress of a research tradition," says Laudan, is to be measured by "the changes in the momentary adequacy of the research tradition during any specified time span."[84] In its earliest phases, is there any doubt that the Galilean research tradition or the tradition of Dalton's atomic theory did not have a rate of progress anywhere comparable to the rate of progress of the Aristotelian theory or the theory of elective affinities, respectively? The permanentists had no major biogeographical response until the 1960s, approximately fifteen years after the issue of the disjunctive distribution of life forms had been raised, discussed, and answered by Wegenerians and other rival theorists. Should these theories, then, have been abandoned in their earliest phases? Do budding, fruitful, and fecund theories continuously exhibit a higher rate of progress over any arbitrary interval of time? Should they be abandoned when in patches they fail to exhibit such a progress? If not, what compelling reason do we have for refusing to pursue a theory whose rate of progress is quite low over its rivals?[85] Parenthetically, when Laudan says that the Aristotelian theory solved problems after Galileans pointed them out, and their solutions smacked of ad hocery, he goes against his own analysis of the acceptability of ad hoc hypothesis.[86]

Finally, consider research work on the problem posed by the disjunctive distribution of life forms. Since the 1920s at least, there were several workers in the field pursuing several different hypotheses, but it was not at all evident that the rate of progress of these hypotheses was the same. If one accepts Feyerabend's *principle of proliferation*, a principle most philosophers of science regard as reasonable, then it is important that scientists actively pursue different theories.[87] Laudan's highly restrictive account cannot explain the espousal of several theories. When Laudan says, "Whether the approach taken here to the problem of 'rational pursuit' will eventually prevail is doubtful,"[88] I concur; what cannot be denied is the utter significance of the problem he treats.

Throughout this discussion an assumption has been made that criteria of theory-choice can be made explicit in the form of rules. As we saw, Laudan proposes rules by using the machinery developed in his idea of problem-solving effectiveness. Kuhn denies the possibility of such an enterprise. In "Objectivity, Value Judgments, and Theory Choice," a chapter in his book, *The Essential Tension*, Kuhn does not militate against rules altogether, for he himself mentions a brief list: a theory should be accurate within its domain; it should be consistent with itself and with the other accepted theories; it should have a broad scope and be simple and fruitful. These criteria may conflict and may rank in a different order of importance in different cases. However, in no situation of significance, argues Kuhn, will this list, or any other, yield a definite choice. "Let me begin by asking," says he, "how philosophers of science can for so long have neglected the subjective elements which, they freely grant, enter regularly into the actual theory choices made by individual scientists."[89]

Although Kuhn does not distinguish the two senses of acceptance being discussed here, it is clear that he is far more interested in the problem of what theory to pursue than he is in the problem of what theory to accept. The oft-noted difficulty with Kuhn's thesis is, of course, that his criteria, either jointly or singly, do not seem to function as a sufficient condition, even less as a necessary condition. If rationality manifests itself in a rule-governed activity, then it is unclear how Kuhn's account helps; or how it can answer the charge, so frequently made against Kuhn, that it has fundamentally irrational overtones. Irrespective of how this conflict is settled between Kuhn and his contemporaries, it is clear that if we are to give a coherent account of the growth and development of science and rationality, we have to solve a nest of unjustly neglected problems surrounding the problem of determining which theory ought to be chosen for further theoretical and experimental research. Pressed to guess, I would say that the methodological tradition evolves more slowly than does the scientific tradition, and that the tradition of method evaluation, namely, the meta-methodological tradition, evolves still more slowly. *Some implicit theory of method from above, and the actual past of scientific theories from below, will provide the necessary constraints to eliminate bizarre methodological traditions.* Any scientist espousing the latter would be deemed irrational. Consequently, when the links between the tripartite traditions have been traced, we will have simultaneously traced the rational development of the history of science and the growth of rationality. It should be evident that this view is simply a generalization of my theory of how to explain a rational decision by a scientist in the history of science.

What the foregoing hints to the historian of science is obvious; but it also has some bearing on the practice of the sociologists of knowledge. Recall Laudan's essentially Lakatosian thesis: the best model of rationality is significant not only for the historian of science but also for empirical scientists such as sociologists and psychologists. What cannot be explained on the best model of rationality is turned over to the domain of the cognitive sociologists of knowledge, who will then explain the irrational beliefs causally in terms of social, political, and economic conditions. Although I have argued that Laudan's thesis fails inasmuch as our best model of rationality does not explicate or explain rational decisions in the history of science, there is a way of saving that thesis, if modified. Once the historian of science has determined the plausible methodological traditions that were currently available in a given historical period, and he finds a scientist of that period deviating from the norm of a plausible method or espousing an implausible method, the historian of science may then proceed in a manner analogous to what Lakatos and Laudan suggest.

5
Alternative Proposal

What alternative view for evaluating methods is left? If not the history of science as an arbitrator between methods, what then? What issues, if any, do extant theories of method neglect? Having examined the various proposals thus far and finding them seriously inadequate, these are the questions one naturally asks. This chapter is an attempt to answer them.

My first thesis is that methods ought to give, and be seen as giving, heuristic advice. Highlighted in the last chapter was the importance of heuristic advice for one trying to explain the growth of knowledge and rationality. Yet, nearly all philosophers of science, surprisingly, fail to accord serious consideration to it. Perhaps the cause of this neglect and unconcern is the tacit suspicion—explicit in Lakatos—that it is not within the province of a method to give heuristic advice, that giving such advice smacks of algorithmic procedures. I shall aver that this suspicion is ill founded. In any event, the denial of this first thesis is incompatible with the insistence on giving heuristic advice to the historians of science whose activities are in all relevant respects similar to the activities of the scientists.

My second thesis is that one way of evaluating methods is by *experimenting* with them. It portrays the proposed theory of method as a *forward-looking view*; a view not hemmed in by the history of science, a view that is far less conservative in its approach than the *backward-looking view*, which looks toward the past or the history of science to arbitrate between currently considered alternative methods. This alternative view explores rival methods and experiments with them; it assumes, for good reasons, that methods that are false, or farther away from the truth, will give wrong heuristic advice. The advice of such a method will lead its followers to dead-ends more frequently than will its competing counterparts; and the usual weeding out process will ensue. The four distinct parts of a method, presented in the first chapter, will lend credence to the conjecture that methods can be experimented with to make informed guesses about their truth-value and effectiveness.

My third thesis is that methods can also be illuminatingly evaluated in a manner analogous, for instance, to the evaluation of theories in ethics. This approach will enable us to explain how we might ideally arrive at our forms of reasoning, and it will provide us a way of justifying those forms. I shall also argue that one ought not to settle methodological conflicts in certain ways and that to evaluate methods, attention should be focused on contemporary science and on the preanalytic judgments of contemporary scientists. This enables me to lay down a fairly precise condition that distinguishes my theory of method from that of most philosophers of science.

My fourth thesis is that a method should account for group rationality. In other words, it should answer the question, What makes a scientific group rational? In the absence of any answer, the first task is one concerning method, not theory of method. Consequently, I have given a preliminary sketch of the solution to the problem. The adequacy of my solution aside, the range and depth of the problems posed and probed in this inquiry will signal their importance and show why a failure to treat them must be regarded as a serious failing in a method. My solution is: a group is rational if, and only if, it is organized in subgroups, each of which adopts a distinct method for pursuing its goals. Brief case studies illuminate the point. The respective goals of the subgroups overlap and interconnect in intricate ways that make the scientific group cohesive. Some of the virtues of this approach share a lot in common with those of the view that advocates the proliferation of theories.

The four theses make up the story I wish to tell, but only in part. For, essentially and in the larger part, my proposal also comprises the central contentions and claims discussed earlier: the pointed difficulties confronting the historically oriented theories of method evaluation; the theory of explaining rational decisions in the history of science; the theory of what makes a scientific agent rational; the framework for methods; the discussion of the logical status of methodological statements; and so on. What has gone before can be fully understood, and regarded as adequately supported by arguments and counterarguments, only with the help and aid of what is now to come; and vice versa.

I. HEURISTIC ADVICE

Odd that a philosopher should hold up his method for acceptance but deny giving heuristic advice.

To evaluate the claim that methods should, or should not, give advice, let us distinguish the following types of advice:

1. Advice about which theory to accept as the best available one.
   I shall refer to this as *theoretical advice.*
2. Advice about which theory to prefer as a guide to practical action.
   I shall refer to this as *practical advice.*
3. Advice about which theory to adopt as a basis for future research (theoretical and experimental).
   I shall refer to this as *heuristic advice.*

Throughout the chapter, these distinctions will be adhered to strictly. While these distinctions are exhaustive, I think, each one could have been more finely honed. For instance, consider heuristic advice. Any number of activities can fall under the rubric "adopting a theory T as a basis for future research": attempting to derive a novel, testable statement from T; attempting to solve a theoretical problem on the basis of T; reconciling theoretical conflicts, using T as a yardstick; trying to show that another theory T' is a limiting case of T; discovering a hypothesis that is consistent with T; and so on. Indeed, a serious and urgent task is to give a taxonomy of scientific problems, and to give an account of their relative importance, since philosophers have emphasized the role of problems in science.

Some philosophers argue that methods do, and ought to, give theoretical advice, but they do not, and ought not, give heuristic and practical advice. This claim stems partly from the fear that heuristic advice can only be algorithmic in nature, and science is known to thrive on decisions that are anything but algorithmic. "I reject Feyerabend's suggestion," says John Worrall, "that if a methodology does not imply advice to scientists about which theories they should work on, then it is empty. Such a methodology will still appraise and rank theories in terms of their present scientific merits, and it will tell a scientist what general features a new theory must have if it is to be even better than any of the existing theories. The fact that these requirements do not indicate how to go about constructing a theory which satisfies them does not mean that these requirements are empty (just as the notion of a proof in a formal system is not empty despite the fact that it does not—in general—indicate how to go about constructing a proof of any particular proposition)."[1] In other words, if we have a welter of theories, our method will tell us what general features the new theory must have in order for it to be better than the others, but it cannot tell us how to arrive at, or, in Bernard Williams's words, *produce* a new theory (presumably, by providing a list of instructions on how to more or less mechanically create a better scientific theory).[2]

No one has recently claimed that a method should provide us with mechanical rules of discovery. Nor was anyone asking what the new theory should look like to be better than its existing rivals. To be sure, that requirement is not empty. Possible ways of meeting it are: T is better than T' if, and only if, T is nearer to the truth than T'; T is better than T' if, and only if, T has greater problem-solving effectiveness than T'. One is in fact entertaining a very different and promising question, the answer to which will deepen our understanding of rationality. The question *(Q)* is: *What theory (theories), if any, should we adopt from the existing competing ones,* T_1, T_2, T_3, . . . , T_n, *which will increase our chances of fashioning a better theory,* T_{n+1}, *by working on it (them)?*

What we are after is best illustrated as follows. Suppose two scientific societies, B and A, adopt the corpuscular theory of light and the wave theory of light, respectively, at a certain time from among the n competing theories available to them. I shall refer to the n theories and the method that each society uses to evaluate the theories as their *state of knowledge* at that time. The two rival theories are in unfinished and rudimentary states when they are adopted. As a consequence of their pursuit, a string of theories is produced from the initial ones. Society A, which began with the wave theory of light, rings in the following sequence of theories: T_{i+1}, T_{i+2}, . . . , T_{i+n}. Society B, which began with the corpuscular theory of light, rings in a different sequence of theories: T_{j+1}, T_{j+2}, . . . , T_{j+n}. Assume that later T_{i+n} is shown to be a far better theory than T_{j+n} or any other theory descendant from any of the original two theories. "Better than" is explained in terms of a common goal, such as truthlikeness, that the two societies share. Our question, then, is not whether there is any mechanical or algorithmic procedure available for moving, let us say, from T_i to T_{i+1} and so on through T_{i+n} but rather whether society *A* could have brought relevant rational considerations to bear for adopting the wave theory of light as opposed to the corpuscular theory in terms of its state of knowledge. We allow for mistakes in the choice we make, so we are not seeking infallible answers; we are, however, seeking plausible answers that enable us to make plausible choices.

It is alleged that any answer to the qustion *(Q)* is based on a mistaken inference. Some philosophers might claim that one ought to adopt the theory that satisfies some criterion *Y* (for Popper that criterion *Y* would be the highest degree of corroboration). The criterion *Y* will be such as to be satisfied by only a single theory. But, so the argument goes, it is invalid to infer from "T is better than T' " that "It is irrational to try to develop T'." Against the proliferationist the argument is easily reformulated. A proliferationist might claim that one ought to adopt those theories that satisfy some criterion *X*. The criterion *X* will be such as to be usually satisfied by many theories. However, it is invalid to infer from "$T_1, T_2, \ldots, T_h$ are better theories than $T_i, T_j, \ldots, T_n$" that "It is irrational to try to develop T_i (or T_j, or . . . T_n)."

Obvious hidden lemmas are operating in the arguments of those who push for single theories as well as in the arguments of those who push for many theories. These hidden lemmas are as follows:

(A1) If further research work is done on the best available theory, *T*, satisfying criterion *Y*, specified by our accepted method, *M*, the chances of arriving at the next best theory are higher than if the work is done on any other theory from the original set, other things being equal.

(A2) If further research work is done on the best available group of theories, $T_1, T_2, \ldots, T_n$, satisfying criterion *X*, specified by our accepted method, *M*, the chances of arriving at the next best theory are higher than if the work is done on any other theory from the original set, other things being equal.

Assumption *(A2)* seems intuitively very plausible—I hold no brief for assumption *(A1)*—because by working on these theories, newer experiments will be fashioned, newer conjectures will be made to account for discrepancies, newer problems will be explored, which together will conspire in the production of a better theory. Implicitly, we also assume that working on poorer alternatives—ones failing to meet the relevant criteria—will not lead to newer and richer problems, that conjectures based on that theory will quickly be falsified, and in general work on that theory will lead to dead-ends. This, too, is a conjecture on our part, and one that is usually made in the adoption of a theory (or a set of theories).

Denial of both *(A1)* and *(A2)* must lead us to assume that

(B) If further research work is done on any available theory, then the chances of arriving at the next best theory are as good, bad, or indifferent as doing research on any other available theory from the original set, other things being equal.

It is well-nigh impossible here either to justify *(A1)* or *(A2)* or to provide a full answer to our original question *(Q)*. However, I shall show that *(B)* reduces to absurdity, and hence lends indirect support to my thesis. Some philosophers argue that there is *no* link between the best theory, or the few good theories, that scientists work on, and the next best theory they produce. A method will simply help a scientist to rank-order scientific theories that are currently held in his field. It would be irrational of the scientist to rank a theory any differently from what the method tells him is the case. The method tells him nothing, however, about which theory he should adopt. The history of science, these philosophers argue, is replete with cases when a theory was adopted on slim evidential support and went on to become enormously successful. Young's wave theory of light is a case in point, they argue. It was not irrational for Young to choose the poorer hypothesis for further basic research, provided he accepted the ranking in which the corpuscular hypothesis was the first. Thus, ***rank-ordering of theories or theoretical advice is severed from the giving of heuristic advice.***

What, then, makes the scientists' choice a wrong choice, once they have admitted to the rank-ordering of theories by a method? Or, what makes the chosen theory, selected with respect to basic theoretical and experimental future research, a wrong choice? Can there ever be a wrong choice? A negative answer to the last question is as incomprehensible as an affirmative answer to the next question, Are all choices equally correct? If the link between the ranking of theories and the giving of heuristic advice is severed, however, then we are forced to give incomprehensible answers and are condemned to protect the "rationality" of astrologers, chiropractors, *vaiyyd* (medicine men), and homeopaths. All that these "scientists" need concede is that contemporary theories in the relevant fields are better than the theories they prefer in practice and adopt for future research. Since the link is severed between the best theory (or theories) satisfying certain criteria and the theory (or theories) scientists should adopt, these "scientists" can adopt *any* theory without being condemned as irrational, if only they take care to concede the ranking. Something is amiss in a view that can be used to defend the rationality of an astrologer (*pace* Feyerabend!).

Young conceded that Newton's theory was the best one (is there any historical evidence for that?) but preferred to work on his own theory. Young's contemporary, Brewster, ranked the wave theory of light above the corpuscular theory because the former theory was very powerful, applicable, and confirmed in vast domains, save in a place or two (such as the phenomenon of inequal refrangibility); yet he adopted the Newtonian corpuscular theory. Little wonder, the argument goes, that there is no connection between ranking of theories and their adoption for further theoretical and experimental development. These examples may be counterexamples to those, if any, who hold *(A1)*, which is implausible anyway; but they are hardly counterexamples to the proliferationist position, wedded as the latter is to assumption *(A2)*. Since there were only two theories, both reasonably powerful, they would have both satisfied the proliferationists' criterion *X*. Consequently, the rationality of the scientists, Brewster and Young in this case, would have been assured. Moreover, astrologers and homeopaths would be correctly labeled irrational in adopting their theories, making the obvious assumption that such theories would fail to satisfy the suggested criterion *X*.

If a method frequently gave the wrong heuristic advice, such that the theories a scientist worked with led to dead-ends, one would be justified in saying that the method was unacceptable: its advice was wrong because its ranking was wrong. If a gap between rank-ordering of theories and the giving of heuristic advice is insisted upon, however, the scientists infringe no normative rules for there are no normative rules to infringe; the rationality of the scientist has no link with the method he uses to evaluate theories; and the method cannot be faulted for the heuristic advice it did not give. In this respect, a method such as the methodology of research programs—unlike the methodology of research traditions—is quite safe from refutation, since it certainly does not run the same high risk as do other methods that give practical and heuristic advice.

It would be incorrect to ask, How shall we know what practical or heuristic advice a method gave to the scientist in the past? How shall we know what its injunctions were? Epistemically speaking, our position with respect to the heuristic and practical advice a method rendered in the past is much better than it is with respect to the method's theoretical advice. A society of scientists is not accurately envisaged as a community of careful log-keepers who rank their theories according to their method and then go about their ways. Thus, to determine what the ranking was, the historian of science usually begins with the theories the scientists in fact adopted or preferred. From that point he proceeds to reconstruct the rules of ranking of the method in question. The degree to which the historian's work is aided by the scientist may vary from a case in which a scientist virtually says nothing about his methods to the one in which he is explicit about them.

For example, consider Geber, Gilbert, and Grosseteste. From Geber's *Summa Perfectionis*, a thirteenth-century alchemical treatise, one may get a well-rounded account of the chemical apparatus and practices used in making gold but no explicit account of his method. Consequently, it is on the basis of the theories Geber used—in discussing and dealing with the composition of metals and in carrying out various chemical procedures, such as sublimation, distillation, and calcination, combined with his refutation of arguments against transmutation—that one can reconstruct the norms Geber must have used in accepting, rejecting, or ranking the various extant chemical theories.[3]

William Gilbert gives the historian a slightly better chance at making a successful reconstruction of his method. The first of the six books of *De Magnete* gives an account of the facts and theories of magnetism known to his contemporaries, together with the discussion about the nature, properties, and behavior of lodestones. In the remaining five books, Gilbert concerns himself with explaining the magnetic movements of coition, declination, variation, direction, and revolution. In the last section of the first book Gilbert proposes his own novel theory about the earth as a large lodestone; hence, the earth has magnetic properties which can be used to explain a variety of terrestrial magnetic phenomena. There is no explicit mention of method. Interestingly enough, however, in his first book Gilbert provided important and useful hints inasmuch as he "marked his own discoveries and experiments with asterisks; larger symbols were used for the more important discoveries and experiments, smaller asterisks for the less important ones."[4]

Grosseteste, at the other end, had worked out his method, his conception of the aim and nature of science, and the mode of scientific explanation which was based on the work of Aristotle. His scientific practice as well as his treatises on optics, astronomy, and specialized scientific problems were deliberately carried out in the light of his method. Grosseteste "seems first to have worked out a methodology applicable to the physical world and then to have applied it in the particular sciences. This methodology may be considered under two headings: first, induction and experiment; and secondly, mathematical physics."[5]

Finally, consider the problem of selecting a historiographical model. The historical conjectures of a historian of science can corroborate or refute the method he uses. If historians use competing methods as historiographical models to write the history of science, we would be able to tell vis-à-vis the successes or failures of their historical conjectures which models are good and which ones are not. In brief, we should be able to rank-order methods serving as historiographical models just as we rank-order scientific theories.

Lakatos claims that his methodology of research programs heads this rank-ordering. This claim is supported by arguing that using his method as a historiographical model not only makes the best sense out of the history of science but also leads the historians to make specific testable claims. Other methods lead to dead-ends and false predictions and force historians of science to say some pretty odd things. In the light of its alleged success, the historians of science are enjoined to adopt or prefer the methodology of research programs as a tool for investigating the history of science. Some very important case histories have been written from the vantage point of Lakatos's method.[6] I shall argue that the heuristic advice that Lakatos gives to historians of science is, at best, inconsistent with his claim that heuristic advice should not be given to scientists in pursuit of interesting theories.

Are the activities of a historian of science and a scientist similar enough in relevant respects to demonstrate inconsistency? They are. Let us suppose that a scientist, such as Galileo, has at his disposal several theories relating to the problem of the nature of light and lenses. He has, in effect, three decisions to make: to pick the theory that is the best in the field; to pick the theory that is good for practical purposes, such as for constructing telescopes; and finally, to pick the theory that would increase his chances of fashioning a better theory.

A historian of science would similarly be faced with making three decisions. Let us suppose that a historian, such as Anthony Hallam, confronts several histories concerning why Wegener adopted his own theory of continental drift for solving problems, problems such as why the continental margins seemed to fit, why related plants and animals were widely scattered across the globe, and how tropical fossils ever found their way to extremely cold climates. The first decision he has to make is to pick the historical account that is the best. The second decision is to pick the account that would effectively serve the purpose of mundane historical investigation—a sort of historian's normal science—such as locating the periodicals Wegener had access to, his academic record, and accounts of Wegener's Greenland expedition of 1906. Finally, the historian has to decide which account, if adopted for more basic research, would increase his chances of writing a better history of science.

The analogy does not end here. Both the scientist and the historian use their methods as a *tool*; the methods themselves do not enter their work or final product directly. The historian of science uses certain normative judgments to write the history of science; it is his implicit or explicit commitment to a method that directs him to certain problems, figures, and places. But, aver Lakatosians, these normative considerations do not enter into the actual writing of the history of science.

Similarly, how a scientist comes to adopt or prefer the best available theory—why he regards certain theories as promising and why he pursues some to the exclusion of others—necessarily reflects some normative criteria used by him (implicitly or explicitly). When he finally gives a solution to the problem, however, or gives a theory that explains most of the known facts, neither the statement of the problem nor the statement of his solution or theory incorporates any normative considerations he had used. Lord Kelvin and other physicists of the nineteenth century considered it fairly settled what the general outline of physical theories would be. The theories would be formulated in differential equations predicting the future world states; it was conceded that minor modifications would be made in this picture, but no basic changes would be necessary. However, Lord Kelvin was bothered by "two small clouds" on the horizon, namely, the problem posed by the negative results of the Michelson-Morley experiments and the failure of the Rayleigh-Jeans law to predict the distribution of radiant energy in a blackbody. David Bohm remarks, "It must be admitted that Lord Kelvin knew how to choose his 'clouds' since these were precisely the two problems that eventually led to the revolutionary changes in the conceptual structure of physics."[7] These changes, as we know, were wrought by the special theory of relativity and the quantum theory. It is clear that, implicitly, Lord Kelvin used some normative judgments to isolate these two particular problems rather than a host of other problems facing physicists then. Neither his statement of the problem of physics nor the solutions to these problems incorporated any methodological considerations. They were out of place in that context.

So there is little doubt that there exists a remarkable structural similarity in the activities of the historians of science and those of the scientists. Yet, most philosophers of science choose to give heuristic advice to the historians of science and argue that no such advice should be given to the scientists. What they are entitled to say is no more than that in order for the historian of science to be rational it is necessary and sufficient that he rank-order the various methods serving as historiographical models in accordance with their favored meta-methodological criterion. Let us suppose that *n* histories, H_1, H_2, H_3, . . . , H_n, have been written on a certain problem from the vantage point of *n* methods, M_1, M_2, M_3, . . . , M_n, respectively, and empirical evidence, considerations of simplicity, and so on, make H_1 better than H_2, H_2 better than H_3, and so forth. The rationality of a historian is guaranteed if he accepts the aforementioned ranking, but his rationality, in some broad sense, is unaffected if he adopts, let us say, H_n, the worst-corroborated historical conjecture. Once the historian of science has accepted the rank-ordering, he can adopt *any* historical conjecture and historiographical model he likes in his future work of investigating historical problems, without being labeled irrational. The parallel to the earlier argument with respect to scientific theories is both complete and perfect. What, then, makes it appropriate to give heuristic advice to historians in their empirical work but not to scientists? What makes it right to say, as some philosophers of science do say, that once a rank-ordering has been established, a historian of science should adopt in his work the model that was used as a tool in writing the best-confirmed history of science? No coherent answer seems possible.

II. METHODS, EXPERIMENT, AND HISTORY

A. C. Crombie:

One of the profoundly influential and fruitful events that made up the scientific revolution of the seventeenth century seems to me to have been the restoration of full contact between science and scientific methodology. In spite of the promising conception of science that began in the thirteenth century, medieval scientists in the end succeeded only in revising some isolated sections of the physics and cosmology they inherited from the Greeks and Arabs. The successful revision by seventeenth century scientists of the whole of the theoretical framework and assumptions of physical science was effected by a close combination of philosophical and technical maneuvers. The conception they formed of scientific method, of the counters available in terms of conceptions of nature, hypotheses, logical procedures and mathematical and experimental techniques, was closely measured by the technical success of the results and by their universality. It was proved by results that the mathematization of nature, the "mechanical philosophy," the use of abstract theories, the experimental method, the conception of functional dependence, the new algebra and geometry, were successful elements in a scientific method. It seems to me that their ability to be good judges of scientific success, and to be impressed by it, is a measure of the distance between the natural philosophers of the seventeenth century and their medieval predecessors with whom they shared so many ideas and aspirations in common.[8]

Dissenting, I. E. Drabkin:

One question we must face (i.e., in assessing significance for the scientific revolution) is the relation of the working scientist to explicit formulations of scientific method. How far is the working scientist actually conscious of such formulations? Is an expert knowledge of such formulations (and a diligent attempt to apply them) any guarantee of scientific discovery? And for one unacquainted with a field of inquiry, not knowing where to start an investigation, are the canons of induction any avail? Is even the possession and use of the practical scientific techniques of mathematics, experimental design and procedure, and all the rest, any guarantee of scientific discovery? My impression is that science often progresses independently of discussions of methodology.[9]

It was not because of any inherent methodological defect, not because of a lack of understanding of experimental method, not because of an exclusive concern with the static and geometric, not because of any inability to distinguish science from philosophy, that Greek science reached

> a deadend. Greek science in antiquity was by and large a poorly organized and precarious enterprise in which relatively few participated, in a society which, except for a few brief periods, was generally indifferent to their work, and which provided few lines of communication and cooperation among them. But after a thousand years or more of arrested development, the achievements of Greek science, thanks to the printed editions, became widely disseminated over an area that enjoyed a flourishing university tradition in which thousands participated, at a time when social and political conditions were favourable to intellectual activity, and the work of the scientist could be highly valued.[10]

The point of juxtaposing these long, important, and contrary paragraphs is not historical but philosophical. They serve to introduce my next thesis in the theory of method I am proposing: *To evaluate methods, experiment*.

Drabkin may be seen as making two claims, one stronger and one weaker. The weaker claim is that methods *in fact* did not influence scientific practice of the sixteenth or seventeenth century, but expanding university tradition, cooperation and open communication among scientists, and the more receptive social and political conditions did. His stronger claim is that methods do not, in principle, have much to do with scientific progress; that is, science can get along very well without method. From his stronger claim follows his weaker claim. It is Drabkin's stronger claim I wish to dispute, and my arguments are intended to buttress, by implication, Crombie's position.

No method can enable one to make discoveries. A method is not to be envisaged as a provider of an algorithm for making scientific discoveries and framing hypotheses. A method can, however, give aid to one seeking theoretical and heuristic advice. A scientist is continuously confronted with an objective methodological problem-situation in which he has to make a choice about which theory to accept or adopt. Given his state of knowledge, that is, his knowledge of the scientific and the methodological traditions, there is a fact of the matter involved. There is a choice to be made of a theory that is distinctly more fruitful than its rivals. What that theory is is not simply a matter of a settling convention. The heuristic advice is quite fallible, and if it is true, or nearer to the truth, of how theories and hypotheses are to be evaluated, it will be successful. But against *this* aspect of method, Drabkin has no argument at all. He has not shown that when scientists make decisions about which theory to accept or adopt, they make no use of method; nor has he shown that such decisions have no impact on the growth of scientific knowledge and rationality.

There is little doubt that a change in method *did* bring about a loosening of the hold that the Aristotelian system had on the thirteenth and fourteenth centuries. Ockham's radical empiricism and his principle of economy, for instance, weakened the Aristotelian argument for the possibility of certain knowledge. Nicholas of Autrecourt went so far as to deny degrees of certainty, and he arrived at an atomistic theory as a more viable alternative to Aristotle's theory of the plenum. Ockham's attack was also leveled against Aristotelian science and metaphysics as much as it had questioned its epistemology. In particular, metaphysical categories of relation, substance, and causation were called suspect in light of his radical empiricism: for instance, Ockham argued that attributes can exist without substance, and vice versa. Ockham rejected Aristotle's basic principle that local motion was a realized potentiality, and he rejected the Aristotelian notions of change in quality and growth.[11] He then proposed his own theory of motion, which was not as widely respected, or as powerful, as the theory of Jean Buridan. While there were Aristotelian adherents, it is not clear that the Aristotelian system was ranked first in the light of the prevailing methods; nor that if it was, it had no serious problems, hitherto unrecognized, to contend with. Yet, the heuristic advice flowing from Ockham's method must have done some damage to science in general, since its instrumentalist stand allowed far too much speculation, with little restraint on the scientific imagination and practice, especially when dealing with the oft-discussed problem of variation in the intensities of qualities and motions.[12] It was to some measure the restraint of realism posed by their methods that proved fruitful for Copernicus and Galileo.

When the methods, and especially their heuristic advice, changed in the sixteenth and seventeenth centuries, the scientific tradition progressed. It was, as Crombie says, the full, delicate, and deliberate interaction of method and scientific practice that altered that tradition. One might say that scientists abandoned old methods of evaluating theories and started experimenting with new ones. What were then regarded as preanalytic intuitions or judgments of the scientists were shelved to see how new ones would fare under actual scientific practice.

In order to decide which of our contemporary methods is sound and better than the rest, I suggest we, too, experiment with the methods we have. To render this suggestion plausible, let me first briefly recapture some of the earlier claims. On the logical status of methodological statements, philosophers are divided: some, such as Ellis and Laudan, maintain that the statements of method are empirical statements; others, such as Popper, argue that they are merely conventions. The discussion on this crucial issue is contorted and confusing, owing to a persistent failure to draw the relevant distinctions. A method is defined by its objective and normative components. One part of the objective component of a method solves logical problems such as the one relating to the problem of verisimilitude; another part of the objective component of a method defines by convention its key terms, such as ad hoc, corroboration, empirically progressive problem-shift, and problem-solving effectiveness. The normative component also has two parts. One significant part of the normative component lays down the conditions of acceptance, pursuit, and adoption of theories, for example, "Reject ad hoc theories." The other part defines rational decision, such as, "It was rational to pursue Harvey's physiological theory because its rate of progress in problem-solving was the highest."[13]

The logical status of a method's statement depends on the part of the method to which it belongs. It would appear that corresponding to the four parts of a method are four distinct ways in which a method can be evaluated. But that, at least, is not obviously true. Methods can be evaluated by making comparisons of their logical claims, as in our comparison of Popper's method with Laudan's method. It is unclear, however, how mere definitions of rival methods can be evaluated. It is also unclear how statements from rival methods defining a rational decision can be evaluated in isolation. In effect, there are precisely two ways in which a method can be evaluated: in terms of its logical claims and in terms of its heuristic claims. We know how to make logical comparisons; but how are heuristic claims of rival contemporary methods to be evaluated? To insist that these claims are conventional is to be left open to the charge that we leave the success of making the right decision a matter of mystery.[14] The truth of these heuristic statements can be evaluated or determined experimentally, which of course does not make them empirical or any less normative.[15] If heuristic claims of a method are true, the method will be successful. Or, the truer they are, the more successful the method will be. Conversely, if a method yields fruitful heuristic decisions, we can conjecture that the method is true. If one method leads to more fruitful decisions than any other method, we can conjecture that it is nearer to the truth than are the other methods.

Examples of the heuristic statements of currently competing methods are:

1. *Popperian heuristic advice:* Adopt the theory that is best corroborated.
2. *Lakatosian heuristic advice:* Adopt the theory that exhibits an empirically progressive problem-shift.
3. *Kuhnian heuristic advice:* Adopt the theory that is simple, consistent, fecund, and so on, and that most responds to the scientists' tutored and practiced intuitions.
4. *Laudanian heuristic advice:* Adopt the theory that exhibits the highest rate of problem-solving effectiveness.
5. *Feyerabendian heuristic advice:* Adopt any theory.[16]

Experiments can be made to determine which heuristic advice—and by implication the method that gives such advice—is better than the rest. The procedure could be as follows. Five groups of able scientists, with adequate resources and so on, are formed. The scientists in each group are trained to make their decisions in accordance with the heuristic advice of a specific method. The first group uses Popper's method, the second group Lakatos's method, the third group Kuhn's method, and so on, while the last group is unstructured and anarchistic as suggested by Feyerabend. Assuming that each of these methods espouses a common goal of seeking truth (which they in fact do not), we may be able to determine which group, in the long run, is able to make more fruitful decisions.

One can view the matter of method evaluation just presented through a thought-experiment. Imagine that all our knowledge about the history of science is forgotten. We know the current theories of general relativity, quantum mechanics, biology, chemistry, geology, mathematics, and so on, but we do not know either their origin and historical development *or* the earlier theories in the same domains. For instance, we know the current theories of electricity and magnetism but not the fact that theories once claimed electricity to be a single, or double, fluid; we have knowledge of the current views of astronomy but no knowledge of the fact that once the earth was thought to be stationary and at the center of the universe with all the heavenly bodies revolving around it;

we know contemporary theories of physiology and medicine but not ones that postulated the existence of phlegm, black and yellow bile, blood, natural spirits, animal spirits, and vital spirits; we are acquainted with the current theories of matter but not with, for instance, Paracelsian *tria prima* (salt, sulphur, and mercury); and so on.

Now even in this imaginary situation, our ongoing scientific practice would force us to make decisions about which theory to accept or adopt. We would continuously find ourselves in a methodological problem-situation and would thus need a method. In light of our need, several methods will be proposed. How would we be able to judge between rival methods? By hypothesis, there are no preanalytic judgments or intuitions of the scientific elite, concerning the rationality or irrationality of accepting or rejecting certain theories in the history of science, with which a method has to square in order to be considered acceptable. In such a situation, it would be inevitable for us to say, "Let us experiment with the methods proposed and see how successful they are. Let us be bold in our conjecture about rationality, as we are sometimes with respect to our theories. Even if we fail we shall have learned a great deal." A Darwinian competition among methods would ensue, until some methods became regarded as sound and stable.

A scientific society formed around a method that violates intuitions others regard as inviolable *can* succeed; and so this approach would enable us to fashion a more radical and deeper method than the current conservative backward-looking view would allow, a view that emphasizes the role of the history of science in arbitration over methods. At least our experimental and forward-looking view does not obviously succumb to the grave difficulties confronting the latter view. It also restores to method the significance it once had in the work and scientific practice of those in the sixteenth and seventeenth centuries, and in the work of Bacon, Grosseteste, Herschel, Whewell, Darwin, and Huxley.

Have we, then, nothing to do with the history of science? Not quite. Among methodologists, there is a remarkably strong, deterministic, and underlying view concerning the growth of knowledge in the history of science. *Progress*, it is assumed, *could not have occurred in any other way than the way in which it, in fact, did.* Feyerabend often argues that if Popper's method had been accepted by the scientists in the history of science, science as we know it would have come to a halt, or its growth would have been seriously impeded. Galileo is his favorite example, and Popper's method, Feyerabend argues, is one with which Galileo would have had little patience, accustomed as Galileo was to counterinductive rules, ad hoc strategems, disregarding rules of consistency, and the like. But this deterministic assumption is probably false. If some rejected theories, such as Aristarchus's heliocentric theory in antiquity, had been developed, science would have progressed more rapidly than it did. Furthermore, we cannot *now* be certain that no new problem of depth and power would have been thrown up by a rejected theory, and that, if it had been, it would have had no effect on practicing scientists, and that no new important theories would have arisen as a result. *Realistic alternatives and possible histories*, I suggest, *must be woven, if methods are to be judged in ways other than the logical and experimental.*

What would have happened if Popper's method had been accepted by scientists in the years between A.D. 500 and 1000, an interval marked by utter stagnation in science? What would have happened if instead of the instrumentalist method adopted in the late Middle Ages, the Lakatosian method had been adopted? What would have happened to the science of chemistry and metallurgy in India in A.D. 1200 had Laudan's method been espoused? Trying to answer these and similar questions would entail imagining realistic possible routes the history of science *could* have taken. Surely, in a hypothetical history, the same theories would not have been adopted, or the same theories rejected, as in the history as-it-occurred. Using a current method for theoretical and heuristic decisions could have meant the destruction of the encyclopedic tradition; or Pitcairn's and Borelli's mechanistic physiological theories could have been adopted, instead of being rejected; or Ptolemy's theory could have been abandoned in favor of the models proposed by ibn-Badia and ibn-Tofail during the twelfth century; or the law of conservation of energy could have been abandoned when the observed energy discrepancy in beta emission decay, which led to the discovery of the neutrino, was accepted as falsifying the conservation law; and so on. If the history imagined is more productive than its factual counterpart, it would lend credence to the method under discussion.

Of the three ways of evaluating methods—logical, experimental, and contrafactual history—the last should be accorded the *least* importance. One significant problem for a theory of method is determining how these criteria are to be weighed. What constraints are to be put on such weaving of tales? To be sure, some constraints are necessary, for we would need to distinguish between realistic and unrealistic alternatives or possible histories; for now, I simply note an interesting problem. It should be enormously evident that this way of method evaluation is no concession to those who would arbitrate among methods by using the actual history of science. What I am suggesting is a *contra*factual, but realistic, account of the development of the history of science as a guide to evaluating methods. Of course, other philosophers would have nothing to do with such possible histories, and rightly so, for otherwise their position would no longer be historically oriented.

III. REASON, PRACTICE, AND REFLECTIVE EQUILIBRIUM

Some philosophers deplore the stability of certain forms of reasoning and, as such, advocate a permanent revolution in reasoning. Such a revolution is unlikely, however, if only because of our biological makeup. Evolution of the ways in which we reason takes place, for sure, but the pace of that change is extremely slow. The task before us is to seek a plausible, if preliminary, explanation of conflicts in reasoning—of how these conflicts are resolved, how, under ideal and appropriately restricted conditions, we would arrive at our forms of reasoning, why these forms of reasoning remain stable for a while before yielding to new forms, and why that change usually occurs slowly and almost imperceptibly.

Our theories of rationality, our forms of reasoning, are like our scientific theories: one can only gauge their importance and their value in practice. We test them, as we do our empirical theories. However, there is no straightforward way of testing our theories of rationality. In the case of empirical theories, there is an independent world out there that the theories describe and predict. If these theories match against the world, we claim we have a true and adequate theory; if not, not. But how does one match the correctness of a heuristic claim against the world (indeed, *what* world?)? The ultimate court of appeal, then, is successful practice. We let rival theories of rationality compete, and they will produce certain results, which in turn will match the world, if only partially, and this will enable us to decide which theories of rationality are adequate and which are not.

The talk about stability is nothing more than talk about reflective equilibrium, one might say; and so it is. To see differently how certain methodological claims are justified and conflicting claims settled, let us begin by seeing briefly how conflicts and claims are settled in other areas: in the areas of logic and so-called inductive inference or inferential strategies.

There are pitfalls in logical reasoning. The typical ones are the informal fallacies and the formal fallacies of affirming the consequent, denying the antecedent, and the like. When informal fallacies are committed, we point out the flaws in such reasoning—for instance, attacking someone's personality does not lend credibility to one's argument (although we are willing to grant that it may produce the desired result). The exposure of fallacy may alter the course of someone's reasoning and make it correct and more effective in the long run.

For example, take a gambler who is convinced that if he is betting on a certain throw of dice that has not come up any time in the past, the chances of that number showing up increase with time and throws. He continues to bet more on the same throw of dice in the hope of recovering his past losses. Someone else then argues that there is no causal connection between the next throw of dice and the past throws, so that there is no reason to believe that past throws will have any effect on future throws. In short, the probability of a particular throw coming up on any toss of the coin continues to remain the same and is independent of past and future tosses of the coin. If the gambler accepts this reasoning, he relinquishes his current belief (which he hitherto regarded as correct) in favor of a more effective rule of inference. In a similar fashion, when asked to draw inferences from evidence and data provided us, we may make mistakes by transgressing the statistical principle encapsulated in the law of large numbers, by ignoring sampling error, or by being insensitive to sample bias, not to mention the mistakes psychologists classify as availability biases in frequency estimation, inappropriate applications of availability heuristics and representativeness heuristics, inappropriate utilization of knowledge structures, and so on. The way in which these errors are rectified range from a commonsensical approach to a sophisticated statistical approach.[17]

"From the standpoint of moral philosophy," says John Rawls, "the best account of a person's sense of justice is not the one which fits his judgments *prior* to his examining any conception of justice, but rather the one which matches his judgments in reflective equilibrium."[18] This is no less true in methodology; more so, if anything.

But, first, what elements rest in reflective equilibrium in method? A scientific theory is in equilibrium with observation statements; particular logical inferences are in equilibrium with a logical theory; particular inductive inferences are in equilibrium with a theory of induction; particular ethical judgments are in equilibrium with an ethical theory. So, in method, particular decisions of accepting or rejecting scientific theories are in equilibrium with the rules of a method. Now these particular decisions or preanalytic judgments of scientists are worthless unless they are accompanied by a reflection on rival methods and unless the relative merits and drawbacks of methods are measured. The scientist arrives at a reflective equilibrium, a stable stand, when the particular decisions or preanalytic judgments he makes in accepting or rejecting theories for further theoretical and experimental tests dovetail with the general rules of the heuristic component of a method; he then accepts that method. These preanalytic judgments, and these only, are worthy of credence when attempting to grind a methodological ax. In effect, the stable relationship between a method and particular judgments of an ideal scientist is achieved in roughly the following fashion.

The scientist recognizes that he needs a proper method by which to make a decision. This need is inspired in part by his actual practice in his field and in part by recognizing the importance of such decision-making. He has inevitably made some judgments insofar as he has been a practicing scientist, but he aims to do better than he has in fact done. He considers a variety of methods available to him, but surely he does not, cannot, and ought not entertain all the methods from Aristotle down that were ever proposed; he considers only viable current methods. He evaluates each method, which partly consists in seeing how methods have in fact fared in his own practice as well as in the practice of other scientists; he considers the conceptual difficulties; and he raises questions pertaining to logical issues. The conceptual and logical difficulties he settles in a different way; but he does not know how to settle competing heuristic claims save by putting them into practice or learning how they have fared when others have put them into practice. This will yield him a range of particular judgments. He then strikes a balance and determines which of the competing methods best conforms to his particular judgments. He espouses what he regards as the best method and then consistently conforms to its methodological dictates. No one can be expected to do better.

Three things are significant to notice. First, a methodological conjecture is on par with a scientific conjecture. The methodological conjecture is proposed to solve methodological problems or to explain particular methodological judgments; the latter do not entail the former any more than observation statements entail scientific theories. Acceptance or rejection of scientific theories is not fully, consciously, and explicitly carried out in terms of an articulated method any more than deciding what to do in a moral dilemma is fully, consciously, and explicitly carried out in terms of a wholly articulated moral theory. But both such theories are needed even if they are nearly always held unconsciously and implicitly.

Second, there is nothing sacrosanct in the method a scientist finally settles upon. In other words, the scientist knows full well that his own future practice or that of others can cast a gloom on his presently held particular judgments, and that fundamental discussion concerning his own method may show serious and intractable difficulties. When such circumstances occur, and they will—notice, the history of science is strewn with methods of yesteryears—he ought to be able to reject his current method in favor of another.

Third, and most significantly, the matter is so complicated that scientists simply will not all evaluate the methods in the same way. Their experiences and their particular judgments will be quite different. We are not as impervious to our particular moral experiences so as to concur, one and all, on the same moral theory as the right one. At least in significant part, our moral conceptions and ideas are formed and fashioned by our practices, our experiences, and our circumstances. Similarly, the experiences and judgments of scientists will be molded by the fields they work in; and these fields will have developed in lopsided ways or, most probably, will have winded along a different path: some scientists will have experienced a revolution in their field (consider the latter half of the nineteenth century in the field of biology), while others may have been working with theories that have long been around (consider the field of mechanics in the eighteenth century); some are straddling between two or more interesting theories (consider the field of paleontology after 1970), while others are languishing to find at least one adequate theory (any social science field will do, perhaps); and so on. Consequently, it is most unlikely that *all* the scientists in a given group or society will have more or less the same preanalytic judgments that will drive them to select or arrive at *one* method which they all regard as the best one.

How are conflicts between scientists concerning the evaluations and weighing of preanalytic judgments and methods to be settled?

Perhaps the primary question should be, How are they *in fact* settled? Some philosophers argue that a conflict between, say, a logician (a cognitive superior or a cognitive conservative) and a nonlogician (a cognitive rebel) is not necessarily a conflict in which contradictory claims are staked. So they view the matter thus: Statements of the form, "Rule *R* is justified," should be analyzed as "Rule *R* accords with the reflective inferential practice of the group of people I think appropriate."[19] These philosophers claim that the "disagreement between the cognitive rebel and the cognitive conservative is, in effect, a dispute over whose reflective judgment ought to be heeded in the issue at hand. On our view, such disputes are not exclusively cognitive disputes. They are better viewed on the model of political disputes whose resolution, like the resolution of other political disputes, is determined by such factors as social power, personal style, and historical accident. There is something a bit radical about the view we are urging."[20]

Let us distinguish between two clear cases. On the one hand, we may have a cognitive dispute between a person outside a given field and persons within that field. This does not make the former a cognitive rebel so much as a cognitive fool. If, despite the urging of a logician, one continues to assert a contradiction, or commit the fallacy of affirming the consequent, or commit the gambler's fallacy, we have an instance of a very uninteresting argument between an expert and a nonexpert. In the judgment of the expert, two elements that were previously in unstable equilibrium ought to be no longer in equilibrium; and he knows which of the two elements should be forgone. However, if we consider disputes between members within a given field on matters of utter importance (for instance, in the field of logic some logicians may defend classical logic against those who advocate relevance logic), then we have an instance of an interesting and important conflict, a conflict, however, in which once again contradictory claims are not necessarily staked. So, if one methodologist says that only the theory with the highest rate of problem-solving effectiveness should be pursued and another claims that only the theory with the highest degree of corroboration should be pursued, and these respective and rival heuristic conjectures do not lead to the same result (as is most likely), it is not clear whether either side has an overwhelming case. What are in equilibrium for one are not for the other, and vice versa. There is nothing radical so much as mistaken about the view that says that this controversy ought to be settled, and should be considered as settled correctly, by power, politics, or illicit persuasion.[21]

I am urging that there is an objective methodological problem-situation to which there is an objective methodological answer. Perhaps the problem calls for a solution that we will never find, or, should we find it, know for certain that it is the correct solution. As in logic or mathematics, so here. Presumably, there is an objectively correct answer to questions such as, Is this logical inference permissible? or, Is this mathematical proof correct? Our only access to the objectively true answer is admittedly what we can accomplish in practice. Hence I take Nelson Goodman in *Fact, Fiction, and Forecast* to be offering an epistemic theory concerning the correctness of deductive and inductive logical inferences. If the rules of inference and our particular judgments are in a reflective equilibrium, then we have good reasons to believe in the soundness of our inference rules. If that reflective equilibrium is disturbed as a result of our practices, then we have good reasons to doubt that we have captured the logical reality (for Goodman this has to be translated into nominalistic terms) in our logical theory. In short, we can be mistaken, and the mere fact of being in reflective equilibrium is no guarantee that we have reached the truth. Correspondingly, I am claiming that when a particular scientific community of reasoners agree, at a given time, that certain heuristic claims are correct, that agreement constitutes neither a necessary nor a sufficient condition for the heuristic claim to be true or correct. Like the truth of mathematical statements, the correctness or truth of heuristic claims is not based on what even the ablest members in the field believe, think, or do. It is based on the objective methodological reality.

Note that in these examples we have communities of reasoners. It is patently not the case that certain communities (of logicians, for instance) reason correctly all the time, while certain others never reason correctly. Is it possible to have a community of the latter sort? What would it be like to live in such a community? How would it be different from ours, and not merely in the way in which they reasoned? (Think of the various examples in *Remarks on the Foundations of Mathematics*, but particularly the one in which the community sells timber at a price that is proportional to the area covered by piles of varying and arbitrary heights. Is it enough to say that such a community has different practices from ours in selling timber, while everything *else* in our respective communities remains the same? Wittgenstein remarks, "Frege says in the preface to *Grungesetze der Arithmetik*: '. . . here we have a hitherto unknown kind of insanity'—but he never said what this insanity would really be like.")[22] It must not be assumed that the community of logicians has all the answers to the questions of reasoning raised by members outside that community, nor must we assume that the results obtained by them are of importance to an equal degree to those outside that community.

It was Hilary Putnam who conjectured what he calls the

> HYPOTHESIS OF THE UNIVERSALITY OF THE DIVISION OF LINGUISTIC LABOR: Every linguistic community exemplifies the sort of division of linguistic labor just described: that is, possesses at least some terms whose associated 'criteria' are known only to a subset of the speakers who acquire the terms, and whose use by the other speakers depends upon a structured cooperation between them and the speakers in the relevant subsets.[23]

If one cannot tell, for instance, the difference between an elm tree and birch tree, says Putnam, it does not mean that when we use the phrase *birch tree*, we are referring indifferently to either a birch or an elm tree. So when ordinary speakers conflict on what the term is referring to, they can settle their controversy by taking their dispute to an expert. But we have experts and experts, of course, and so those who are experts in one field are laymen in others, and vice versa. In some sense, the linguistic labor is divided by nearly everyone.

Presumably, then, when conflicts arise between individuals who are outside the communities of logicians, statisticians, and methodologists, respectively, concerning the correctness or propriety of a particular piece of inference or reasoning, they settle the dispute by invoking expert advice. However, just as we get by with what we are doing without constantly referring to the expert to tell us whether something is elm or birch, aluminum or molybdenum, and our mistakes frequently go unrecognized, so also we get along even though our errant reasoning may frequently go unnoticed. But the possibilities of resolving conflicts or uncertainties in our reasoning are present, and they provide checks and balance between reasoners, ensuring that our ordinary tasks and travails are not noticeably affected or endangered. This picture—and it is no more than a picture—may enable us to see how forms of reasoning may be propagated from a community of experts to others until, over an interval of time, they permeate the whole society.

At this juncture, one ought to ask, How does this view differ from that of Imre Lakatos, Larry Laudan, and others, who emphasize the role of preanalytic judgments in the evaluation of methods, also? There is a vast difference, which can be put in a nutshell, thus: their theories of method take into account the preanalytic judgments concerning episodes in the history of science that are far removed in time from the scientists now engaged in their activities; my view confines these judgments to those of contemporary scientists. These are judgments that the scientists may not fully be able to articulate and explain, but their convictions, as expressed in these judgments, are born and nurtured in their practice. Unless a practicing scientist happens to be an astute historian of science (such as Mach), his views on whether or not certain decisions in the history of science were rational are quite worthless. One needs a deeper appreciation of the theoretical, metaphysical, and methodological heritage of the past scientists, not to mention of the contemporary social, political, and economic conditions and circumstances in which they were placed, to arrive at what *would* have been their preanalytic judgments, and then pronounce on whether *their* particular decisions to accept or reject *their* specific theories were rational or irrational. But this is hard to do, as any historian knows. It is plainly not enough to simply rattle off claims such as, the Copernican theory was better than the Ptolemaic theory, Harvey's theory was better than Galen's theory, Darwin's theory was better than Lamarck's theory, and so on. Anyone can do *that*. A future historian of science will have as much difficulty in appreciating what we currently regard as plausible; he will have to wear our thinking cap, in Herbert Butterfield's immortal phrase, and try to understand *our* scientific, methodological, and metaphysical legacy.

In short, in evaluating contemporary methods, I invoke a certain class of preanalytic judgments, in particular those that range over decisions of contemporary science, and hence this view is sharply distinguishable from the other theories of method. The difference among our rival theories of method is best understood by asking, Does the view presented here transgress the principle of parity as do the other views?[24] If the answer is, no, it does not, then the difference will have been firmly established.

Let me finally sketch one more approach. Rawls places rational, self-interested, moral agents in a hypothetical position, known as the original position, in which the agents, one and all, have general knowledge about their society, know the social sciences such as moral psychology, and so on; but they do not know what their race, sex, parentage, talents, property, or their natural and acquired advantages and disadvantages are. In short, they do not know anything about themselves or their society that is arbitrary from a moral point of view. The question in the original position facing the moral agents is, By what principles ought they to govern and regulate their society? The agents consider one conception of justice after another, including varieties of utilitarian, teleological, intuitionistic, and egoistic conceptions, and Rawls's own two principles of justice. Rawls then shows by what manner and mode of reasoning the agents in the original position will select his two principles of justice, namely, everyone should have the most extensive liberty compatible with the like liberty for all; and, social and economic inequalities are to be permitted provided that they are to the mutual advantage of everyone. These, and not others, are the moral principles, moral agents in the original position will agree, on which to found their society.

Robert Nozick suggests an alternative way of showing how the moral agents will arrive at the Rawlsian principles, a way which when adapted and modified to suit our circumstances partially illuminates and deepens our own problem and solution.[25]

Let the moral agents in the original position in which Rawls places them, says Nozick, be *Stage 1* of the argument. At this stage they arrive at some principles that are not Rawls's. They step out of the hypothetical original position and conduct their affairs and govern their society in accordance with the principles, say *P*, arrived at in the *Stage 1* original position. The actual putting of these principles into practice will yield much tacit moral knowledge, will develop their sense of justice, and will inculcate correct moral dispositions (attitudes toward others, themselves, and animals, for instance) in a way that no amount of mere formal discussion could. For a while their particular ethical judgments and principles *P* will be in a reflective equilibrium, until their practices affect their social, political, and economic arrangements and affairs in a way that upsets that equilibrium. As a consequence of their practice, they will come to regard certain actions and economic arrangements, for instance, as morally wrong and unjust, which they would not have regarded as being so if they had been living in a society founded on principles other than *P*.

Place these same individuals in the original position, and this will be *Stage 2* of the argument. They know why they want to discard principles *P*, and they engage anew in a process of reasoning which yields a different set of principles, say, *P′*. Once again they return from the hypothetical original position, this time to conduct their affairs and govern their society on the moral principles, P'. These moral agents will develop further their sense of justice and acquire newer moral attitudes, until they begin to see serious, if partial, defects in P', and they return to *Stage 3* original position to reconsider new alternative moral principles, and espouse P''. And so on.

If we iterate this process, says Nozick, we shall eventually converge on the Rawlsian principles of justice, or the Rawlsian principles will be chosen at every *Stage n* if they are chosen at *Stage n-1*, or each stage of the argument will yield different principles from the ones that went before, with no convergence or final solution in sight.

Imagine, then, that at *Stage 1* rational knowledge-seekers are in an original position to decide which heuristic norms to use to govern their scientific practices. They have, one and all, knowledge of the social sciences, such as the psychology of discovery, the sociology of knowledge, and the sociological and economic basis of scientific institutions, for such knowledge will inform them of the side-constraints to be imposed on methods.[26] Most important, however, they are acquainted with their state of knowledge (as defined in section I), namely, they know what the theories, methods, and decisions of the recent past were, what parts of science developed significantly, and which parts fell quickly by the wayside. But they do not know anything about themselves, their commitments, their personal role in developing particular theories, whether they are in this field or that, whether for fame or fortune as well as knowledge, and so on; in short, they do not know anything about themselves or their society that is arbitrary from a methodological point of view.

In the original position of *Stage 1*, they consider rival methods, compare their relative merits, and arrive at *M* as the best method. They step out of the hypothetical original position and conduct their scientific affairs in the light of the method *M*. The actual putting of this method into practice will yield much tacit knowledge concerning the evaluation of theories, develop their sense of rationality in science, both of persons and theories, and inculcate certain dispositions (attitudes toward ad hoc hypotheses, necessity for tolerating and nurturing fledgling theories and up to what point, and so on), in a way that no amount of formal methodological discussion could. For a while their particular decisions concerning the acceptance or rejection of theories and the heuristic principles or advice offered by *M* will be in a reflective equilibrium, until the actual execution of their scientific practice guided by *M* leads to particular judgments that disturb that equilibrium. As a consequence of their practice, they may come to regard certain heuristic advice—for instance, to continue to adopt a theory even where it has repeatedly failed independent tests—as irrational or incorrect. They could not have regarded this advice as irrational as forcefully if they had not been conducting their affairs in accordance with the heuristic rules of *M*.

These knowledge-seekers find themselves, hence, in the *Stage 2* original position. They know why *M* will not serve their practice well, and so they reconsider newer methodological alternatives and settle on *M′* as the next best method. Once again, they return from the original position, this time to conduct their scientific affairs and actions in terms of *M′*, to test *its* efficacy. As a result of their new practices, these knowledge-seekers will develop some more their sense of rationality, gain further tacit knowledge of the correct conditions under which theories should be accepted or rejected, until they begin to see defects in *M′* as well, defects that disturb their reflective equilibrium; and they return to reconsider still newer methodological alternatives in the *Stage 3* original position. There they will espouse a new method, *M″*, as the best method. And so on. The process is repeated until *the* best method is found or until each successive stage leads them to converge on the best method. If they find themselves oscillating between two methods in distinct stages, or if they find that there is neither convergence nor the possibility of arriving at the best method (there is merely a displacement of one method by another), they will give up the problem of deciding which is the best method as hopeless or unsolvable.

This ideal procedure enables us to explain how scientists might arrive at the best method, the best form of reasoning in science, with which to experiment. Procedures of this sort take time before the scientists come to recognize that the vices of a method far outrun its virtues; hence, we can explain why the change in our forms of reasoning is allowed to occur only slowly.

What is more, the framework for methods enables us to see precisely what parts of a method can be supported in this way and what parts cannot. Neither the logical parts of a method nor the conventional parts can be so supported; only the evaluative part of a method is solely dependent on the heuristic part, so that such a view can be used only to confirm or confute the heuristic advice given by a methodology. This should also strengthen my claim that the methodological problem of deciding which is the best theory, or which theory should be accepted as the best for practical purposes, pales into insignificance in comparison with the problem of deciding which should be accepted for further theoretical and experimental purposes. It is answers to this latter problem, I contend, that will enable us to glimpse the real movers and shakers in the growth and development of scientific knowledge.

While the concept of reflective equilibrium and the notion of the original position are quite as useful in discussing methodology as they are in discussing ethical theories, it is not a matter of simply translating the important results of one philosophical domain into another. A fuller account of this technique and notion, as used in methodology, must take into consideration a significant difference. The problems in ethics arise because the resources are scarce, and self-interested rational agents prefer more of these resources rather than less. What one moral agent acquires, the other cannot rightfully have without proper consent or contract.

In methodology, by contrast, rational knowledge-seekers have a common goal, namely, more and more knowledge. No rational knowledge-seeker in the original position will decline the proposal that what is sought or discovered by one should be made accessible to all, or is a common property of all. In short, at no stage will anyone accept a proposal that forbids him to partake of the discovery of others; nor will he forbid others to partake of the discoveries made by him. If he threatens to block others from knowing what he has found or discovered, then he will run the risk of coming under a similar threat. Nor in the original position will a knowledge-seeker agree to purchase knowledge from others, since in that state he does not know what his economic background is, and thus whether he will be able to afford the price at which the knowledge is being bought and sold. The knowledge-seekers will agree that pieces of knowledge should be treated unlike pieces of property, real estate, shares, and bonds, which can be bought and sold on the open, free market. These knowledge-seekers know that a lack of free, easy, and open access to scientific knowledge and discovery can seriously hamper scientific growth.

Now, we can make the assumption that resources are in a common pool or that knowledge-seekers are to put a certain amount received from patents or products consequent upon their discovery into a common pool, which is then to be distributed among knowledge-seekers so as to promote and produce the maximum advantage for science; and this has little to do with individual rights over property. Or we can make the assumption that the growth and development of science, to the extent that it is dependent on the distribution of resources, is a matter to be decided only by knowledge-seekers who have contributed to the pool *and* by staying within, say, the libertarian theory of rights. For the purpose of seeking knowledge, it may be rational to distribute the resources suggested by the first alternative; to be moral, it may be imperative to let already-distributed resources remain in a particular way or distribute them as suggested by the second alternative. A lover of paradox might put the point thus: one can be rational in the arrangement of the affairs of science if one distributed the resources to ensure only the growth and development of science, but one would thus be irrational in a moral sense. Or, one can be rational in arranging the economic and political affairs in a way that will not violate the rights of individuals, but then one would be irrational in the sense in which it matters for science.

Whatever the resolution of the paradox, a deeper philosophical theory, insofar as it concerns itself with heuristics, must in the ultimate analysis take scarce resources into account, inasmuch as the distribution of these resources can either hinder or help in the growth and development of science. Some theories will need greater resources for experimental and testing purposes than others, in effect taking the resources away from other theories for *their* testing and experimenting. But what is primarily at stake here is *knowledge*, not individual property rights. No knowledge-seeker in the original position would prevent more resources from going into one field of science, say, genetics, than into another, say, weed science (even if the latter happens to be his own), if the increment of growth and the importance of knowledge would be far greater than it would if the resources were distributed otherwise.

Finally, and most importantly, it is inevitable to ask what form of society rational knowledge-seekers would agree to in the original position. In the sphere of morality, Rawls has argued that they would select only one set of principles of justice. Would the scientists, then, at any stage in the original position (save the last), select only *one* single method to guide their practices in the hope of achieving their goals?

I think not.

IV. A THEORY OF GROUP RATIONALITY

What I wish to propose is a problem: what is it that makes a scientific group rational? I would like to offer the sketch of a solution. The problem—especially if seen against the background of issues pertinent to scientific method—is, I think, fruitful. It opens up new, unexplored philosophical areas, problems and prospects that have a deep bearing on questions of rationality. I commence the discussion of this problem by delineating an overview of philosophy of science set squarely in the tradition of Paul Feyerabend, Thomas Kuhn, Imre Lakatos, Larry Laudan, Karl Popper, Hilary Putnam, and others. The traditional view, substantial and deep-rooted, is referred to as *the classical view*—better expressed as the classical picture of rationality. To be sure, much is important and useful in this view, but there is also a radical flaw in it which leads to considerable, and hitherto unnoticed, difficulties. I then sketch an alternative view, *the view of multiple methods*. Two case studies from the history of science are presented as illustrations of that view; and, before concluding, I indicate how a scientific group, envisaged by such a view, will remain stable; how that group has a better chance of making more rapid progress in the accumulation of knowledge than a group envisaged on the classical view; and, finally, why the view of multiple methods is adequately placed to explain how and why aims or goals change and grow.

The Classical View

In the classical picture, the view of rationality we are offered is this: if an individual scientist wishes to reach a goal of truth or verisimilitude, of solving problems, and the like, he ought to act in accordance with the method a philosopher in this tradition suggests. To take Popper as an example, a scientist ought to act in accordance with the dictates of the method of falsificationism: propose testable theories; do not investigate ad hoc theories; select the theory, for further theoretical and practical purposes, that is best corroborated; accept a simpler hypothesis because it is more testable than a less simple theory; and so on. Popper does not claim to offer an infallible method, but he does believe that his method will give us a better chance to achieve the goal of verisimilitude.

It is true, of course, that the classical picture can be presented in two ways that in all *essentials* of approach are similar in spirit. These two views I shall christen *the single-theory approach* and *the many-theories approach*, respectively. On the single-theory approach, such as that of Popper, a method specifies the best of the available theories, and the scientists are enjoined to accept and adopt that theory until it is in more trouble than at least one extant theory. In that case the latter theory should then be accepted. For any scientist to violate that norm would be to act irrationally.

On the many-theories approach, such as that of Lakatos, who advocates proliferation of research programs, a method specifies a set of theories (ranked or otherwise), and the scientists are enjoined to adopt any theory that is an element of that set. The goal of the many-theories approach is to engage the scientific community to work on a host of scientific theories (specified by the method in question) and not to be confined to adopting a single theory. To mention a few of the real advantages of this approach: each proposed theory will pose new problems that are missed by its rivals; they will propose newer solutions, which will lead to the investigation of newer phenomena; and each rival theory will provide a vantage point from which to judge and select other theories. On the lines of Feyerabend: in order to make progress, we need to find out what is wrong with the existing theories so that better ones can be proposed; and it is easier to discover the faults of a theory in the presence of its rivals.

This approach has so many advantages over the single-theory approach that its close affinity to the latter has gone unnoticed. For instance, both versions of the classical picture assume that the scientific activity of *all* individuals in a group ought to be guided by the norms of a *single* method. Laudan would persuade us that a scientific community of astronomers, biologists, chemists, zoologists, geologists, sociologists, and so on should use the methodology of research traditions as a yardstick by which to measure the success of their theories, and that each scientist in the hypothetical community should use the criterion of the rate of progress defined in terms of problem-solving effectiveness to decide which theory to pursue further and which theory to abandon. While theories may proliferate in a single domain, the *method* by which the theories in any domain are measured in that scientific community should be the same.

It is this crucial assumption that I want to question and that will provide me with a springboard for presenting an alternative view. Both versions of the classical picture have a lot to commend them; but I want to show that they are not nearly enough. Indeed, they are seriously wanting in that they altogether ignore a distinction I now want to make, a distinction that was inspired by John Rawls's *A Theory of Justice*.[27]

Rawls draws a distinction between the principles that govern individual justice and the principles that govern just institutions. As he says, "The principles of justice for institutions must not be confused with the principles which apply to individuals and their actions in particular circumstances."[28] To put the matter tersely, Rawls's theory of justice as embodied in his two principles (i.e., the principle of equal liberty and the difference principle) will enable us to judge whether a given social institution, understood as a public system of rules that defines offices and positions with their rights and duties, powers and immunities, and the like,[29] is just or unjust. Similarly, I draw *a distinction between the principles that govern individual rationality and the principles that govern group rationality*. The principles that determine the rationality of a scientific group must not be confused with the principles that determine the rationality of individual scientists who, in their particular historical circumstances, are engaged in the task of, among other things, deciding whether to pursue or reject a given theory. Briefly, a theory of group rationality, such as the theory of multiple methods, will enable us to judge whether a given scientific society as defined, for instance, by its methods and practices of evaluating theories, is rational or irrational. Again, just as Rawls claims that the primary subject of justice is the basic structure of society,[30] so I claim that *the primary subject of rationality in science ought to be the basic structure or form or organization of the scientific community whose members are engaged in the pursuit of shared goals.*

Neither version of the classical picture nor any of the theories of rationality commonly offered draw the foregoing distinction. Thus far, the methods or the classical theories of rationality have been engaged in dealing with problems that relate to the evaluation of theories at a certain time, the evaluation of theories over an interval of time, the evaluation of a particular action or decision of an individual scientist at a certain time, and the evaluation of an individual (concerning his rationality) over an interval of time. By no means kept separate in the classical tradition, let us briefly touch on each of these distinctions.

Initially, the problem that was most important for Popper was formulated as one of determining the characteristic a theory had to possess to be regarded as scientific at any given time. For Popper, that characteristic was testability: if a theory was testable, then it was scientific; if scientific, then testable. As Popper points out, Marxist theory of history was at one time scientific (and indeed shown false because it did not pass its tests) and later metamorphosed into a metaphysical system because its testability had been choked.

For Lakatos, Laudan, and Kenneth Schaffner,[31] what is important is not merely what the status of a theory is at a given time but also how it has progressed over an interval of time. Lakatos's method refers to theories as being in a progressive problem-shift, degenerating problem-shift, and so on, where these terms apply to the performance of a theory over an interval of time. The evaluation of Bohr's old quantum theory is made in the light of its evolution from 1913 onwards. It began with the problem of explaining the stability of Rutherford's atoms. It explained the wavelengths of hydrogen's line emission spectrum. The theory predicted not only the then-known Balmer series (1885) and Paschen series (1908) but also the series subsequently discovered by Lyman (1914), Brackett (1922), and Pfund (1924). A modification of the old quantum theory made possible the prediction of the Pickering-Fowler series, which for a time had proved anomalous for the theory. Calculating the elliptical orbits of the electrons, Sommerfeld in 1915 discovered the fine-structure of the spectrum. Later when, based on Sommerfeld's sophisticated models, certain predicted lines were not forthcoming, Pauli's exclusion principle accounted for the gaps, revised the shell theory, and predicted some unknown facts. Bohr's old quantum theory, according to Lakatos, was a clear case of a research program in a progressive problem-shift.[32]

The problem of evaluating a particular action or decision of an individual scientist at a certain time has likewise engaged the methodologist. Popper advocates adopting a testable theory in favor of a nontestable one; Laudan advocates accepting the theory with the highest degree of problem-solving effectiveness; and so on. Hence a methodologist would be interested in asking, for instance, if Descartes was rational in rejecting Harvey's essentially Aristotelian physiological theory of the heart and replacing it with his mechanical theory. He would ask if Spallanzani was irrational in rejecting the theory of spontaneous generation; if Michael Servetus was rational in accepting the prevailing Galenic theory of anatomy and physiology of the arterial system. Clearly, the evaluation of the rationality of a decision on the part of a scientist is crucially dependent on the evaluation of the theory at a given time or over an interval of time, although the converse is not true.

Finally, it is important to decide whether an individual scientist is rational and not simply whether he acted rationally in a specific situation. But what constitutes his rationality? I have conjectured that a consistent adherence to his adopted method and his ability to change the norms of his method under specific scientific and nonscientific pressures will yield insight into the rationality of an individual scientist.[33] This view enables us to make testable conjectures.

Although these four problems are major ones that any theory of rationality or method must confront, they are very different from the problem, *What makes a group rational*?

Perhaps, a tacit assumption of the classical view may be that group rationality is nothing more than a summation of individual rationality. In other words, to ensure the rationality of a group, it is sufficient to ensure the rationality of its individual members. However, it seems to me that even this tacit assumption must be denied. Aside from the fact that it commits the fallacy of composition, the assumption needs rejection for a number of reasons, some of which are the following.

Consider the many-theories approach first. On this view, a single method, M, is accepted as defining the current practice of the members of a scientific group. According to M, p theories out of the q theories currently proposed ought to be adopted for further theoretical and experimental investigations; this is, of course, the widely shared principle of proliferation. In effect, M says that any member of the group may adopt any theory from p (instead of being confined to a single theory as in the other classical approach). Let us consider an example from the field of paleontology. One of the as yet not satisfactorily solved problems is what caused the massive extinctions of organisms in the Cretaceous-Tertiary period approximately 65 million years ago. Organisms that were destroyed were microscopic floating animals and plants, calcareous planktonic foraminifers, calcareous nanoplanktons, ammonites, mollusks, marine invertebrates, marine reptiles, flying reptiles, and both orders of dinosaurs, whereas land plants, crocodiles, snakes, mammals, and several species of invertebrates were unaffected. A scientist in this field, according to M, can adopt any of the several theories proposed for explaining the massive extinctions of organisms. Currently competing hypotheses to explain this puzzling fact are: the gradual or rapid changes in the condition of oceans, climate, and atmosphere occasioned by a random or a cyclical coincidence of causal factors; a reversal of the magnetic field during that period; a nearby supernova; the flooding of the ocean surface by freshwater from a supposed arctic lake; and, finally, the impact of a large earth-crossing asteroid.[34]

The classical view leads to a curious result. Let *T* (the hypothesis of the earth-crossing asteroid) be a theory in *p*, and to make matters simple, assume with the majority of paleontologists that *T* is the best-confirmed theory (where the requisite degree of confirmation is defined by *M*). Suppose that every member of the group decides to adopt *T*. It follows that according to *M* every member is rational inasmuch as each member acted in accordance with the dictates of *M*. But something has now gone wrong: there is no proliferation of theories! No reasonable norm of *M* would, however, enjoin each member of the group to work on each theory of *p*, or on a fairly large subset of *p*, just to ensure that there is proliferation of theories in the group. If, as seems reasonable, no such injunction ought to be made, then the method preserves the rationality of each individual and yet allows the principle of proliferation to be violated. This is odd and puzzling.

The situation can be saved *only if* we make the distinction between individual rationality and group rationality. It is clear that that distinction casts a different light on the principle of proliferation. It is no longer viewed as a principle that governs individual rationality but rather a principle that governs group rationality. We *do* want to say that if all or a very large majority of paleontologists working in this field were to adopt the hypothesis of the earth-crossing asteroid, then that group of scientists would be irrationally organized (inasmuch as it violates the principle of proliferation).

The argument against the single-theory approach can proceed analogously. According to the Popperian method, scientists ought to accept and adopt, for practical purposes as well as for further theoretical and experimental investigations, the theory that is best corroborated. On the Popperian view, if an individual scientist adopted a poorer theory, one concerning, let us say, the reversal of the magnetic field, *no matter what the other scientists in the group were doing*, that scientist would be irrational. Such a view might be defended by saying that there is no restriction on what theory to test or research so long as the theory can be put to a severe test. The more severely it is testable, the better are its credentials. This defense is inconsistent with the Popperian heuristic advice.[35] To be sure, it is a necessary condition that the accepted theory is a testable theory, but it is not a sufficient condition. The necessary and sufficient condition for a scientist to be rational, on Popper's method, is to accept and adopt the best of all corroborated theories.

The single-theory approach can be criticized from a perspective different from the one used to criticize the many-theories approach. At a certain time, t, a community of scientists whose practice is defined by Popper's method might be supposed to have the following theories, T_1, T_2, T_3, . . . , T_n, to choose from. Each of these theories has a different degree of corroboration, where corroboration is defined as the compact history of the severe tests a theory has undergone. Let us say that the series has been arranged in the order of decreasing degree of corroboration so that T_1 is the best theory.

Later at t', T_1 is in serious trouble since most of its independent testable conclusions have been falsified, and T_2 is better corroborated than T_1. The series of existing theories has to be reordered in the following way: T_2, T_3, T_1, . . . , T_n. But this has the absurd consequence that *no* new theory can be proposed and adopted for research and experimental tests *until* we have first exhausted all the alternatives we had available at t and each of them has been found wanting at t'. Furthermore, it calls for a clear index of the degree of confirmation below which a theory cannot fall; otherwise, we will be forever stuck with our initial alternatives!

Laudan's method of research traditions advocates a distinction between the *context of acceptance* and the *context of pursuit*. Which theory or research tradition should one accept? "The choice of one tradition over its rivals," writes Laudan, "is a progressive (and thus a rational) choice precisely to the extent that the chosen tradition is a better problem-solver than its rivals."[36] But it is a different tale when it comes to the problem of which theory should be pursued. "It is always rational to pursue any research tradition which has a higher rate of progress than its rivals (even if the former has a lower problem-solving effectiveness)."[37] Thus, in our previous example of the large-scale extinction of organisms in the Cretaceous-Tertiary period, if the earth-crossing asteroid theory exhibits the highest rate of progress compared with its rivals, it would be rational to pursue it but irrational to pursue any other theory. However, since the 1960s at least, there have been several paleontologists in the field who have been *pursuing* different hypotheses, such as the hypothesis of the reversal of the magnetic field during this period, or the hypothesis of a nearby supernova. It is clear that on Laudan's view, with respect to the question of pursuit, it would be irrational to proliferate theories (unless their rate of progress were identical and highest!). Or, to use Laudan's own examples, if it is irrational to pursue theories that have a lower rate of progress than some of their rivals do, then how can we explain why Aristotelianism or the theory of elective affinities had a substantial following for a long period of time when the rate of progress of these theories was not, by Laudan's own hypothesis, the highest? If, however, it is rational to pursue theories with a poor progress report, then it is unclear how Laudan avoids the extreme view he attributes to Lakatos—and which Feyerabend so wholeheartedly endorses—namely, that any theory can be pursued as rational.[38]

The constraints of the single-theory approach on scientific practice are very serious, and they are, I think, a direct consequence of a failure to draw a clear distinction between individual and group rationality. In the work of Popper and Laudan, this failure is far more obvious than in the many-theories approach.

The View of Multiple Methods

How should a society of scientists be organized in order that goals of its members can be most effectively reached? Alternatively, and simply, *What is the rational structure of a scientific group*? One might propose the following.

Imagine a scientific society to be divided into several subgroups, where a subgroup is defined by the method it adopts for making decisions. The totality of these subgroups, which are interlocking and well-knit, we shall refer to as the group. The situation ideally envisaged is this. *Engaged in a joint enterprise to pursue a set of shared (partially overlapping?) goals, there will be relatively few, stable, competing, and conflicting subgroups,* G_1, G_2, G_3, . . . , G_n *in a continuously shifting equilibrium, pursuing science under the rubric of different methods,* M_1, M_2, M_3, . . . , M_n, *respectively*. Members of subgroup G_i will use M_i to decide what scientific theories to accept and adopt and what theories to reject. The structure of such a group is referred to as one exemplifying the pursuit of science through multiple methods (fig. 1); and the strucure is rational. Let us enlarge the picture and examine, or fill in, the details.

It is quite difficult, if not impossible, at this stage of the investigation, to pin down the precise number of subgroups that must compete at any given time or time interval to preserve the rationality of the group.

However, it is not a difficulty peculiar to the view of multiple methods. For instance, a corresponding difficulty faces those who opt for the principle of proliferation of theories; they do not specify any precise number of theories to adopt at any given time. This is left to the situation at hand. In significant part, the number of subgroups will be controlled by various side-constraints in the form of economic, social, political, and moral factors.

A subgroup is stable if it is reasonably successful in developing interesting problems, in solving some of these problems, and in producing better and better theories. Since the subgroup acts in accordance with the dictates of its methods, the success of the group is partially, at least, indissolubly linked to its adopted method. I say "partially" advisedly. Contemporary methodologists interested in the problem of method evaluation have assumed that the success of right decisions is to

THE VIEW OF MULTIPLE METHODS

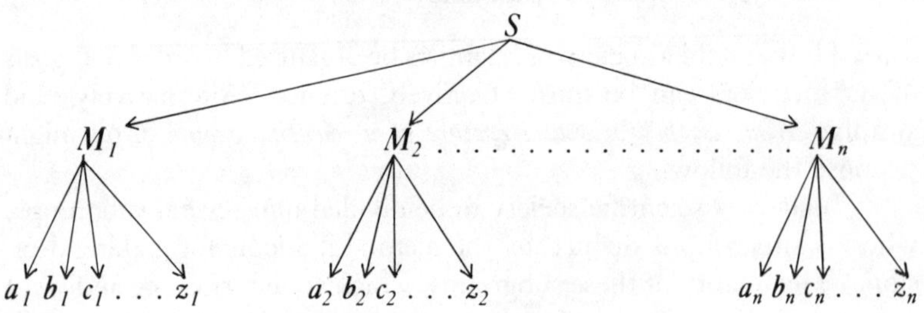

KEY: S = Group

M_i = Subgroup *i* governed in its scientific activity by method *i* (i = 1, 2, 3, . . . , n).

x_i = individual *x* belonging to subgroup *i*
(i = 1, 2, 3, . . . , n)
(x = a, b, c, . . . , z)

Figure 1

be solely attributed to the method in question. But clearly this may not be true. The success may have a lot to do with extraneous factors, such as talent, ability to create new theories, adequate resources, and luck. On the view of multiple methods, the small number of competing and conflicting subgroups will consist of stable subgroups.

Why competing and conflicting subgroups? The rationale for the group to be governed by a set of competing and conflicting subgroups is best explained by analogy with the rationale for the many-theories approach. The dovetailing of the view of multiple methods and the *experimental* approach with the evaluation of methods is intentional. When scientists are confronted by a methodological problem-situation in which they are forced to make a decision about which theory to adopt, there is a fact of the matter involved. Some decisions are truer than others; that is, heuristic advice given by some methods is better than that given by other methods. Such a claim will enable us to understand why some methods are effective and others are not. One important way of deciding which method yields the better, more effective, truer heuristic advice is to let diverse methods compete and find out which method leads to more fruitful results in the long run. If science is pursued in the way suggested, we shall learn more about the weaknesses and strengths of a method by measuring it against the successes and failures of its rivals; we shall confront deeper methodological problems; we shall permit ourselves more radical methods than if science is pursued on the basis of a single method as in the classical approach (fig. 2).

Here we leave aside some important and interesting questions. For example, what constitutes the identity of a method, given that it may make adjustments and revisions in its various dicta? Since methods can easily conflict—for instance, when the dictum of one method conflicts with the dictum of another method—how different must methods be from one another before they can be allowed individually to govern subgroups and together to govern a group? How successful must a method be before it is allowed to govern a subgroup?

Serving strictly the purposes of illustration, and *not* of evidence, consider two brief cases from the history of science.

Illustration 1. Examining ancient theories of optics and vision—the intromission, extramission, and mediumistic theories—we find one historian of science remarking that "these three kinds of theories defined

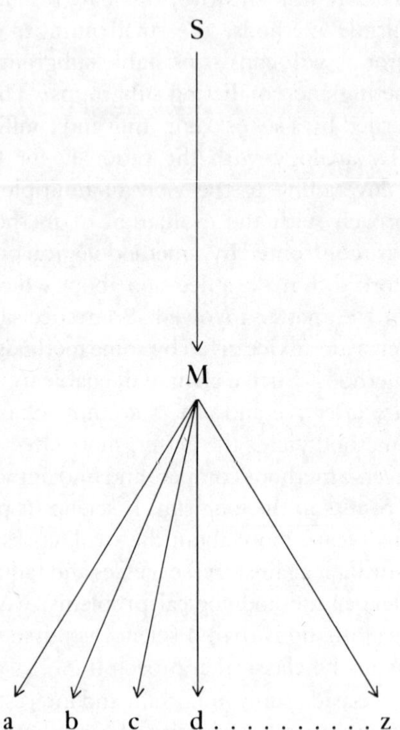

KEY: S = Group

M = Method adopted by every member of the subgroup. In effect, a group that has only one subgroup.

x = individual belonging to the group (subgroup), (x = a, b, c, . . . , z).

Figure 2

the principal battle lines with visual theory."[39] The debate within the various groups "was not merely a debate over the direction of radiation, *for it was thoroughly intertwined with basic questions about the aims and criteria of optical theory*."[40]

The first subgroup, advocating the intromission theory, consisted of atomists (Epicurus, Lucretius) who argued that atoms emanated from a visible object in all directions, retaining their configurations as they entered the eye of the observer. To receive this convoy of atoms (*simulacra*, *eidola*) was to receive a visual impression of the object itself. While spewing atoms, the object did not diminish, because other atoms took the place of those that left. In a version ascribed to Democritus, the pupillary image was given a prominent role inasmuch as images of objects were mirrored in the cornea, which in turn was regarded as essential to the visibility of an object. While members of this subgroup espoused different variations of the theory, they shared not only a common core of the theory but also a common family of problems. Problems they were faced with were, How could the *eidola* of a very large object shrink to enter the observer's eye, without distorting the size of the object when perceived? How could *eidola* pass through one another without interference, when they lay on the line of sight of two or more observers?

The second subgroup, advocating extramission theory, comprised mathematicians (Euclid, Ptolemy) who argued that radiation emanated from the observer, in order to "feel" the object; when the radiation fell on an opaque object, by an unexplained mechanism the perception was signaled back. The group maintained that the radiation from the eye of the observer issued forth in the form of a cone, with the apex centered on the eye and the base on the object. The radiation proceeded in straight lines unless reflected or refracted. Their concern with developing a mathematical theory of vision caused them to neglect problems pertaining to the nature of radiation as well as those related to the physiological and psychological aspects of vision, common concerns of their rivals. Against this theory, Aristotle, a member of the third subgroup, objected to the impossibility of a physical ray issuing from an eye to reach the fixed stars, and that, too, in a bare instant.

The third subgroup, advocating the mediumistic theory, consisted of those interested in discovering physical causes of vision (Aristotle, Galen), who argued that a medium brought the perceived object into contact with an observer. Colored bodies produced qualitative changes in the transparent medium, such as air, and these transformations were transmitted to the transparent humors of the eye of the observer. The eye was colored green by a green object, and this color acquisition constituted seeing. The eye became the visible object.

What is noteworthy for our purposes is that each subgroup had its own distinct way of appraising a theory. The basic purposes of an extramission theory was to offer a geometrical account of space and to develop a mathematical theory of perspective in which the localization of an object was a function of the visual cone, just as the apparent size and shape of an object was a function of its distance from the observer and its orientation with respect to the line of sight. By its practitioners, the theory was not judged in terms of the criterion of physical plausibility. For instance, in the hands of Euclid, the theory, without any physical explanation, claimed that the clarity of perception directly varied with the number of angles under which an object was seen; he acknowedged the influence of external light on vision but was silent about the nature of that influence. No member of this subgroup would have accepted the mediumistic theory, for the latter would have failed completely on mathematical grounds. Yet, to the members of the mediumistic subgroup, this failure would have been inconsequential. Their theory offered a plausible causal explanation of some observations and, hence, met their method's criteria of acceptance and pursuit. What were regarded as serious objections to one theory by one group were not thought to be objections by another group; their incongruous evaluations can only be explained in terms of their differing purposes and goals embodied in their respective methods.

There was proliferation of theories in the field of optics because there were multiple methods. Because these methods, espoused by the subgroups, led to the acceptance of some theories and the rejection or modification of others, the strengths and weaknesses not only of the theories but also of the methods revealed themselves over time. Thus, the Aristotelian Alhazen developed a powerful method, as well as theories of the anatomy and physiology of the eye and visual perception that satisfied that method. This method incorporated the best elements of the methods of the three competing schools, drawing together the physical, mathematical, and physiological criteria so as to obliterate old distinctions and forge new methodological traditions.

Illustration 2. Three distinct schools or subgroups formed the society of physicians in antiquity: Methodists, Empiricists, and Dogmatists or Rationalists. While we may recognize the leech as being distinct from the physician (as constituting the fourth subgroup), the distinction was by no means clear-cut. What proved important for the leech was his eventual adherence to a school, which not only gave him a certain status but improved his practice of treating the sick.[41]

The practitioners of the Methodist school (Thessalius) opposed the medical theories of the Dogmatist and the Empiricist schools on methodological grounds. They distrusted experience and accepted the skepticism of Pyrrho. They rejected the idea of progress and did not conduct etiological research and experiment; they sought to infer directly from the symptoms of the disease, without the aid of theory, the state of the body which they explained as either tense or relaxed. As a consequence of their methodological stance, they had no use for drugs, which were regarded as very important by other schools or subgroups. Indeed, the dietetic physician (Herodicus) who attempted to cure internal diseases—those that affect the whole man—by regulating food, drink, work, rest, and exercise, used neither drugs nor surgery.

While the Empiricist school, the second medical subgroup, emphasized experience, advised the practicing physician to rely on his experience and that of others and to supplement analogical reasoning in new and novel cases, it banned theoretical research or search for hidden causes, an activity fundamental to the next school. The Empiricist school denied the possibility of knowledge or that nature was understandable, and so they thought that theories could be dispensed with. Only observations of the symptoms of the disease, of evident causes, like hunger and thirst, rest and fatigue, and of the effects of remedies, mattered in medicine. What was regarded as a cure, or an observation of a constant conjunction between symptoms and disease, they insisted upon being repeatedly tested before it could be considered reliable.

The Dogmatist school, the subgroup whose members were Herophilus, Erasistratus, and of course Galen, stressed the role of theory, speculation, and research, and the possibility of knowledge and the growth of knowledge. Partly this buttressed their claim that the Empiricists' method was wrong. Constant conjunction was unreliable, even when frequently tested. What certified knowledge was a theory, say the humoral theory, which posited a deeper underlying mechanism to explain the nature of disease. The consequences of a proposed theory had to be tested. It is interesting to note that Galen's arguments against various conjectures of Asclepiades, Erasistratus, and others on the role of kidneys in the production of urine can be understood better in terms of his method.

Given the role of theory and experiment, the Rationalist insisted on the importance of anatomical dissection, pharmacology, and physiological experiments. Logical reasoning was regarded as very important; equally so was the learning of the nature and number of diseases, together with their species and genera. To be sure, analogical reasoning must have been involved, since most of the experiments were performed on monkeys and animals and the results transferred onto the human anatomy and system. There was a fundamental belief in the growth and progress of knowledge, but its nature was more on par with mopping-up operations, rather than with scientific revolutions. Thessalius had argued that other schools had very little to contribute, that physicians of the past were full of errors, and that only his school had the right answers, answers he presumed he could teach in six months.[42] Galen, however, supposed that while those in the past had made useful contributions to medical knowledge, they had not exhausted it. He believed that he had made considerable progress, and that others would make further progress, too. (It is claimed that Galen knew more about the anatomy of the Barbary ape than we do.)

After the third century, the sects were no longer vigorously active, and slowly the Methodist and the Empiricist schools perished, with the latter transformed into the rather weak school of the Empirics. Until Paracelsus, Galen's theories were to hold sway for approximately 1,300 years. The state of the craft declined; at best, it stood where it had been during that period. What prompted this sterility in the study and practice of medicine, it might be explained, was the lack of the proliferation of methods, just as the success of Galen's scientific theory was in significant part due to the better method on which it was nurtured.

We now turn to the next element in the theory of group rationality; we need to explain why the subgroups will be in a continuously shifting equilibrium. Feyerabend observes that "Methodology is a means for moving from one historical stage to another."[43] Each group is using the norms of its adopted method to make various decisions at each stage: to decide what theories to test, what theories to teach, what theories to adopt and articulate; and it is these decisions that determine in a complex and interesting way the successive stages—the continuous shifts—in the history of the craft of the respective subgroups and, hence, of the entire group.

Since each subgroup is continuously advancing forward—not an inevitable process—it is undergoing a continuous change. This change is usually toward a new equilibrium from an old one. The equilibrium of a subgroup is defined in terms of the stability of the rival subgroups and the conditions, natural and social, surrounding them.

The subgroups, as we said, are interlocked and well-knit because they are united by a shared set of goals. Each subgroup can assess, over an interval of time, its success or failure with respect to the problem-set it worked with and the solutions it offered. In short, it can gauge to what extent its *experiment* with its method has succeeded. If a subgroup is unsuccessful relative to other subgroups, that is, if a subgroup is unstable, its members will move out and join the more successful subgroups. The group disequilibrium has been removed by the group moving toward a new equilibrium in which the competing, stable subgroups have been diminished by one. Popper says, "Some aim must precede any particular instance of the trial and error method. This does not mean that our aims are not in their turn subject to this method. Any particular aim can be changed by trial and error, and many are so changed. (We can change the setting on our thermostat, selecting by trial and error one that better satisfies some aim—an aim of a different level.) And our system of aims not only *changes*, but it can also *grow* in a way closely similar to the way in which our knowledge grows."[44] Assuming we understand Popper correctly, the view of multiple methods may be a first step toward a conjecture of how goals, like theories, may compete, grow and improve. Inasmuch as methods aim at certain basic goals, a failure of a method may reflect the failure of fundamental goals. How *else* can fundamental goals be adjudged?

Another way in which a subgroup can experience a disequilibrium is if the external conditions, either natural or social, change dramatically, in which case practical problems may take priority, with an unanticipated outcome on theoretical problems and results. In such an unstable environment, persisting subgroups will be those that attack primarily practical problems and alter their basic theoretical and experimental researches in the light of those problems. The recent demand for developing new energy resources has led many scientists *into* such areas as solar energy, wind and wave energy, geothermal energy and *away from* other groups presiding over other fields of scientific research. Exploring these avenues, who can predict what impact such ventures, guided by practical concerns and motives, will have on our theoretical knowledge of the sun and on the sciences of meterology, oceanography, and geology?

Does the view of multiple methods avert the problems that confronted the classical view? One of the problems facing the classical view was that if every individual scientist, using the same method, adopted the best theory *T*, the net result would be no proliferation of theories, and yet everyone would be rational. It might be argued that the present view does not avoid that problem. Let us suppose that the group is governed by *n* subgroups. Each subgroup entertains a theory *T*, among others in the relevant domain; and by the respective method used by each subgroup, it is quite rational for any member in any subgroup to accept *T*. If every member does accept *T*, we are led to the same anomalous result that faulted the classical view.

This is a logically possible but utterly unrealistic case. It is unlikely that each subgroup will entertain *T* among other theories no matter what historical stage it is at. Since the initial set of theories a subgroup will commence with is different for each subgroup, the vastly different heuristic advice of the rival methods will chart a vastly different history of the growth and development of theories for each subgroup. Thus, over an interval of time, the major competing theories in each subgroup will be far different than is envisaged in the hypothetical case.

Furthermore, the diverse and incompatible fundamental goals and aims of each subgroup render the acceptance of the same theory, *T*, by all the subgroups even more unlikely. This was evident in the case of the theories of optics in antiquity and in the Middle Ages: the mathematical criteria for appraising a theory of optics used by the members of one group was not used or favored by another group using the criteria of plausible causal connections. Similarly, the Dogmatist clan in the history of ancient medicine used criteria for theory appraisal considerably different from the criteria used by the schools of Methodists or Empiricists. Indeed, from the vantage point of Feyerabend, the view of multiple methods would seem best to capture his intentions. For what Feyerabend is advocating is that theories should conflict in a more fundamental way if the principle of proliferation, as envisaged by him, is to be satisfied and the promise of an accelerated growth of knowledge fulfilled. After all, Aristotelians can propose rival optical theories while sharing goals and a method in common; but that sort of conflict is not nearly as deep, or nearly as interesting, as the conflict of theories that would result when non-Aristotelians propose alternative optical theories. The latter case of conflict is a clear consequence of the view of multiple methods.

Perhaps it may be argued that there is really no distinction between the many-theories version of the classical view and the view of multiple methods. Any situation that is accurately described in the vocabulary of multiple methods is equally accurately redescribable as one in which there are competing theories and a single method whose goals are abstractly specified values capable of being differently interpreted and differently weighted by different subgroups. Thus, what I see as a rational society, it might be pointed out, is simply one that proliferates rival metaphysical research programs, not methods. There are rival optical theories beause there are rival metaphysical programs in which the optical theories are embedded. So the classical one-method view should suffice to explain, and justify, the deep theoretical diversity.[45]

The structure and framework for methods, however, together with the historical examples and examples of methods I urged we should experiment with, should convince us that it is in fact not the case of having one method whose various parts are being differently emphasized by rival subgroups. If the point is merely one of claiming that the description of the situation of any scientific society is underdetermined by historical fact, then it is not a special worry; it is an old one. However, enough has been said by virtue of which we can distinguish rival goals of methods, their distinct ways of appraising theories, and their radically different heuristic advice. I have tried to argue for the primacy of method. Other philosophers have accorded the pride of place to metaphysics, and still others to scientific theories; but I think we all agree that all three should be considered. There is a close and intricate connection between a metaphysical theory and the scientific theory it fosters and nurtures. A method, however, enables us to select theories, and theories reflect the (in)adequacies of metaphysical research programs; hence, a method indirectly, but no less forcefully, has an impact on the growth and development of metaphysics. If I am right, the role of method in the history of science can be shown to be far more important and significant than the roles of metaphysics and theories in the growth and development of knowledge. This does not diminish the fact—indeed it only highlights it—that the tie between the trio of method, metaphysics, and scientific theories is complex and intricate. Nor does it diminish the fact that methods do not solely legislate over the other two but that metaphysics and scientific theories influence methods as well, if less persistently and pervasively.

Another objection to this view may be the argument that a group with several competing and conflicting subgroups would be unstable. Once the methods espoused by the subgroups are rank-ordered, so the argument might go, most scientists would flock to the subgroup whose method ranked first. Such an influx of scientists into that subgroup would result in other subgroups being nearly without members, and so the group as a whole would have a strong and continuous tendency to be a group with a single subgroup (the classical view). In order to be sound, this argument needs to establish that the difference between the best subgroup and the rest is too wide for membership to be sustained in the other subgroups. But this is scarcely established. The basic goals and aims of the members of a subgroup are not easily relinquished; the power and significance of these fundamental goals cannot be evaluated in a short time; and so the evolution of a subgroup, and its subsequent extinction, is likely to be a long, drawn-out process. Moreover, the passing away of a single subgroup does not signal the end of others. Nor does it dictate that the members of that subgroup will enter a single subgroup rather than disperse over several extant ones. In any event, even if the number of methods supported by subgroups happens to be very small (but, at least, greater than one), the chances of producing the desired results—which those who stipulate the principle of proliferation of theories hope for—are better on the proposed view of group rationality than on any alternative theory of rationality.

The problem of group rationality is a genuine one, and not one that can be settled by a mere convention. The solution to the problem presented does not simply and arbitrarily determine the rationality of a scientific group any more than the classical view arbitrarily determines the rationality of an individual scientist. What excuses the brevity with which the issue of group rationality has been treated—and I know how sketchy that treatment has been—is that the claim of the proposed theory of method, namely, that a method must offer a solution to the problem of group rationality, cannot be made plausible without at least attempting to show the significance of the issue. At present our intuitions about group rationality are weak, at best. Our task is the familiar one in which a theory is engaged in sharpening those intuitions that will subsequently lead us to change and alter that very theory. We are presented with the dual interplay between, respectively, our intuitions of individual rationality and those of group rationality. The more cognizant we are about the philosophical problems and issues surrounding the notion of group rationality, the better we may understand the notion of individual rationality. Clearly, mine is not a Nozickian way.[46]

In a flight of speculative fancy, we may imagine a remarkable unity. If the group is rational, then each subgroup is rational, for the group has several competing, conflicting, and stable subgroups. Each subgroup is rational since it is pursuing its respective goals from the vantage point of its method. If the subgroup is rational, then scientists under its rubric are rational, since the rationality of the scientist consists in consistently adhering to the norms of the method he espouses. If a scientist is rational, then the rationality of an individual scientist is in the last analysis determined by the rationality of the group structure. The unity would persist under mildly disturbing circumstances. Thus, if an individual scientist in a subgroup is not rational, that would not make the subgroup, of which he is a member, irrational. If some subgroup is not rational, that would not make the group, of which it is a member, irrational.

Any solution to the problem of group rationality will naturally lead, I suspect, to the awakening of the dormant tradition of fashioning utopias. It will lead us to ask: What is an ideal scientific society? What goals and aims best flourish in a society, or what society would best nurture the goals toward which we aspire? What is the nature of man that marks the perimeter for defining such an ideal society?[47] What deeper impulses lie behind scientific activity,[48] in what society can they best be tapped, and what transformations will they wreak? How do goals linked to the pursuit of knowledge and learning attune to social ends and goals? What principles will enable us to resolve a conflict between these goals? In short, how could a just and a good society exist in harmony with an ideal scientific society? Answers to these questions, and others cast in a similar spirit, will vitalize much of the philosophy of science where it seems arrested by its exclusive concern with individual scientists and their theories.

What is often forgotten, in reading Francis Bacon's celebration of his utopia in the half-completed *New Atlantis*, is that his utopia was also a celebration of his method. The social utopia was intricately woven with what might be called the scientific utopia. Among members of Salomon's House, a miniature society of scientists, are depredators and mystery men, collectors of various experiments in all the books; miners, charged with trying nôvel experiments; dowry men, supervisors of these experiments employed to elicit useful knowledge from them; lamps, scientific think-tanks engaged in designing more intriguing experiments; inoculators, the executors of such designs; merchants of light, scientific emissaries who went abroad in search of more exotic knowledge; and finally, those that raise the former discoveries by experiments "into greater observations, axioms and aphorisms." These were called interpreters of nature. Working in perspective houses, engine-houses, a mathematical house, chambers of health, parks, half-mile high towers, deep caves, brew- and bake-houses, dispensatories or shops of medicines, perfume-houses, sound-houses and their ilk,[49] the members executed their tasks, presumably, in the light of Bacon's method, his Tables of Investigation, tasks oriented toward inaugurating and sustaining the great instauration.

We smile at reading Bacon's conception of an ideal society, as we do in reading the ideals of a Campanella or a Harrington. The methods that informed their utopias, from *our* vantage point, appear overly neat and quaint. But in a way that altogether surprises, the classical view is like theirs: they both offer a single method with which to make and govern decisions in a scientific society. Their vision, if narrow, is an outcome of that view. We ought not to neglect the study of utopias as the philosophers of science of at least the last one hundred years have. We should enlarge our conception of the issues of rationality, for we will deepen our knowledge of our methods as a consequence. We should deepen that knowledge, for nothing less than the nurturing and the growth of our conception of the world and ourselves may be at stake. We should focus on the structure of a scientific society as we do, and must, on the theoretical products of that group, for we shall learn more about what a reasonable society should be. There are risks of wasted efforts; but unless these tasks are antecedently and almost conclusively shown to lead to mire and misshaping of issues, we must embark on such ventures.

(Mustn't we?)

Notes

1: A FRAMEWORK FOR METHODS

1. This is the least understood of our reasons. No one has proposed a halfway interesting solution to the problem although very many have raised the issue from varied angles: Jay F. Rosenberg, *Linguistic Representation*, especially, pp. 142–145, and Larry Laudan, *Progress and its Problems*, pp. 223–225.

2. John Farley, *The Spontaneous Generation Controversy: From Descartes to Oparin*, chap. 2.

3. Joseph Agassi, *Towards an Historiography of Science*.

4. Imre Lakatos, "History of Science and Its Rational Reconstructions," *Philosophical Papers*, vol. 1. This view is now a commonplace. "It is the historian's intellectual—even moral—obligation not only to be self-conscious about the kind of norms he is applying, but also to see to it that he is utilizing the best available set of norms" (Larry Laudan, *Progress and its Problems*, p. 165). Of course, Lakatos regards the methodology of research programs as the best historiographical model, and Laudan would argue that the best model in question is his own, namely, the methodology of research traditions. A clear earlier statement of this position is found in Karl Popper; see below, chap. 4 n. 53.

5. Roy Porter, "The Industrial Revolution and the Rise of the Science of Geology."

6. Laudan, *Progress and Its Problems*, especially pp. 198, 208–209.

7. Imre Lakatos, "Rational reconstruction or internal history is primary, external history only secondary, since the most important problems of external history are defined by internal history," *Philosophical Papers* 1:118.

8. While the procedure is quite plausible in the area of ethics, it leads to quite incongruous results in the area of methodology. Even in methodology,

however, my objection is to the specific way in which such procedure is used, not with the procedure itself. In a later work, I shall use this procedure myself, based on different assumptions and aims. But a rather brief preview of it can be gleaned from the last chapter, Sec. III.

9. Lakatos, *Philosophical Papers*, 1:91.

10. Thomas S. Kuhn, *The Essential Tension*, pp. 272, 277.

11. Karl Popper, "Normal Science and Its Dangers," pp. 57–58.

12. Larry Laudan, "The Philosophy of *Progress*."

13. The title of one of his books should suffice: *Against Method*.

14. "Methodological rules are closely connected with other methodological rules. . . . But the connection is not strictly a deductive or logical one" (Karl Popper, *The Logic of Scientific Discovery*, p. 54).

15. David Miller, "Popper's Qualitative Theory of Verisimilitude," and Pavel Tichy, "On Popper's Definitions of Verisimilitude."

16. Imre Lakatos, *Philosophical Papers*, 1:33–34.

17. Imre Lakatos, "Replies To Critics," pp. 178, 180.

18. Hilary Putnam, *Meaning and the Moral Sciences*, p. 19.

19. Ibid., p. 20. But on this topic also see Karl Popper's unjustly neglected paper, "The Aim of Science," in *Objective Knowledge*, especially, pp. 197–202.

20. Putnam, *Meaning and the Moral Sciences*, p. 21.

21. See Michael Devitt's unsparing objections in his "Critical Notice," a review of Putnam's book, *Meaning and the Moral Sciences*, especially, pp. 396–399.

22. Larry Laudan, "A Confutation of Convergent Realism," especially pp. 33, 39. Parts of Laudan's paper are criticized in my "In Defence of Truth."

23. The objections against the Putnam-Kripke causal theory of reference are far too varied and far too numerous to list.

24. Charles Darwin espoused the method of Herschel and Whewell, while his avid supporter, Thomas Huxley, espoused the method of Mill. As is well known, Mill and Whewell clashed over the claim that consilience is the definitive mark of truth.

25. Problems of similar nature and complexity abound in philosophy. A stock problem in meta-ethics is to provide a way of determining the truth-conditions of ethical statements. But a more instructive comparison is with mathematical statements. Because the use of mathematics has led to remarkably successful scientific theories, we account for that success by assuming that mathematical statements are true. This in turn leads us to postulate mathematical entities and to worry over the conditions under which mathematical statements are true. Hartry Field has argued that this Quine-Putnam view can be dispensed with. There is no need to assume that mathematical statements are true, or that there are mathematical entities. In any event, invoking such entities brings forth the difficulty of explaining how we can have knowledge of such nonspatio-temporal entities since there can be no causal connection between them and ourselves.

Mathematical theories, so Field urges, can be good without being true, provided that they are conservative, that is, consistent with every internally consistent nominalistic theory. But, its conservativeness notwithstanding, mathematics is useful and efficacious since it aids in simplifying deductions. See Hartry Field, "Realism and Anti-Realism About Mathematics," and *Science Without Numbers.*

Is there a way of using Field's strategy to show the efficacy of methodological statements without assuming them to be true? Without asking what terms of a method refer and what do they refer to? Are methodological theories usually conservative? Are they theoretically dispensable, too?

26. Lakatos, *Philosophical Papers*, 1:52–53.

27. Popper has claimed that "there is no clash between my theory of non-induction and either rationality, or empiricism, or the procedure of science" (*Objective Knowledge*, p. 5). In Russell's words, which Popper quotes, on Hume's solution to the problem of induction, "*there is no intellectual difference between sanity and insanity*. The lunatic who believes that he is a poached egg is to be condemned solely on the ground that he is in a minority. . . ." But, unless Popper advocates that a severely tested theory is one we should rely on in the *future*, we see no intellectual difference between a sane man who accepts such a theory and an insane man who accepts the least corroborated theory.

So, it is unhelpful to be told by Popper that "there is no 'absolute reliance'; but since we have to choose, it will be 'rational' to choose the best-tested theory. This will be 'rational' in the most obvious sense of the word known to me: the best-tested theory is the one which, in the light of our *critical* discussion, appears to be the best so far, and I do not know of anything more 'rational' than a well-conducted critical discussion" (*Objective Knowledge*, p. 22). Both Hume and a sane man can readily grant that the critical discussion of a theory will tell us how it has fared in the *past*; but, Hume will argue that since the critical discussion, or the notion of corroboration, says nothing about the *future* performance of the theory, why should one not accept the *least* corroborated theory for practical purposes, rather than the theory with the highest degree of corroboration. On Popper's view, as on Hume's, the man who espouses the poorly tested theory will be condemned solely on the grounds that he is in a minority. Consequently, it is difficult to see why there is no clash between Popper's theory of non-induction and rationality.

For a recent cogent discussion, see Wesley Salmon's, "Rational Prediction." Putnam had raised similar objections earlier, but briefly, in "The 'Corroboration' of Theories," in *Philosophical Papers*, vol. 1, see especially pp. 251–252 and 268–269. For a defense against Putnam's other criticisms, see Karl Popper, *The Philosophy of Karl Popper*, pp. 993–999, and my paper, "Putnam's Schemata."

28. Adolf Grünbaum, "Can a Theory Answer More Questions than One of Its Rivals?"

29. Popper, *Objective Knowledge*, pp. 52–53.

30. See John Watkins, "Corroboration and the Problem of Content-Comparison," especially, pp. 360–363, among other responses to Grünbaum.

31. Thomas Kuhn, "Reflections on My Critics," p. 237.

32. "Some of the principles deployed in my explanation of science are irreducibly sociological, at least at this time" (ibid.). Recently, in his Foreword to Ludwik Fleck's *Genesis and Development of a Scientific Fact*, Kuhn wrote, "In 1950 and for some years thereafter I knew of no one else who saw in the history of

science what I was myself finding there. Very probably also, acquaintance with Fleck's text helped me to realize that the problems which concerned me had a fundamentally sociological dimension" (p. viii). But my view of Kuhn is not generally shared. For instance, see Ian Hacking's recent disclaimer in the introduction to his *Scientific Revolutions*, pp. 4–5.

33. Robert Nozick, *Anarchy, State, and Utopia*, p. 6.

34. E. R. Leach, *The Political Systems of Highland Burma*, p. 182.

35. Cited in Robert K. Merton, *The Sociology of Knowledge*, p. 17.

36. David Bloor, *Knowledge and Social Imagery*, especially, chaps. 5, 6.

37. Ludwik Fleck, *Genesis and Development of a Scientific Fact*, p. 116.

38. Ibid., p. 106.

39. Michael Ruse, *The Darwinian Revolution: Science Red in Tooth and Claw*, pp. 250–261; neither Ruse nor I subscribe to the view, and the example is only meant to illustrate it.

40. Popper, *Objective Knowledge*, p. 261. Of course, there is no guarantee that even a true theory would lead to our survival, for the theory may well lead us to conclude that our end is imminent.

41. I am under no illusion that to speak of a method as explaining the history of science is to speak perspicuously. I am merely paying lip-service to an ongoing, widely shared tradition which I shall criticize later, especially in chap. 4, sec. III-V.

42. Robert Nozick, *Anarchy, State, and Utopia*, pp. 7–8.

43. Ibid., p. 8.

44. Paul Feyerabend, *Against Method*, especially chaps. 6, 7.

45. In this connection it is quite interesting to note what Robert Stalnaker says in his paper, "A Theory of Conditionals," p. 178.

46. Nozick, *Anarchy, State, and Utopia*, pp. 28–30. Needless to add, the analogy is not perfect in all respects.

47. This account is indebted to Herbert Ginsburg and Sylvia Opper, *Piaget's Theory of Intellectual Development*, chap. 4.

48. Studying speech and hearing defects, Tadanobu Tsunoda arrived at an astonishing theory that Japanese brains function differently from Caucasian brains: this difference is accounted for not in terms of genetics or conditioning but rather in terms of the peculiarities of the Japanese language. One of the peculiarities is that the Japanese language, like the Polynesian language, is rich in vowels. The Japanese process vowels in only one hemisphere; they deal with all the vowels in the left hemisphere while Westerners handle isolated vowels in the right hemisphere. Tsunoda found that the language one learns as a child affects the way in which the two hemispheres of the brain develop their special talents. As a consequence, the Japanese psychological profile—they are less analytical, more emotional, and have a greater sense of harmony—is different from the profile of their Western counterpart. See Atuhiro Sibatani's, "The Japanese Brain."

It is tempting to speculate what changes or effects are marked in the brain by learning a specific scientific theory (language). How do these changes or effects channel and control subsequent behavior of the scientists, and what impact would this in turn have on the growth and development of science? What special talents of a hemisphere are inhibited or developed as a result of learning one theory rather than another.

49. See Ginsburg and Opper, *Piaget's Theory of Intellectual Development*, pp. 212–216.

50. As a complement to the present approach, see Alvin I. Goldman's useful article, "Epistemics: The Regulative Theory of Cognition."

2: POPPER'S THEORY OF METHOD

1. Karl Popper, *Conjectures and Refutations*, p. 137.

2. "Just as we may *seek* for absolutely true propositions in the realm of facts or at least for propositions which come nearer to the truth, so we may *seek* for absolutely right or valid proposals in the realm of standards—or at least for better, or more valid, proposals" (Karl Popper, *The Open Society and Its Enemies* 2:385–386).

3. Ibid., 2: 383.

4. Popper, *Conjectures and Refutations*, p. 136. Jonathan Barnes appears to share Popper's enthusiasm when he says, "The Presocratic philosophers had one common characteristic of supreme importance: they were rational" (*The Presocratic Philosophers*, vol. 1, *Thales to Zeno*, p. 4). But were they rational in Popper's sense, i.e., were they scientists who proposed falsifiable theories? Barnes's reply to that question is more cautious than Popper's; for instance, see pp. 4–5, 49–52. Also see the quite reasonable reservations expressed in F. M. Cornford's, "Was the Ionian Philosophy Scientific?" especially, pp. 30–31.

5. See Barnes, *The Presocratic Philosophers*, vol. 1, *From Thales to Zeno*, p. 24, where it is suggested that the Leibnizian Principle of Sufficient Reason was first proposed, if implicitly, by Anaximander.

6. Popper, *Conjectures and Refutations*, p. 127.

7. Popper is generally regarded as holding such a view on the basis of passages such as the following: "I shall require that the logical form of a scientific system shall be such that it can be singled out, by means of empirical tests, in a negative sense: it must be possible for an empirical scientific system to be refuted by experience" (Karl Popper, *The Logic of Scientific Discovery*, p. 41). Clearly, logical form, like consistency, is an objective property of a proposition. See also n. 20 below.

8. Popper, *Conjectures and Refutations*, p. 151.

9. Popper, *The Open Society and Its Enemies*, 1:62–63.

10. Ibid., p. 58.

11. Ibid., pp. 62–63.

12. Ibid., pp. 68–73.

13. Popper *does* speak of seeking. One should, of course, never claim to have found the absolutely right or valid proposal; see n. 2 above.

14. Popper, *The Open Society and Its Enemies*, 2:386.

15. Ibid., 1:23.

16. Ibid., p. 68.

17. Ibid., p. 62.

18. Karl Popper, *The Poverty of Historicism*, pp. 152–159.

19. Popper, *The Logic of Scientific Discovery*, p. 55.

20. But see, Adolf Grünbaum, "Is Freudian Psychoanalytical Theory Pseudo-Scientific By Karl Popper's Criterion of Demarcation?" Does the criticism against Popper stand if one invoked not merely the logical form of the theory to pronounce it scientific, but also took into account the neglected second-order tradition? See n. 7 above.

21. For some interesting details, see Clark Glymour, *Theory and Evidence*, pp. 91, 282–283.

22. Popper, *The Logic of Scientific Discovery*, p. 52.

23. See chap. 4, sec. I.

24. See chap. 4, sec. I.

25. Larry Laudan, "The Philosophy of *Progress*," sec. 3.3. Far from regarding the problem of demarcating scientific theories from metaphysical ones as a pseudoproblem, Laudan appears not only to recognize the problem but to embrace Popper's solution as well. That is, Laudan claims that the distinction between individual theories in a research tradition and that tradition itself is this: "individual theories constituting the tradition will generally be empirically testable for they will entail (in conjunction with other specific theories) some precise predictions about how objects in the domain will behave. By contrast, research traditions are neither explanatory, nor predictive, nor directly testable" (*Progress and Its Problems*, p. 81; also see, pp. 71–72). Why should this not be regarded as a Popperian way of distinguishing, with the help of the principle of testability or falsification, between a research tradition and the individual theories embedded in it? Why isn't Laudan's solution, even if non-Popperian, a solution to a genuine problem of demarcation?

26. Popper, *Conjectures and Refutations*, pp. 193–200.

27. Hilary Putnam, *Philosophical Papers* 1: 268, 270–304. Hilary Putnam, *Reason, Truth, and History*, pp. 106–108, 111, 124–126, 188–194, particularly the claim attributed to Arthur Burks on p. 192.

28. See John Watkins, "Between Analytic and Empirical." The dispute is only meant to illustrate my point.

29. Popper, *Conjectures and Refutations*, p. ix. My emphasis.

30. For the notion of progress, which concerns us here, among early scientists and philosophers, see E. R. Dodds, *The Ancient Concept of Progress and Other Essays on Greek Literature and Belief*, chap. 1.

31. Popper, *Conjectures and Refutations*, p. 151.

32. P. Schilpp, *The Philosophy of Karl Popper*, p. 978.

33. Popper, *Conjectures and Refutations*, p. 75 n. 16.

34. Karl Popper, "The Rationality of Scientific Revolutions," p. 89.

35. For a reluctant defense of Quine, see the interesting difficulty raised by Michael Hooker in his, "Peirce's Conception of Truth," pp. 132–133.

36. Popper, *The Logic of Scientific Discovery*, p. 37. My emphasis.

37. Ibid., p. 52.

38. Ibid.

39. Popper, *Conjectures and Refutations*, p. 314. My emphasis.

40. Ibid., p. 322.

41. Karl Popper, "Normal Science and Its Dangers," p. 57.

42. Popper, "The Rationality of Scientific Revolutions," p. 83. My emphasis.

43. Ibid., p. 88.

44. Ibid., p. 85.

45. Ibid. My emphasis.

46. Popper himself speaks of the possibility of "a bad idea inspiring many good ones"; see *Conjectures and Refutations*, p. 8.

47. See Popper, *Objective Knowledge*, especially, pp. 162–168.

48. Popper, *The Logic of Scientific Discovery*, p. 40. Also see *Objective Knowledge*, p. 193, where Popper says that some of his methodological proposals are "fully in keeping with the *actual practise* of the theoretical sciences." My emphasis.

49. P. Schilpp, *The Philosophy of Karl Popper*, p. 981.

50. Ibid., pp. 979, 984–985.

51. Ibid., pp. 1187–1188 n. 81.

52. Indeed, see ibid., p. 1026.

53. John Worrall, "The Ways in Which the Methodology of Scientific Research Programmes Improves on Popper's Methodology," pp. 46–47.

54. Popper, *The Logic of Scientific Discovery*, p. 52.

55. Thomas Kuhn, *The Structure of Scientific Revolutions*, pp. 64–73.

56. Brian Ellis, *Rational Belief Systems*, p. v.

57. Ibid., p. 12.

58. My illustration is deeply dependent on Steven Stanley's marvelous book, *The New Evolutionary Timetable*. I have also profited from parts of his more technical book, *Macroevolution: Pattern and Process*, and from the now-classic article by Niles Eldredge and Stephen Jay Gould, "Punctuated Equilibria: An Alternative to Phyletic Gradualism."

59. To get a balanced picture, what follows has to be read in conjunction at least with Secs. II and III of chap. 5.

60. Popper, *Objective Knowledge*, pp. 170–180.

61. Karl Popper and John Eccles, *The Self and Its Brain: An Argument for Interactionism*, p. 41.

62. David L. Hull, *Philosophy of Biological Sciences*, p. 49.

63. Popper, *The Logic of Scientific Discovery*, p. 54.

64. Or the chapter could have ended with the following remark of Popper's: "As an epistemologist I have only one interest—to find out the truth about the problems of epistemology" (*Conjectures and Refutations*, p. 6).

3: LAKATOS'S THEORY OF METHOD

1. Paul Feyerabend, "Problems of Empiricism," p. 277.
2. Thomas Kuhn, *The Structure of Scientific Revolutions*, p. 1.
3. Imre Lakatos, *Philosophical Papers*, vol. 1, chaps. 2, 3, respectively.
4. Ibid., p. 145.
5. Ibid., p. 144 n. 8.
6. Ibid., p. 102.

7. Quoted in Mary Hesse's, "Hermeticism and Historiography: An Apology for the Internal History of Science," pp. 136–137.

8. Quoted in ibid., pp. 139–140. I have also profited from reading Edward Rosen's, "Was Copernicus a Hermetist?" While we are alike in having borrowed our examples from others, we differ in the use to which we put these examples to work.

9. Lakatos, *Philosophical Papers* 1: 118, 119, 120, respectively.

10. Ibid., p. 125.

11. Ibid.

12. This is quite a genuine question, and not simply a rhetorical one. Lakatos *allows* inconsistent research programs. Would he also allow an inconsistent theory of method? An inconsistent historiographic model?

13. Imre Lakatos, "Replies to Critics," p. 179.

14. Ibid., pp. 179–180.

15. Heinz Post, "Novel Predictions as a Criterion of Merit," pp. 493–494. Indeed, at one point, Lakatos does speak of the basic value judgments of the "leading scientists" (*Philosophical Papers* 1:132).

16. Lakatos, *Philosophical Papers* 1: 134, 132, 114, respectively.

17. Richard Hall, "Can We Use the History of Science to Decide between Competing Methodologies?," p. 157.

18. Ibid., pp. 157–158.

19. Larry Laudan, *Progress and Its Problems*, p. 162. By implication, Ernan McMullin makes the same claim as do Hall and Laudan when he says, "The best methodology will thus be the one which goes furthest in reducing history of science to 'internal' history" (Ernan McMullin, "Philosophy of Science and Its Rational Reconstructions," p. 221).

20. Lakatos, *Philosophical Papers* 1:114, 134, 152 n. 4, respectively.

21. See pt. (II) of the solution in the appendix.

22. See pt. (I), and in particular pt. (III), of the solution in the appendix.

23. See pt. (I) (ii) of the solution in the appendix.

24. See pt. (III) (i) of the solution in the appendix.

25. Lakatos, *Philosophical Papers* 1:132.

26. Ibid.

27. Owsei Temkin, *The Double Face of Janus and Other Essays in the History of Medicine*, pp. 167–168; and Lynn White, jr., "The Ecology of Our Science," p. 75.

28. Paul Feyerabend, "On the Critique of Scientific Reason," p. 116; also see his paper, "In Defense of Aristotle: Comments on the Condition of Content Increase," pp. 162–164.

29. See p. 82, this volume.

30. White, "The Ecology of Our Science," pp. 75–76.

31. Ernan McMullin, "The History and Philosophy of Science: A Taxonomy," p. 33.

32. McMullin, "Philosophy of Science and Its Rational Reconstructions," pp. 225–226, 227–228.

33. Ibid., p. 226.

34. Lakatos, *Philosophical Papers*, 1: 133.

35. McMullin, "Philosophy of Science and Its Rational Reconstructions," p. 224.

36. Noretta Koertge, "Rational Reconstructions," pp. 359, 366, respectively.

37. Ibid., pp. 364, 365, respectively.

38. Garland Allen, *Life Science in the Twentieth Century*, p. 48.

39. Peter Hutchinson, *Evolution Explained*, pp. 69–72.

40. Allen, *Life Science in the Twentieth Century*, p. 48.

41. Koertge, "Rational Reconstructions," p. 366.

42. Thomas Kuhn argued (?) this long ago in *The Structure of Scientific Revolutions*, pp. 8–9, 207, and the distinction has been recently questioned by Hilary Putnam in *Reason, Truth, and History*, especially chap. 6.

43. Quoted in Gerald Holton, *The Scientific Imagination: Case Studies*, p. 272.

44. It is interesting to note that when earlier Koertge commented on Lakatos's "History of Science and Its Rational Reconstructions," she claimed that there were "serious shortcomings (in Lakatos's theory) when viewed as a comprehensive theory of scientific growth." Lakatos replied that these so-called shortcomings were in fact the virtues of his theory since he agreed with Popper's criticisms of the possibility of a (scientific) theoretical history ("Replies to Critics," p. 179). Koertge, in "Rational Reconstructions," merely repeats some of her earlier claims without answering Lakatos's earlier defense.

45. The following works proved useful: Frank Dawson Adams, *The Birth and Development of the Geological Sciences*; W. N. Edwards, "Robert Hooke as Geologist and Evolutionist," pp. 96–97; Sir Archibald Geikie, *The Founders of Geology*; John C. Greene, *The Death of Adam*; and, A. P. Rossiter, "Hooke as Geologist," p. 455.

46. This chapter is a much expanded and thoroughly revised version of a crude earlier paper which appeared under the title, "Imre Lakatos' Meta-Methodology: An Appraisal." I am grateful to the publisher for allowing me to use that paper.

4: LAUDAN'S THEORY OF METHOD

1. Larry Laudan, *Progress and Its Problems*.

2. R. Collingwood, *The Idea of History*, p. 283, and *The Principles of Art*, p. 164f. These are Popper's own references in his acknowledgment to Collingwood (see Karl Popper, *Objective Knowledge*, pp. 186–187n, 167, respectively). Of course, their manner of treating problems is vastly different as, for instance, in their theory of understanding.

3. Thus, see Karl Popper, *The Logic of Scientific Discovery*, especially the one-page Preface to the First Edition, 1934, and pp. 15, 16, 22. It is evident that the idea of problems dominates *Objective Knowledge* more than it does *Conjectures and Refutations*. While compared to the latter, its role in *The Logic of Scientific Discovery* is not nearly as central.

4. Karl Popper, *Conjectures and Refutations*, p. 222. Also, Popper, *Objective Knowledge*, pp. 287–288.

5. Popper, *Objective Knowledge*, p. 177.

6. Ibid., p. 170.

7. "The growth of knowledge—or the learning process—is not a repetitive or cumulative process but one of error elimination. It is Darwinian selection, rather than Lamarckian instruction. This is a brief description of epistemology from an objective point of view. . . . But although it describes the growth of the third world, it can be interpreted as a description of biological evolution. *Animals, and plants, are problem-solvers*. And they solve their problems by the method of competitive tentative solutions and the elimination of error" (Popper, *Objective Knowledge*, pp. 144–145). My emphasis.

8. Hilary Putnam, *Meaning and the Moral Sciences*, p. 20.

9. Popper, *Objective Knowledge*, p. 192.

10. Laudan, *Progress and Its Problems*, p. 127.

11. David Miller, "Popper's Qualitative Theory of Verisimilitude," and Pavel Tichy, "On Popper's Definitions of Verisimilitude." Curiously, neither is mentioned by Laudan. I learn from J. N. Hattiangadi's paper, "The Structure of Problems," Part I, pp. 346–347, that as early as 1970, Carl Hempel had already proved that the notion of verisimilitude was severely problematic and incoherent. Hattiangadi's paper emphasizes the role of problems as much as does Laudan without, I think, being susceptible to the kind of objections that confront Laudan's method. It would be quite useful to compare the two rival approaches.

12. David Miller, "The Accuracy of Predictions."

13. In particular, see Laudan, *Progress and its Problems*, chaps. 5, 6.

14. Ibid., pp. 16–17. Some of the examples are my own.

15. I adopt Popper's ontology to facilitate making the point; see Popper, *Objective Knowledge*, especially, pp. 116, 118.

16. Laudan, *Progress and Its Problems*, p. 17.

17. Ibid., pp. 22–23.

18. Ibid., p. 25.

19. Ibid.

20. Larry Laudan, "The Philosophy of *Progress*," sec. I.

21. Laudan, *Progress and Its Problems*, p. 17.

22. Ibid., pp. 19–20. This is clearly an overstatement. It *may* be plausible about interesting cases like Trembly's polyp (*Chlorohydra viridissima*), which refused to be pigeon-holed into the then generally accepted classification of things into animal, plant, and mineral. It is scarcely true of every unsolved problem posed, for instance, by the motion of projectiles, fossils, composition of stars, and so on.

23. Ibid., p. 21.

24. Ibid., p. 68.

25. Ibid.

26. I revert to Laudan's way of speaking: theories entail statements of problems.

27. Laudan, *Progress and Its Problems*, p. 30.

28. Such a claim has been made by D. H. Mellor in his paper, "Some Problems about Solving Problems"; it is also a claim that is obvious for Popper to make.

29. Laudan, "The Philosophy of *Progress*."

30. Popper, *Objective Knowledge*, p. 22. Indeed, in the recently added app. 2 of his book, Popper says, in response to the difficulty of content comparison, that content should be relativized to the *relevant* problems, that is, to problems regarded as relevant by practicing scientists. Clearly, only a finite number of problems can be considered in such a case.

31. This was pointed out to me by David Miller. However, such an objection can be made against Popper, too. Has the latter given us a way of individuating severe tests? If not, how shall we measure the degree of corroboration of a theory, given that the degree of corroboration is defined in terms of the number of severe tests a theory has passed?

32. This was, of course, a very significant problem that was solved by Lord Rayleigh. As a matter of fact, the law is called, 'Lord Rayleigh's blue-sky law.'

33. For instance, D. H. Mellor, "Some Problems about Solving Problems," pp. 525–526.

34. Laudan, "The Philosophy of *Progress*," p. 545 n. 7.

35. Laudan, *Progress and Its Problems*, p. 109.

36. The situation is really much worse than I portray it: unlike Laudan (*Progress and Its Problems*, pp. 19–20), T^* is no respecter of scientific boundaries or domains, and will single-mindedly 'solve' problems in atomic physics, sociobiology, medicine, and so on.

37. It is important that theories be consistent. Consider T^* and T, where the former is inconsistent and the latter is consistent and complete. They both solve every problem, by hypothesis, but the problem-solving effectiveness of T^* is zero while that of T is greater than zero.

38. Laudan, *Progress and Its Problems*, p. 162.

39. Except for very minor changes, this section is similar to my paper, "Truth, Problem-Solving, and Methodology," and I gratefully acknowledge the permission of the publisher to use it here. Laudan, among others, has responded to it, and my reply can be found in "The Defence of Truth." If I have not altered the text to take account of the exchange, it is in the belief that the views expressed in this section are still essentially correct.

40. Laudan, *Progress and Its Problems*, p. 158. For a similar distinction see Imre Lakatos, *Philosophical Papers* 1:121 n. 1; also, Henry Guerlac, *Essays and Papers in the History of Modern Science*, p. 27.

41. Laudan, *Progress and Its Problems*, p. 160.

42. Ibid.

43. Laudan says that "it is a *necessary condition* of any acceptable model of rationality that it square with (at least some of) our PIs" (ibid., pp. 160–161). My emphasis. It is unfortunate, therefore, that Laudan does not show precisely and clearly how the methodology of research traditions squares with even *one* of the aforementioned PIs. Could it be that these are only *sufficient conditions* after all?

But it, too, does not settle the question whether the PIs are jointly or individually sufficient.

44. Laudan, *Progress and Its Problems*, p. 161.

45. Ibid.

46. This is the view adopted by Gerhard Wichler in his *Charles Darwin*, especially, pp. 50–57.

47. Ernst Mayr, "Lamarck Revisited," in *Evolution and the Diversity of Life: Selected Essays*, pp. 241–242.

48. For two other examples of where Lamarck flip-flopped, see Michael Ruse, *The Darwinian Revolution: Science Red in Tooth and Claw*, pp. 6, 7.

49. For a strong pro-Lamarckian view, see H. Graham Cannon's *Lamarck and Modern Genetics*. Between the two extreme views on Lamarck represented by Cannon and Wichler (see n. 46), respectively, is a superb, well-balanced, and wide-ranging work on Lamarck by Richard W. Burkhardt, Jr. entitled, *The Spirit of System*; see especially chap. 6.

50. Laudan, *Progress and Its Problems*, p. 165.

51. Ibid., p. 185. It is a measure of the tenacity of the classical theory of explanation that even Laudan falls prey to it. On his own view, (1) will express a law, (2) and (3) will express initial conditions, and the conclusion will describe the event, action, or decision to be explained.

52. Ibid., p. 186.

53. "It is the historian's intellectual—even moral—obligation not only to be self-conscious about the kinds of norms he is applying, but also to see to it that he is utilizing the best available set of norms. How can he make that choice? By accepting that model of rationality (or perhaps those models if we can find more than one satisfying the appropriate conditions) which does the greatest justice to our PIs about HOS_1" (ibid., p. 165).

Ever since Popper suggested the zero-method, philosophers of science have proposed various doctrines as variants on that method. Popper claimed that in most social situations there is an element of rationality involved. If an agent was perfectly rational, he would make optimal use of all available information to attain whatever goals he has. Nearly always, however, an act of the agent will fall short of ideal or complete rationality. By the zero-method Popper meant, "the method of constructing a model on the assumption of complete rationality (and perhaps also on the assumption of the possession of complete information) on the part of all individuals concerned, and estimating the deviation of the actual behaviour of the people from the model behaviour, using the latter as a kind of zero-coordinate" (*Poverty of Historicism*, p. 141). What cannot be accounted for on the basis of the zero-method must be explained on the basis of causes, such as the influence of traditional prejudice (Popper's example). Lakatos, of course, made an analogous claim for the historiography of science, as does Laudan now. However, Laudan's view is more interesting and more fully developed than any other view I am familiar with.

54. Laudan, *Progress and Its Problems*, p. 187.

55. Ibid., p. 188.

56. Ibid.

57. Ibid., p. 202.

58. Ibid., p. 200. To determine the candidates, Laudan urges that cognitive sociologists of knowledge use the best model of rationality, namely, his own.

59. My example leans heavily on Clifford M. Will's, "Gravitation Theory," and I am grateful to him for checking my illustration.

60. Popper, *Objective Knowledge*, p. 176.

61. Edward Grant, *Physical Science in the Middle Ages*, pp. 13–15.

62. Imre Lakatos, *Philosophical Papers* 1:114.

63. Robert S. Westman, "Three Responses to the Copernican Theory: Johannes Praetorius, Tycho Brahe, and Michael Maestlin," p. 339.

64. Ibid., p. 303, but also see pp. 314–315 n. 69.

65. Thomas Kuhn, *The Copernican Revolution: Planetary Astronomy in the Development of Western Thought*, p. 71.

66. The dispute between instrumentalists and realists was far from being a mere metaphysical quibble, especially in the context of astronomy. *The metaphysical position adopted profoundly affected and influenced the decision whether to accept an astronomical model or not*. Pierre Duhem's *To Save the Phenomena* is still the single best piece illustrating the remark of this note.

67. Laudan, *Progress and Its Problems*, p. 130.

68. Paul Feyerabend, *Science in a Free Society*, p. 41.

69. Laudan, *Progress and Its Problems*, pp. 158–159. Here Laudan is arguing against Ronald Giere, who thought that such a distinction may prove fruitful and who claimed plausibly that it is the recent history of science (history of quantum mechanics, molecular biology, and contemporary psychology) that ought to be used as a yardstick for measuring methods. I am unclear what Giere's arguments are to support this claim. My own view of the matter can be found in the next chapter (see especially Secs. II, III).

70. Laudan, *Progress and Its Problems*, p. 203.

71. Ibid., p. 187.

72. Ibid., p. 170. Also see, pp. 79, 92, 124, 128, 187.

73. Gerd Buchdahl, "History of Science and Criteria of Choice," pp. 204–230.

74. At this point, I urge the reader to consult, and keep in mind, the chart in the chapter on Popper; see p. 43.

75. I am indebted to Henry Frankel's, "The Paleobiogeographical Debate Over the Problem of Disjunctively Distributed Life Forms," pp. 211–259.

76. Gustav Scherz, "Stensen, Niels," pp. 32–33.

77. Laudan, *Progress and Its Problems*, p. 113.

78. Ibid., pp. 112–113.

79. Ibid., p. 109.

80. "*Research traditions are neither explanatory, nor predictive, nor directly testable*. Their very generality, as well as their normative elements, precludes them from leading to detailed accounts of specific natural processes. It is for just this reason that the objective evaluation of any research tradition is crucially linked with the problem-solving process. The very idea that an entity like a research tradition could be objectively evaluated may seem paradoxical. But nothing could be further from the case, for we can say quite simply that a successful research tradition is one which leads, via its component theories, to the

adequate solutions of an increasing range of empirical and conceptual problems" (ibid., p. 81–82).

81. Ibid., pp. 83–84.

82. Ibid., p. 83.

83. Paul Feyerabend, *Against Method*, pp. 185–186.

84. Laudan, *Progress and Its Problems*, p. 107.

85. In short, Laudan has failed to make "explicit what has been implicitly described in scientific usage as 'promise' or 'fecundity' " (ibid., p. 112).

86. Ibid., pp. 112, 114–118.

87. For the real progenitor of the principle of proliferation, see Popper's conjecture in P. Schilpp, *The Philosophy of Karl Popper*, p. 1187, n. 80.

88. Laudan, *Progress and Its Problems*, p. 113.

89. Thomas Kuhn, *The Essential Tension*, pp. 325–326.

5: ALTERNATIVE PROPOSAL

1. John Worrall, "Thomas Young and the 'refutation' of Newtonian Optics," pp. 163–164. Worrall's view is shared by a large majority of philosophers. Here is a passage from John Watkins's forthcoming book: "I personally hold that while a methodologist or philosopher of science may have something worthwhile to say about the comparative appraisal of the products of scientific research, it is not his business to advise scientists how to go about their research. In particular, it is not for him to tell them what they should or should not work on. I personally find the idea that a methodology should give heuristic advice rather ridiculous, a partial reversion to the exploded idea of scientific method as an organon of discovery; I liken it to the idea that it is the business of art critics to give painters advice on how to paint good pictures." A far more detailed defense of the thesis that the proper function of a method is not only to appraise theories but also to yield heuristic advice is contained in my paper, "Methodological Appraisals, Advice, and Historiographical Models" (Copyright © 1980 by D. Reidel Publishing Company, Dordrecht, Holland). I am grateful to the publisher for allowing me to use a small, revised portion of that article here.

2. I cite Williams only because he *seems* to come as close as anyone has ever come in recent years to claiming that scientific methods are algorithmic devices which, when correctly applied, produce scientific theories; see Bernard Williams, *Descartes: The Project of Pure Inquiry*, especially, pp. 38–39, 42–43, 45–46.

3. A. C. Crombie, *Augustine To Galileo* 1: 147–148.

4. Susan Kelly, "Gilbert, William," p. 397.

5. A. C. Crombie, "Grosseteste's Position in the History of Science," p. 101. The theme of this paragraph is central to Crombie's book, *Robert Grosseteste and the Origins of Experimental Science*.

6. See, for instance, nearly all the articles in *Method and Appraisal in the Physical Sciences: The Critical Background to Modern Science, 1800–1905*, Colin Howson, ed.

7. David Bohm, *Causality and Chance in Modern Physics*, p. 68.

8. A. C. Crombie, "The Significance of Medieval Discussions of Scientific Method for the Scientific Revolution," pp. 95–96.

9. I. E. Drabkin, "Commentary on the Papers of A. C. Crombie and Joseph T. Clark," p. 143.

10. Ibid., p. 147.

11. A. C. Crombie, *Augustine to Galileo* 2: 47, 75–79.

12. Edward Grant, *Physical Science in the Middle Ages*, p. 34.

13. For details, see chap. 1, pp. 8–12.

14. See chap. 1, pp. 12–14; chap. 2, pp. 58–62.

15. On the classical view, the truth of a mathematical statement is dependent on an objective mathematical reality, a reality we discover and conjecture about. However, whether such a statement is true or not can be known experimentally or a posteriori. But our ability to know that statement experimentally would not in itself make the logical status of a mathematical statement empirical; see Saul A. Kripke, *Naming and Necessity*, pp. 35–37, 159. Analogously, the truth of a normative statement, encased in a statement of heuristic advice, is dependent on an objective methodological reality—a reality partly defined by the prevailing methodological tradition and problem-situation. Our ability to know its truth-value experimentally is not sufficient to render the logical status of such a methodological statement empirical.

16. The point is not exegetical. Any method failing to give heuristic advice is already shown to be very weak. Therefore, it is more constructive and interesting to consider these methods *as if* they gave such advice. We can then have an additional way of evaluating them.

17. See Richard Nisbett and Lee Ross, *Human Inference: Strategies and Shortcomings of Social Judgment*, for numerous examples and experiments.

18. John Rawls, *A Theory of Justice*, p. 48. My emphasis.

19. Stephen P. Stich and Richard E. Nisbett, "Justification and the Psychology of Human Reasoning," p. 201. See how odd this analysis appears when it is applied in the realm of ethics.

20. Ibid.

21. Nor is the suggestion new; see Thomas S. Kuhn, *The Structure of Scientific Revolutions*, pp. 93–94.

22. Ludwig Wittgenstein, *Remarks on the Foundations of Mathematics*, p. 44e. See especially pars. 142–151.

23. Hilary Putnam, *Philosophical Papers* 2: 228.

24. For the principle of parity and the discussion leading up to it, see pp. 122–125.

25. Robert Nozick, *Anarchy, State, and Utopia*, pp. 212–213.

26. See chap. 1, pp. 22–26.

27. I earnestly hope that when the issues relating to group rationality in science are more fully discussed and explored that social and political philosophy will benefit, too, from *its* new results and researches. One branch of philosophy will then have paid its debt to another branch. I gratefully acknowledge the permission of the publisher to use here my paper, "A Theory of Group Rationality."

28. Rawls, *A Theory of Justice*, p. 54.

29. Ibid., p. 55.

30. Ibid., p. 3.

31. Kenneth Schaffner, "Outlines of a Logic of Comparative Theory Evaluation with Special Attention to Pre- and Post-Relativistic Electrodynamics," pp. 311–373.

32. Imre Lakatos, *Philosophical Papers* 1: 55–68.

33. For a theory of what constitutes the rationality of a scientist and how his individual decisions are to be explained, see particularly chap. 4 Secs. III and IV.

34. Several others could be listed: racial senescence; an intrinsic depletion of genetic vigor; extrinsic causes such as epizootics and trace element concentration changes; metastasy (movement of the entire crust of the earth as a unit over the mantle) causing large-scale environmental and climatic changes; transgressions and regressions of epeiric seas; see Luis W. Alvarez et al., "Extraterrestrial Cause for the Cretaceous-Tertiary Extinction," and John F. Simpson, "Evolutionary Pulsations and Geomagnetic Polarity."

35. Karl Popper, *Objective Knowledge*, pp. 13, 15, 22; also, Karl Popper, *The Logic of Scientific Discovery*, pp. 49–50, 53–54, 55 n. 3.

36. Larry Laudan, *Progress and Its Problems*, p. 109.

37. Ibid., p. 111.

38. Ibid., p. 113. Some of the criticisms of Laudan have been repeated for the sake of continuity and completeness.

39. David C. Lindberg, "The Science of Optics," pp. 341–342.

40. Ibid., p. 342. My emphasis. What follows relies heavily on the work of Lindberg, especially on his *Theories of Vision from Al-Kindi to Kepler*.

41. Owsei Temkin, *The Double Face of Janus and Other Essays in the History of Medicine*, pp. 138–139, 147. It is clear that the leech belonged to a distinct, but inferior, group of practitioners; what Temkin leaves unclear is why he was called "leech."

42. Owsei Temkin, *Galenism: Rise and Decline of a Medical Philosophy*, pp. 31–32. This illustration is indebted to the works of Temkin cited here and in the preceding note.

43. Paul Feyerabend, *Against Method*, p. 18 n. 5.

44. Karl Popper, *Conjectures and Refutations*, p. ix.

45. This was voiced by Philip Quinn.

46. Nozick emphasizes our intuitions about individual or micro situations, unlike Rawls who claims that his principles of justice are applicable only to macro situations, namely, the basic structure of society; hence, micro situations cannot be cited as counterinstances to the Rawlsian difference principle (Robert Nozick, *Anarchy, State, and Utopia*, pp. 204–205). I suppose it is the way with intuitions: the stronger ones tend to dominate the weaker ones *and* our theories. This is no reason to give in. A larger picture may enhance the detail and make it more engaging. Attempting to draw such a picture may also be the only way in which our weak intuitions may cease to be weak. Translated: a view of group

rationality, admittedly based on (for the moment) toddling intuitions, can enhance and deepen our view of the particular cases of individual rationality.

47. "Recipes for the Good Society," writes Martin Hollis, as he begins his book, *Models of Man*, "used to run, in caricature, something like this—

(1) Take about 2000 hom. sap., dissect each into essence and accidents and discard the accidents.
(2) Place essences in a large casserole, add socializing syrup and stew until conflict disappears.
(3) Serve with a pinch of salt.

Such recipes have produced many classic dishes in political theory." However, Hollis in this delightful opening of his book is not as skeptical about theorizing about the Good Society as he is about trying to do it without some clear and cogent conception of human nature. Two pages later, he says, "Every social theory needs a metaphysic, I shall contend, in which a model of man and a method of science complement each other." I am contending that what is true of the needs of a social theory is true of the needs of a theory of a Good Society, Just Society, or an Ideal Scientific Society—or a society that comes to be all three so far as is possible.

48. See chap. 1, n. 1, and the text corresponding to it.

49. Francis Bacon, *New Atlantis*, pp. 129–137.

Bibliography

Adams, Frank Dawson. *The Birth and Development of the Geological Sciences*. New York: Dover Publications, 1954.

Agassi, Joseph. *Towards an Historiography of Science. History and Theory*. Supplement 2. Middletown: Wesleyan University Press, 1967.

Allen, Garland. *Life Science in the Twentieth Century*. Cambridge: Cambridge University Press, 1978.

Alvarez, Luis, et al. "Extraterrestrial Cause for the Cretaceous-Tertiary Extinction." *Science* 208, no. 4448 (June 1980): 1095–1108.

Bacon, Francis. *New Atlantis*. In *The World's Great Classics: Ideal Commonwealths*, rev. ed., vol. 33. New York: The Colonial Press, 1901.

Barnes, Jonathan. *The Presocratic Philosophers*. Vol. 1. *Thales to Zeno*. London: Routledge & Kegan Paul, 1979.

Bloor, David. *Knowledge and Social Imagery*. London: Routledge & Kegan Paul, 1976.

Bohm, David. *Causality and Chance in Modern Physics*. Philadelphia: University of Pennsylvania Press, 1957.

Buchdahl, Gerd. "History of Science and Criteria of Choice." In *Historical and Philosophical Perspectives of Science*, edited by Roger H. Stuewer, pp. 204–230. Minneapolis: University of Minnesota Press, 1970.

Burkhardt, Richard W., Jr. *The Spirit of System*. Cambridge: Harvard University Press, 1977.

Cannon, H. Graham. *Lamarck and Modern Genetics*. Westport: Greenwood Press, 1975.

Collingwood, R. *The Idea of History*. Oxford: Clarendon Press, 1966.

———. *The Principles of Art*. Oxford: Clarendon Press, 1965.

Cornford, F. M. "Was the Ionian Philosophy Scientific?" In *Studies In Presocratic*

Philosophy. Vol. 1. *The Beginnings of Philosophy*, edited by David J. Furley and R. E. Allen. New York: Humanities Press, 1970.

Crombie, A. C. *Augustine to Galileo*, 2d rev. and enlarged ed., vols. 1, 2. Cambridge: Harvard University Press, 1979.

———. "The Significance of Medieval Discussions of Scientific Method for the Scientific Revolution." In *Critical Problems in the History of Science*, edited by Marshall Clagett, pp. 97–101. Madison: The University of Wisconsin Press, Ltd., 1969.

———. "Grosseteste's Position in the History of Science." In *Robert Grosseteste: Scholar and Bishop*, edited by D. A. Callus. Oxford: Clarendon Press, 1953.

———. *Robert Grosseteste and the Origins of Experimental Science, 1100–1700*. Oxford: Clarendon Press, 1953.

Devitt, Michael. "Critical Notice." *Australasian Journal of Philosophy* 58, no. 4 (December 1980): 395–404.

Dodds, E. R. *The Ancient Concept of Progress and Other Essays on Greek Literature and Belief*. Clarendon: Oxford University Press, 1973.

Drabkin, I. E. "Commentary on the Papers of A. C. Crombie and Joseph T. Clark." In *Critical Problems in the History of Science*, edited by Marshall Clagett, pp. 141–152. Madison: The University of Wisconsin Press, Ltd., 1969.

Duhem, Pierre. *To Save the Phenomena: An Essay on the Ideal of Physical Theory from Plato to Galileo*. Chicago: The University of Chicago Press, 1969.

Edwards, W. N. "Robert Hooke as Geologist and Evolutionist." *Nature* 137, no. 3455 (January 18, 1936): 96–97.

Eldredge, Niles, and Gould, Stephen Jay. "Punctuated Equilibria: An Alternative to Phyletic Gradualism." In *Models in Paleobiology*, edited by Thomas J. M. Schopf. San Francisco: Freeman, Cooper and Co., 1972.

Ellis, Brian David. *Rational Belief Systems*. New Jersey: Rowman and Littlefield, 1979.

Farley, John. *The Spontaneous Generation Controversy: From Descartes to Oparin*. Baltimore: The Johns Hopkins University Press, 1977.

Feyerabend, Paul. "In Defence of Aristotle: Comments on the Condition of Content Increase." In *Progress and Rationality in Science*, edited by Gerard Radnitzky and Gunnar Andersson, pp. 143–180. Dordrecht: D. Reidel Publishing Co., 1978.

———. *Science in a Free Society*. London: NLB, 1978.

———. "On the Critique of Scientific Reason." In *Essays in Memory of Imre Lakatos*, edited by R. S. Cohen et al., pp. 109–143. Dordrecht: D. Reidel Publishing Co., 1976.

———. "Problems of Emipiricism." In *The Nature and Function of Scientific Theories*, edited by Robert Colodny, pp. 275–353. Pittsburgh: University of Pittsburgh Press, 1970.

Field, Hartry. "Realism and Anti-Realism about Mathematics." Manuscript.

———. *Science Without Numbers*. Princeton: Princeton University Press, 1980.

Fleck, Ludwik. *Genesis and Development of a Scientific Fact*. Chicago: The University of Chicago Press, 1979.

Frankel, Henry. "The Paleobiogeographical Debate over the Problem of Disjunctively Distributed Life Forms." *Studies in History and Philosophy of Science* 12, no. 3 (September 1981): 211–259.

Geikie, Sir Archibald. *The Founders of Geology*. London: Macmillan and Co., 1905.

Ginsburg, Herbert, and Opper, Sylvia. *Piaget's Theory of Intellectual Development*. Englewood Cliffs, N. J.: Prentice Hall, Inc., 1969.

Glymour, Clark. *Theory and Evidence*. Princeton: Princeton University Press, 1980.

Goldman, Alvin I. "Epistemics: The Regulative Theory of Cognition." *The Journal of Philosophy* 75, no. 10 (October 1978): 509–523.

Goodman, Nelson. *Fact, Fiction, and Forecast*. Cambridge: Harvard University Press, 1955.

Grant, Edward. *Physical Science in the Middle Ages*. Cambridge: Cambridge University Press, 1977.

Greene, John C. *The Death of Adam*. Ames: The Iowa State University Press, 1959.

Grünbaum, Adolf. "Is Freudian Psychoanalytic Theory Pseudo-Scientific By Karl Popper's Criterion of Demarcation?" *American Philosophical Quarterly* 16, no. 2 (April 1979): 131–141.

———. "Can a Theory Answer More Questions than One of Its Rivals?" *The British Journal for the Philosophy of Science* 27, no. 1 (March 1976): 1–23.

Guerlac, Henry. *Essays and Papers in the History of Modern Science*. Baltimore: The Johns Hopkins University Press, 1977.

Hacking, Ian, ed. *Scientific Revolutions: Oxford Readings in Philosophy*. Oxford: Oxford University Press, 1981.

Hall, Richard. "Can We Use the History of Science to Decide Between Competing Methodologies?" In *PSA 1970: In Memory of Rudolf Carnap*, edited by Roger C. Buck et al., pp. 151–159. Dordrecht: D. Reidel Publishing Co., 1971.

Hattiangadi, J. N. "The Structure of Problems, Part I." *Philosophy of the Social Sciences* 8, no. 4 (December 1978): 345–365.

———. "The Structure of Problems, Part II." *Philosophy of the Social Sciences* 9, no. 1 (March 1979): 49–76.

Hesse, Mary. "Hermeticism and Historiography: An Apology for the Internal History of Science." In *Historical and Philosophical Perspectives of Science*, edited by Roger H. Stuewer, pp. 134–162. Minneapolis: University of Minnesota Press, 1970.

Hollis, Martin. *Models of Man*. Cambridge: Cambridge University Press, 1977.

Holton, Gerald. *The Scientific Imagination: Case Studies*. Cambridge: Cambridge University Press, 1978.

Hooker, Michael. "Peirce's Conception of Truth." In *The Philosophy of Wilfrid Sellars: Queries and Extensions*, edited by Joseph C. Pitt. Boston: D. Reidel Publishing Co., 1978.

Howson, Colin, ed. *Method and Appraisal in the Physical Sciences: The Critical Background to Modern Science, 1800–1905*. Cambridge: Cambridge University Press, 1976.

Hull, David. *Philosophy of Biological Science*. Englewood Cliffs, N. J.: Prentice Hall, Inc., 1974.

Hutchinson, Peter. *Evolution Explained*. London: David & Charles, 1974.

Kelly, Susan. "Gilbert, William." In *Dictionary of Scientific Biography*, edited by Charles Coulston Gillispie, 5: 396–401. New York: Charles Scribner's Sons, 1972.

Koertge, Noretta. "Rational Reconstructions." In *Essays in Memory of Imre Lakatos*, edited by R. S. Cohen et al., pp. 359–369. Dordrecht: D. Reidel Publishing Co., 1976.

Kripke, Saul A. *Naming and Necessity*. Cambridge: Harvard University Press, 1980.

Kuhn, Thomas S. *The Essential Tension: Selected Studies in Scientific Tradition and Change*. Chicago: The University of Chicago Press, 1977.

———. "Notes on Lakatos." In *PSA 1970: In Memory of Rudolf Carnap*, edited by Roger C. Buck et al., pp. 137–146. Dordrecht: D. Reidel Publishing Co., 1971.

———"Reflections on My Critics." In *Criticism and the Growth of Knowledge*, edited by Imre Lakatos and Alan Musgrave. Cambridge: Cambridge University Press, 1970.

———. *The Structure of Scientific Revolutions*, 2d ed., enlarged. Chicago: The University of Chicago Press, 1970.

———. *The Copernican Revolution: Planetary Astronomy in the Development of Western Thought*. Cambridge: Harvard University Press, 1957.

Lakatos, Imre. *Philosophical Papers*. Vol. 1. Edited by John Worrall and Gregory Currie. Cambridge: Cambridge University Press, 1978.

———. "Replies to Critics." In *PSA 1970: In Memory of Rudolf Carnap*, edited by Roger C. Buck et al., pp. 171–182. Dordrecht: D. Reidel Publishing Co., 1971.

Laudan, Larry. "A Confutation of Convergent Realism." *Philosophy of Science* 48, no. 1 (March 1981): 19–49.

———. "The Philosophy of *Progress*." In *PSA 1978*, vol. 2, edited by Ian Hacking. East Lansing: Philosophy of Science Association, 1981.

———. *Progress and Its Problems: Towards a Theory of Scientific Growth*. Berkeley, Los Angeles, London: University of California Press, 1977.

Leach, E. R. *The Political Systems of Highland Burma*. London: Bell, 1954.

Lindberg, David C. "The Science of Optics." In *Science in the Middle Ages*, edited by David C. Lindberg. Chicago: The University of Chicago Press, 1978.

———. *Theories of Vision from Al-Kindi to Kepler*. Chicago: The University of Chicago Press, 1976.

McMullin, Ernan. "Philosophy of Science and Its Rational Reconstructions." In *Progress and Rationality in Science*, edited by Gerard Radnitzky and Gunnar Andersson, pp. 221–252. Dordrecht: D. Reidel Publishing Co., 1978.

——— "The History and Philosophy of Science: A Taxonomy." In *Historical and Philosophical Perspectives of Science*, edited by Roger H. Stuewer, pp. 12–67. Minneapolis: University of Minnesota Press, 1970.

Mayr, Ernst. *Evolution and the Diversity of Life: Selected Essays*. Cambridge: Harvard University Press, 1976.

Mellor, D. H. "Some Problems about Solving Problems" In *PSA 1978*, vol. 2, edited by Ian Hacking. East Lansing: Philosophy of Science Association, 1981.

Merton, Robert K. *The Sociology of Science: Theoretical and Experimental Investigations*. Chicago: The University of Chicago Press, 1973.

Miller, David. "The Accuracy of Predictions." *Synthese* 30, nos. 1/2 (February/March 1975): 159–191.

———"Popper's Qualitative Theory of Verisimilitude." *The British Journal for the Philosophy of Science* 25, no. 2 (June 1974): 166–177.

Nisbett, Richard, and Ross, Lee. *Human Inference: Strategies and Shortcomings of Social Judgment*. Englewood Cliffs, N. J.: Prentice Hall, Inc., 1980.

Nozick, Robert. *Anarchy, State, and Utopia*. New York: Basic Books, Inc., Publishers, 1974.

Popper, Karl. *Objective Knowledge: An Evolutionary Approach*, rev. ed. Oxford: Clarendon Press, 1979.

———. "The Rationality of Scientific Revolutions." In *Problems of Scientific Revolution: Progress and Obstacles to Progress in the Sciences; The Herbert Spencer Lectures 1973*, edited by Rom Harré. Oxford: Clarendon Press, 1975.

———. "Normal Science and Its Dangers." In *Criticism and the Growth of Knowledge*, edited by Imre Lakatos and Alan Musgrave, pp. 51–58. Cambridge: Cambridge University Press, 1970.

———. *Conjectures and Refutations: The Growth of Scientific Knowledge*. New York: Harper & Row, 1968.

———. *The Open Society and Its Enemies*, vols. 1 and 2. London: Routledge & Kegan Paul, 1962.

———. *The Poverty of Historicism*. New York: Harper & Row, 1961.

———. *The Logic of Scientific Discovery*. New York: Harper Torchbooks, 1959.

Popper, Karl, and Eccles, John C. *The Self and Its Brain: An Argument for Interactionism*. New York: Springer International, 1977.

Porter, Roy. "The Industrial Revolution and the Rise of the Science of Geology." In *Changing Perspectives in the History of Science*, edited by Mikuláš Teich and Robert Young, pp. 320–343. London: Heinemann, 1973.

Post, Heinz. "Novel Predictions as a Criterion of Merit." In *Essays in Memory of Imre Lakatos*, edited by R. S. Cohen et al., pp. 493–495. Dordrecht: D. Reidel Publishing Co., 1976.

Putnam, Hilary. *Reason, Truth and History*. Cambridge: Cambridge University Press, 1981.

———. *Meaning and the Moral Sciences*. Boston: Routledge & Kegan Paul, 1978.

———. *Philosophical Papers*, vols. 1 and 2. Cambridge: Cambridge University Press, 1975.

Rawls, John. *A Theory of Justice*. Cambridge: Harvard University Press, 1971.

Rosen, Edward. "Was Copernicus a Hermetist?" In *Historical and Philosophical*

Perspectives of Science, edited by Roger H. Stuewer, pp. 163–171. Minneapolis: University of Minnesota Press, 1970.

Rosenberg, Jay F. *Linguistic Representation*. Dordrecht: D. Reidel Publishing Co., 1974.

Rossiter, A. P. "Hooke as Geologist." *Nature* 137, no. 3463 (March 14, 1936): 455.

Ruse, Michael. *The Darwinian Revolution: Science Red in Tooth and Claw*. Chicago: The University of Chicago Press, 1979.

Salmon, Wesley. "Rational Prediction." *The British Journal for the Philosophy of Science* 32, no. 2 (June 1981): 115–125.

Sarkar, Husain. "In Defence of Truth." *Studies in History and Philosophy of Science* 14, no. 1 (March 1983): 67–79.

———. "A Theory of Group Rationality." *Studies in History and Philosophy of Science* 13, no. 1 (March 1982): 55–72.

———. "Truth, Problem-Solving and Methodology." *Studies in History and Philosophy of Science* 12, no. 1 (March 1981): 61–73.

———. "Imre Lakatos' Meta-Methodology: An Appraisal." *Philosophy of the Social Sciences* 10, no. 4 (December 1980): 397–416.

———. "Methodological Appraisals, Advice, and Historiographical Models." *Erkenntnis* 15, no. 3 (November 1980): 371–390.

———. "Putnam's Schemata." *Philosophical Topics* 10, no. 1 (Spring 1979): 125–137.

Scherz, Gustav. "Stensen, Niels." In *Dictionary of Scientific Biography*, vol. 13, edited by Charles Coulston Gillispie, pp. 30–35. New York: Charles Scribner's Sons, 1970.

Schilpp, P. A., ed. *The Philosophy of Karl Popper*, vols. 1 and 2. La Salle: Open Court, 1974.

Sibatani, Atuhiro. "The Japanese Brain." *Science 80* 1, no. 8 (December 1980): 22–27.

Simpson, John. "Evolutionary Pulsations and Geomagnetic Polarity." *Geological Society of America Bulletin* 77, no. 2 (February 1966): 197–204.

Stalnaker, Robert. "A Theory of Conditionals." In *Causation and Conditionals*, edited by Ernest Sosa. London: Oxford University Press, 1975.

Stanley, Steven M. *The New Evolutionary Timetable: Fossils, Genes, and the Origin of Species*. New York: Basic Books, Inc., 1981.

———. *Macroevolution: Pattern and Process*. San Francisco: W. H. Freeman and Co., 1979.

Stich, Stephen P., and Nisbett, Richard E. "Justification and the Psychology of Human Reasoning." *Philosophy of Science* 47, no. 2 (June 1980): 188–202.

Temkin, Owsei. *The Double Face of Janus and Other Essays in the History of Medicine*. Baltimore: The Johns Hopkins University Press, 1977.

———. *Galenism: Rise and Decline of a Medical Philosophy*. Ithaca: Cornell University Press, 1973.

Tichy, Pavel. "On Popper's Definitions of Verisimilitude." *The British Journal for the Philosophy of Science* 25, no. 2 (June 1974): 155–160.

Watkins, John. "Corroboration and the Problem of Content-Comparison." In

Progress and Rationality in Science, edited by Gerard Radnitzky and Gunnar Andersson, pp. 339–378. Dordrecht: D. Reidel Publishing Co., 1978.

———. "Between Analytic and Empirical." *Philosophy* 32, no. 121 (April 1957): 112–131.

Westman, Robert S. "Three Responses to the Copernican Theory: Johannes Praetorius, Tycho Brahe, and Michael Maestlin." In *The Copernican Achievement*, edited by Robert S. Westman. Berkeley, Los Angeles, London: University of California Press, 1975.

White, Lynn, jr. "The Ecology of Our Science." *Science 80*, Premier Issue (November/December 1979): 72–76.

Wichler, Gerhard. *Charles Darwin: The Founder of the Theory of Evolution and Natural Selection*. New York: Pergamon Press, 1961.

Will, Clifford. "Gravitation Theory." *Scientific American* 231, no. 5 (November 1974): 25–33.

Williams, Bernard. *Descartes: The Project of Pure Inquiry*. London: Penguin Books, 1978.

Wittgenstein, Ludwig. *Remarks on the Foundations of Mathematics*. Cambridge: The MIT Press, 1967.

Worrall, John. "The Ways in which the Methodology of Scientific Research Programmes Improves on Popper's Methodology." In *Progress and Rationality in Science*, edited by Gerard Radnitzky and Gunnar Andersson, pp. 45–70. Dordrecht: D. Reidel Publishing Co., 1978.

———. "Thomas Young and the 'refutation' of Newtonian Optics: Case Study in the Interaction of Philosophy of Science and History of Science." In *Method and Appraisal in the Physical Sciences: The Critical Background to Modern Science, 1800–1905*, edited by Colin Howson, pp. 107–179. Cambridge: Cambridge University Press, 1976.

Name Index

Subject Index

Designer: UC Press Staff
Compositor: Trend Western
Printer: McNaughton & Gunn
Binder: McNaughton & Gunn
Text: Janson
Display: Janson